Confronting Rape

Confronting Rape documents two decades of anti-rape activism. From grassroots efforts to the institutionalization of state-funded rape crisis centers, the movement has changed public thinking significantly about sexual assault. Activists in rape crisis centers across the US have created a feminist success story, although not always as they would have chosen. *Confronting Rape* explores how the state has reshaped rape crisis work by supporting the therapeutic aspects of the anti-rape movement's agenda and pushing feminist rape crisis centers toward conventional frameworks of social service provision, while submerging the feminist political agenda of transforming gender relations and preventing rape.

Through a rich comparative history of six organizations in Los Angeles, Nancy Matthews explores the complexities within a movement that includes radicals, moderates, women of color, lesbians – all working within varying frameworks. Originally critical of the state's handling of rape and distrustful of co-optation, most rape crisis centers eventually came to rely on state funding for organizational survival. But have the resulting compromises gone too far? *Confronting Rape* reveals significant, often covert, local level resistance and struggle against the mainstreaming of rape crisis work. Bureaucratic routines and discourses are both the tools through which the state redefines rape crisis work and the terrain of activists' resistance.

Nancy A. Matthews is Visiting Assistant Professor at the Department of Sociology, Oberlin College, USA.

International Library of Sociology
Founded by Karl Mannheim

Editor: John Urry
University of Lancaster

Confronting Rape

The Feminist Anti-Rape Movement and the State

Nancy A. Matthews

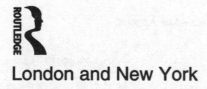

London and New York

First published 1994
by Routledge
11 New Fetter Lane, London EC4P 4EE

Simultaneously published in the USA and Canada
by Routledge
29 West 35th Street, New York, NY 10001

© 1994 Nancy A. Matthews

Typeset in Times by LaserScript, Mitcham, Surrey
Printed and bound in Great Britain by
Mackays of Chatham PLC, Chatham, Kent

British Library Cataloguing in Publication Data
A catalogue record for this book is available from the British Library

Library of Congress Cataloging in Publication Data

Matthews, Nancy A., 1957–
  Confronting rape : the feminist anti-rape movement and the State /
Nancy A. Matthews.
  p. cm. – (The International library of sociology)
  Includes bibliographical references and index.
  ISBN 0–415–06491–0 : $45.00. – ISBN 0–415–11401–2 (pbk) : $12.95
  1. Rape victims – Services for – Political aspects – California –
Los Angeles.
  2. Rape victims – Services for – California – Los Angeles.
  I. Title. II. Series.
  HV6568.L67M37 1994
  362.88'3'0979494–dc20   93–49037
                                                              CIP

For Lisa

Contents

Acknowledgements

Studying the anti-rape movement over the past several years has influenced profoundly my outlook and understanding of political processes. I am deeply grateful to all the women I interviewed who generously shared their experiences and observations. Their story here appears through the lens of my particular sociological imagination, but I hope that they find it a worthy contribution to the important work they have done. Several people helped in significant ways. Without my friend Claire Kaplan, I might not have been introduced to the dilemmas of the anti-rape movement in the 1980s. Her insights and help in gaining entry to doing the research were invaluable. Patty Giggans, Executive Director of the Los Angeles Commission on Assaults Against Women, and Rochelle Coffey, Director of the Pasadena YWCA Rape Crisis Service, provided access to helpful archival material in addition to allowing me to interview them.

Many people have contributed in large and small ways to this work. Sylvia Walby was present at the project's conception, and her belief in the work was crucial to its completion as a book. Joan Mandle, Jane Mansbridge, Kay Mohlman, and Kate Gilbert read parts of this manuscript or related work and offered helpful comments and encouragement. Patricia Yancey Martin and Myra Marx Ferree invited me to the Feminist Organizations conference in 1992, which was a stimulating and inspiring experience. They have read work not directly from this book, but their feedback has influenced my thinking here as well. Exchanges with the other scholars at that meeting have been valuable as well, in particular Verta Taylor, Robin Leidner, Ronnie Steinberg, and Claire Reinelt. Kimberle Crenshaw and Carol Tavris each sought out my manuscript, and their enthusiastic responses reassured me that the work would be of interest to feminists outside of sociology.

I am very grateful to two people who took the time to read the entire manuscript closely. Hester Eisenstein offered her knowledge of feminist history and valuable insights about feminist engagement with the state. Tim Diamond's grasp of the kind of sociology I do helped me strengthen and better articulate my arguments. Neither of them of course bears responsibility for the final product.

Writing this book has spanned three major geographical moves, but I have been fortunate to find support from friends and colleagues in Los Angeles, Hamilton, New York, Chicago, and Oberlin, not to mention the far-flung members of my intellectual, political, and emotional community. Gail Dubrow, who was my "dissertation buddy" through this work's earlier incarnation, has continued to offer invaluable humor and support. Kay Mohlman has cheered me on, read parts of the manuscript, and shared many ups and downs and new recipes. I have benefited from enthusiasm, interest, and sage advice from Wendy Kozol, Bill Gibson, Mindie Lazarus-Black, Sara Schoonmaker, Mary Moran, and Ayofemi Folayan at various points in the process.

A couple of people have helped me keep bread on the table through hard times. Elizabeth Mertz, whose project on language and law school I worked on at the American Bar Foundation during the writing, was unfailingly supportive and encouraging. She is a model of creating a feminist workspace and intellectual environment. Arlene Kaplan Daniels took me under her administrative wing at Northwestern University by inviting me to be a Visiting Scholar in Women's Studies, giving me access to resources, both material and symbolic.

My family has continued to be understanding and supportive, even though this project, just like graduate school, seemed to take longer than made sense. I thank my parents, Bill and Norma Matthews, especially for valuing education, and understanding my commitment to it. I'm grateful to Lisa Frohmann for moral and practical support all through the years of this project, and for her boundless faith in my work.

An earlier version of much of Chapter 7 appeared in *Gender and Society*, December 1989.

Abbreviations

Alliance	Southern California Rape Hotline Alliance
BAWAR	Bay Area Women Against Rape
CETA	Comprehensive Education and Training Administration
Coalition	California State Coalition of Rape Crisis Centers
Compton	Compton YWCA Rape Crisis Center
East LA	East Los Angeles Rape Hotline
FAAR	Feminist Alliance Against Rape
LACAAW	Los Angeles Commission on Assaults Against Women
LEAA	Law Enforcement Assistance Administration
NCPCR	National Center for the Prevention and Control of Rape
NIMH	National Institutes for Mental Health
OCJP	Office of Criminal Justice Planning
Pasadena	Pasadena YWCA Rape Crisis Service
RCC	Rape Crisis Center
Rosa Parks	Rosa Parks Rape Crisis Service
SAC	Sexual Assault Services Advisory Committee (OCJP)
SCLC	Southern Christian Leadership Conference
SCWAR	Santa Cruz Women Against Rape
Valley	San Fernando Valley Rape Crisis Service
VOCA	Victims of Crime Assistance
WASA	Women Against Sexual Assault
YWCA	Young Women's Christian Association

Introduction

Twenty years after the first speak-out against rape, we are still grappling with the meaning and extent of sexual violence in women's lives. Violence against women became a fundamental issue for the new feminist movement that began in the late 1960s, and became the focus of a distinct, parallel anti-rape movement. Today, rape crisis centers are ubiquitous in the U.S.; found in cities of all sizes and in many rural counties, they offer counseling and a variety of other services to survivors of sexual assault. What began as an anti-rape movement has developed into a collection of organizations that provide a range of services. The *movement* aspect of anti-rape work is now less apparent than its character as a network of social service agencies, which are often integrated into the very institutions the early movement opposed.

This book is about the struggles and fortunes of the anti-rape movement during its first two decades of work. I begin with its birth in collectivist, radical feminism and the invention of a new service, rape crisis work. I trace the development of a new organizational form that combined politics with service provision, and its transformation as the movement matured, new opportunities arose, and rape crisis centers became more integrated into existing social service networks. The movement confronted a number of state agencies at various points – from its early critique of the state for not addressing male violence to its later reliance on state funding for organizational survival. The story of this changing relationship between the anti-rape movement and the state is central to understanding how rape crisis work has developed and helps us understand more about states and social movements in general.

This study is animated by a concern for understanding a movement that has had a profound impact on our society, yet is all but invisible, as a movement, to the broader public. How did it begin? What were its goals? What has been gained or lost? How did the context of the movement's genesis affect its perspectives, goals, and actions? How has the changing political climate affected its impact and ongoing work? How has society responded to the anti-rape movement? In attempting to answer these questions, one of my aims is to chronicle a history that risks being lost by virtue of having been made by people whose lives have not in the past been routinely documented. I also hope to illuminate a central dilemma of activists in our time: how do we engage the powers that we wish to change? My focus is the specific political struggles, contingencies, and accomplishments of a local anti-rape movement linked to a wider movement and to centralized state agencies.

A CHANGING MOVEMENT AND THE STATE

The anti-rape movement was founded on two notions: first, the radical political insight that violence against women is a fundamental component of the social control of women, and second, that women should try to do something to turn victims into survivors. Early activities included confrontations with individual rapists, street theater, and pressing the police in public forums. The movement tended to be anti-state, stemming both from its roots in the leftist counter-culture and the particular violations of rape victims by the police and criminal justice system. Nevertheless, over the first decade of the movement, anti-rape groups became increasingly oriented toward providing services to individual women.

One important strand in this story is the anti-rape movement's changing relationship to the state. The fact that the movement addresses violence meant almost inevitably that the state would be involved. Feminists' anger about inadequate law enforcement action on behalf of women victims of male violence led to an ambiguous stance toward the state. From the beginning, the failure of law enforcement effectively to prevent, control, or punish rape was a target of the movement's activity, but at the same time, many feminist anti-rape activists saw their work as an alternative to relying on or being involved with the criminal justice system. Skepticism toward the state extended to careful scrutiny of possible funding sources – early activists often refused money that required too close a relationship with suspect state agencies, particularly law enforcement. This changed, and over time, increased reliance on state funding has had a contradictory effect on the movement, both effectively promoting the movement's survival and contributing to its transformation from grassroots activism to professionalized social service provision.

A second strand in this story is the dynamics of feminist movement organizations. The anti-rape movement's genesis in the radical, counter-cultural feminism of the early 1970s meant that its earliest form of organization was collectivist. These feminists' critique of how unequal power relations are embedded in institutional structures led them to create alternatives. Early rape crisis centers were egalitarian, non-hierarchical, and attempted to operate by consensus. But as a result of internal processes of development and external pressures to conform, conventional organizational structure supplanted the early collectives. Today rape crisis centers have a variety of organizational forms. Some are part of larger institutions, including hospitals, community mental health centers, and even district attorneys' offices; some are located in YWCAs or other community organizations, others are in women's centers on college campuses, or are projects of battered women's shelters; some are free-standing organizations. The common structure, though, is some version of the private, not-for-profit corporation. They often look more like social service agencies than social movement organizations.

Paralleling structural change has been the professionalization of rape crisis work. In keeping with their roots in the counterculture, early activists were suspicious of authority and expertise, and in an effort to respect and empower the women they aided, they emphasized the ability of any woman to do rape crisis work. Peer counseling has been partially replaced by professional counseling and this is still a matter of debate within the movement. Ironically, these anti-professional activists developed expertise which in part drew on the professional skills of social workers and other human service workers who were part of the movement. In turn, these professionals worked to legitimize what they were learning and developing within their professions, creating a specialty in treating sexual assault that has gained recognition and furthered the understanding of the related phenomena of rape, child sexual abuse, and battering. The legitimation of concepts such as rape trauma syndrome, which is now sometimes used in rape trials to explain victims' behavior, are part of this process. Professionalization of rape crisis work thus has occurred in two related senses: one is what social movement theorists observe about the increase in paid, "professional" movement leaders, and another is the adoption of some of the work the anti-rape movement started by established professionals, who locate it within their niche, as work they have special and exclusive claim over.

While rape crisis work originated as an expression of the new feminist politics, today it is also a manifestation of a therapeutic society. The framework of therapy has become a mode for dealing with numerous social problems in the late 20th century United States and has thus become a mixed blessing. For all their liberatory potential, therapeutic frameworks often disguise social ills as personal trauma (Polsky 1991). Connecting the emergence of professionalized rape crisis work with funding of such services by the state, I argue that state agencies prefer and promote the individualized treatment model of addressing rape, rather than the more political analyses developed by early activists. State sponsorship of services and the related ascendancy of service-provision are a conservatizing influence on the movement because they shift the focus to therapeutically managing the aftermath of rape rather than to changing social relations in order to prevent rape.

The choice of certain kinds of action comes to characterize a movement; movements are identified by their services, lobbying, educational work, or civil disobedience. The chosen work itself embodies demands that influence other decisions and frame subsequent choices. The selection of hotlines as the centerpiece of their work had consequences for the anti-rape movement, in that it produced hybrid organizations that were both political and service-oriented. Recruitment of volunteers to staff these hotlines meant drawing in people who did not necessarily share the political analysis of the founders, which helped tip the scale toward service. The process of professionalization and increasing dependence on external funding also pushed the movement's identity away from a political orientation as the work became shaped by the social service and bureaucratic concerns of the state. An understanding of the tension between politics and service helps to explain ongoing tensions in the movement.

Internal factors converged to make the hotline and counseling services the centerpiece of their projects. These factors included the activists' value on bringing the political down to the personal level; the way in which counseling drew on traditionally feminine skills; the reliance on voluntary labor; and the many social workers who were involved. The political environment was a further catalyst to these groups' transformation from social movement organizations into social service agencies because the state was the most likely source of needed financial help; the state, in response to increasing demands for services, had an interest in having volunteer groups provide them at relatively low cost; and adopting the structure of non-profit status was necessary in order to participate in the state's grant economy.

Reliance on state grants constituted a new structural relationship to the state: these groups were partially absorbed into the network of service organizations existing on the periphery of the state. As a result, rape crisis services have become a contested terrain on which organizational and ideological autonomy are disputed with the state agencies that now claim such services as their own. Oppositional ideology is maintained through the educational programs the groups offer (both the intensive training of volunteer members and public workshops). These struggles have implications for our understanding of the state's relationship to women, and to feminism, which are developed in the final chapter.

RAPE CRISIS SERVICES TODAY

Rape crisis services have evolved considerably since they were first started, but the core activities have remained constant. Although rape crisis centers vary in their organizational location quite a bit, they are associated with a surprisingly consistent set of services (Gornick, Burt, and Pittman 1985; Byington, Martin *et al.* 1990), although what is actually delivered may vary. The rape crisis centers in this study have the following kinds of services in common: they offer crisis intervention through a 24-hour telephone hotline and face-to-face counseling for rape victims and their families and friends. Trained volunteers take calls, which are forwarded to their homes, during four to six hour shifts. Women may call the hotline soon after an assault, or they may wait years before calling. The hotlines follow up after the first contact, and sometimes this results in the rape survivor coming to the center for in-person counseling, being referred to a private counselor, or joining a support group organized by the center. In addition, rape crisis volunteers or staff provide accompaniment and advocacy services; they will go with the caller to the hospital, the police, through court-related appointments, or appointments with other agencies, and if necessary intervene with these agencies on their behalf.

In addition to crisis intervention services, rape crisis centers organize and provide community education about sexual assault. Members go to schools, churches, community groups, and businesses to do workshops on rape and rape prevention. Some organizations have more elaborate programs that specialize in teaching women self-defense. A major project of the anti-rape movement in southern California for the past decade has been to develop a training and certification program for women self-defense instructors. This has been important to women in the movement because they are able to teach a feminist approach to rape prevention that emphasizes empowering women rather than merely protecting them. Self-defense instruction also has been an avenue for reaching new communities. For example, deaf women first became involved in Los Angeles' oldest rape crisis center through this training in 1988.

Direct services to women and community education about sexual assault are the basic activities of all the rape crisis centers. In recent years some have expanded and diversified their programs to address related issues, such as child abuse prevention. Some also serve battered women, but in most of Los Angeles, those services are offered by separate organizations. The uniformity in services among hotlines is a product of both the movement's evolution and specification of standards by the state funding agency.

THE RESEARCH

Unlike other studies that focus on a population of extant rape crisis centers at a given time (e.g. Burt, Gornick, and Pittman 1984; Gornick, Burt, and Pittman 1985; Byington *et al.* 1991; Martin *et al.* 1992; Martin 1993),[1] this study follows the development of a few organizations over a long period of time. In Los Angeles the movement could be studied in microcosm. Los Angeles County is a large area of 8 million people encompassing diverse racial and cultural communities, a wide array of individuals and groups with differing ideologies and politics, and yet which is related geographically, politically, and socially. Certainly there are unique features to how the anti-rape movement and rape crisis centers developed there, as there are in any city, but the range of problems, solutions, debates, successes and failures of the movement there largely mirror what has been found in the national scene. I pay careful attention to the particularities of the situation in Los Angeles, and in California. Indeed I wish to emphasize that local conditions affect the choices activists can and did make in organizing their movement. My emphasis is on the process of change and active creation of an institution over time within a particular context, but at more than the usual case study level. By studying several related organizations that share place and time, I can offer a more comparative analysis than a case study, and exhibit a more realistic picture of the range of work that was done by anti-rape activists. On the other hand, I offer a more richly detailed, historical, and processual view of these organizations than a large-scale national study could.

I study six organizations in detail, which are listed in Table 1 along with their dates of founding. The first four are movement organizations by virtue either of their explicit ideological grounding in feminism or their time of origin. The last two organizations started later and were

Table 1 Founding dates of rape crisis centers in Los Angeles

Center	Date
Los Angeles Commission on Assaults Against Women (LACAAW)	1973*
Pasadena YWCA Rape Crisis Service (Pasadena)	1974
East Los Angeles Rape Hotline (East LA)	1976
San Fernando Valley Rape Crisis Service (Valley)	1980
Rosa Parks Rape Crisis Service (Rosa Parks)	1984
Compton YWCA Rape Crisis Center (Compton)	1984

Note: *The Anti-Rape Squad that was a precursor to LACAAW started in 1972

less directly products of the feminist anti-rape movement, but emerged from organizations in the Black community, and thus had a more activist orientation than more establishment RCCs that originated at the same time. Individual organizations have their own political and institutional histories – who founded them, when, with what resources, but all of them have been affected by the broader movement, even those whose founding was not directly from the grassroots movement. I did not include rape crisis centers whose origins were more institutionalized; in Los Angeles, primarily those located in hospitals.[2] Selection of organizations followed an inductive method, which was historically sensitive, so some organizations that could have been included were not – smaller

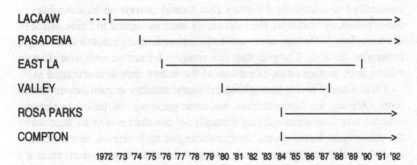

Figure 1 Period of operation of rape crisis centers in Los Angeles
Note: The East Los Angeles Rape Hotline was reorganized in 1990 into a multi-purpose organization called Avance, which provides bilingual Spanish–English AIDS-related services in addition to rape crisis services and other community work.

RCCs farther from the geographical center of Los Angeles, or those that were more active long before I commenced my study.[3] Figure 1 shows the time periods for the groups I studied.

Human agency, and especially women's activism to change the conditions of their lives, figured prominently in the questions I asked and the methods by which I sought to answer them. I thus set out to analyze the variety of experience among communities – mediated by gender, race and ethnicity, and geography – at the points of connection to a particular issue. The issue – rape – was not chosen for abstract theoretical reasons, although it has theoretical implications, but because there were concrete events, the social fact of a movement and its resulting organizations that posed compelling questions. In studies of violence women are commonly conceived as victims, both of individuals and of social forces; my study approaches them as social actors, resisting and reshaping the social relations that constitute their lives. Thus, I was interested in what people did in those communities about the issue of rape, what happened as a result of what they did, and how it was affected by events and processes outside and within those communities.

While institutionalized structures document themselves as a side effect of how they are organized, emergent structures, such as social movements, are "recorded primarily in the memories of the participants" (Roy 1989). The data were collected primarily through in-depth interviews with participants in the movement and officials of the Office of Criminal Justice Planning. I also examined archival materials from the organizations studied, and conducted field research, attending meetings, special events, and conferences related to the movement. I was committed to recording a history that would otherwise be invisible. In the oral history tradition, the interviews were designed to "give voice to the voiceless" (Di Leonardo 1987: 3), recording rich detail that would otherwise be lost. I hoped that the women I interviewed would view telling their stories as an extension of the action they had engaged in.

I was acutely aware throughout the study that the women I interviewed were offering an interpretation, an understanding, of their experience, which I was then reinterpreting through my construction of an account of the movement, based on my understanding of their stories. My method is rooted in the interpretive and feminist epistemologies that embrace reflexivity, a self-consciousness about how we are embedded in social relationships even as we conduct research (Oakley 1981; Emerson 1983). The identities I brought with me to the research and those of the women I interviewed mediated the interaction. Being a white, middle-class, academic, feminist, activist woman facilitated my access to some kinds of information/understanding and precluded access to other kinds. Feminist critiques of the masculine bias in sociology (e.g., Epstein 1974; Oakley 1981; Stacey and Thorne 1985) have extended to reconceptualizing the discipline from women's standpoint (e.g., Devault 1986; Smith 1987). I share the work toward creating an alternative paradigm for research that acknowledges the social relationships involved in research, that recognizes the interestedness of the researcher in her topic, and attempts to mitigate the hierarchical and exploitative relations that characterize traditional social science research.

Certain interview passages contained dense description of pivotal events and organizational processes and these became the focal points from which I wrote the story of the movement. That these passages form the backbone of the story will become apparent in the substantive chapters that follow.

The interviews

I interviewed women from six rape crisis centers, and staff members at the Office of Criminal Justice Planning (OCJP). The interviews took place in the interviewees' offices or public places, and usually lasted about two hours. The individuals and their affiliations are listed in Appendix A. The number of people interviewed from each organization varied with the age of the organization; I interviewed more people from the older groups in order to collect accounts from the several different periods of the organizations' existence. The semi-structured interviews covered the individual's experience in the anti-rape movement, her recollection of events and processes in the movement's history, and her account of how the organization worked. The interviews were tape-recorded and later transcribed, in full or in part. The interview schedule and the two-step consent form I used are included in Appendix B.

Access

Two related experiences opened the doors to the women I wanted to study. The first was my friendship with a woman who was a volunteer at LACAAW since 1981, and a staff member there from 1986 to 1989. We became acquainted as activists in another political organization. Her stories about ongoing debates and changes at LACAAW raised many issues pertinent to my interests in social movements, and feminism in particular, political processes within organizations, and involvement of the state. This woman became my key informant in the early stages of research; her experience provided me with an initial "who's who" of the movement locally. Her position as a valued and reputedly diplomatic member of the movement meant that her "seal of approval" hastened my access to many people in the rape crisis organizations.

A second experience also facilitated my access. In the summer of 1986 I became involved in a coalition that organized a "Take Back the Night" march to protest a series of unsolved murders of women of color in Los Angeles. I was attracted to the coalition because it focused on the intersection of gender, race, and class. Many of the women in the coalition were from the anti-rape movement. My participation gave me an opportunity to meet some of the women I would later interview, but more importantly, it marked me as an insider – someone whose interests corresponded with theirs.

Documents

The second major source of data for this study were various movement and organizational documents and government documents that define the relationship between the OCJP and rape crisis centers. I had access to the history files of the Los Angeles Commission on Assaults Against Women, the oldest anti-rape group in Los Angeles, and of the Southern California Rape Hotline Alliance, as well as miscellany given to me by people I interviewed. The movement documents ranged from formal meeting minutes to handscrawled lists, flyers about events, and resolutions presented to conferences. Later documents included public relations literature, forms used for record-keeping, training schedules, educational booklets, and statements of purpose. Many of these materials were also artifacts resulting from particular relationships (e.g., the forms used for collecting data for the OCJP; booklets produced with special grants). I also gathered several publications of the OCJP that govern and describe the relationship between that agency and the rape crisis centers it funds. They also included historical references to relevant legislation. In addition I collected other OCJP publications (brochures, newsletters, reports) that gave me a broader picture of the agency and thus the context within which its Sexual Assault Program operates. The materials I had access to were those in use in 1988.

The documents were a valuable supplement to the oral accounts. Documents, like interviews, are also produced by social processes (*cf.* Smith 1974, 1990). Part of interpreting their meaning is to look for clues to what the context was. Is a piece of writing produced by a movement organization? Whom does it address: other members of the movement? Members of the public? State officials? Whether something is typed on stationery or handwritten may tell something about the material resources of the organization. A sequence of documents may reveal valuable information about the social processes that produced them. What do the papers say about the members' concerns at the time?

HOW THIS BOOK IS ORGANIZED

In Chapter 1 I address theoretical issues that are woven through the story in the subsequent chapters, including feminist theory about violence against women, feminism as a movement, and how I approach the state in this study. Chapter 2 offers a brief overview of the national context in which local anti-rape organizing arose. Chapter 3 is primarily a historical chapter which recounts the founding of the earliest three rape hotlines in Los Angeles. In this context I discuss the origins of different strands in the movement which generated ongoing tensions. Chapter 4 covers four major issues that confronted each organization after founding: leadership and decision-making style; recruitment and training; funding; and external relationships. I examine how the different conditions of founding and interpretive frames affected the course taken by each organization in resolving these issues and argue that choice of the hotline as the main tactic was a powerful force in shaping them all, regardless of differences in style and politics.

A watershed period of transformation is the subject of Chapter 5, which examines the internal and external sources of crisis and change during a two-year period that saw the formation of the Rape Hotline Alliance, the near-folding and resuscitation of two older groups, and the founding of a new radical hotline. Chapter 6 discusses the emergence of substantial state funding and how that contributed to the resolution of the movement's crisis and consolidated a social service agency orientation in rape crisis centers. I analyze the political forces at work in the state, the means of cooptation it used, including political processes and bureaucratic requirements, and resistance from movement activists.

Chapter 7 looks at some of the results of those developments, especially the expansion of racial and ethnic diversity in the movement. I explore the racial dynamics in feminism and the anti-rape movement and examine the emergence of two additional hotlines in the mid-1980s in Black communities, founded with OCJP funding. I discuss how these differ from other hotlines and the particular issues that confront them because of their relationship to the state and their communities. In Chapter 8 I discuss two ongoing sources of tension in the movement that relate to its ideology and practice: how feminists view the relationship between violence and the state, and feminist ambivalence about the state's bureaucratic mode of operating. I close by considering the contributions this study of the anti-rape movement makes to the sociological understanding of social movements, feminism, and the state.

Chapter 1

Feminism, the state, and the anti-rape movement
Theoretical underpinnings

Before beginning the story of the Los Angeles anti-rape movement, consideration of some definitions and theoretical questions is in order. This study contributes to two theoretical dialogues. One is the question of what the anti-rape movement can tell us about the larger new feminist movement of which it was a part. How shall we characterize and analyze feminist organizations? What distinguishes them from other movement organizations? I discuss below some of the models that have been developed by feminist scholars in the past and how well they apply to the anti-rape movement. The second set of issues I raise below have to do with developing an understanding of the relationship between social movements generally, and feminism in particular, and the state. I outline the model of the state I draw on in this study, and discuss how the professionalization of reform connects movements and the state. Then there's the question of developing a gendered theory of the state. Does the state have a distinctive place in the maintenance of gender inequality? Is the state male?

FEMINISM AND THE ANTI-RAPE MOVEMENT

Recent social movement scholars developing the resource mobilization perspective have emphasized organization over ideology. Applying this focus to feminism, scholars noted two branches in the new feminist movement, primarily differentiated by style and structure. The older branch was composed of conventionally structured organizations such as the National Organization for Women and the National Women's Political Caucus, while the younger, "small group" branch operated through looser networks of activists (Hole and Levine 1971; Freeman 1975; Evans 1979; Ferree and Hess 1985). Ferree and Hess refer to these as the "bureaucratic" and "collectivist" strands, and summarize the two ideal types:

> The bureaucratic organization . . . is characterized by a formal division of labor, written rules, universal standards of performance, hierarchical offices, impersonal relationships, technical expertise, and individualistic achievement norms. In contrast, the ideal type of collectivist organization is a community of like-minded persons, with minimal division of labor, rules, or differential rewards. Interaction among staff is holistic, personalized, informal, and designed to achieve consensus.
>
> (Ferree and Hess 1985: 49)

The collectivist strand of the movement was composed of networks constructed through personal contacts and publications.

Jo Freeman argued that a group's structure is decisive in its survival. Bureaucratic feminist organizations were more likely to succeed at mobilizing sufficient resources to continue doing work, even while undergoing transformation, including radicalization. While the collectivist groups were fertile ground for innovation, they also had a tendency to be ineffective, short-lived, oligarchical, and conservative, Freeman argued. She suggested that the more bureaucratic feminist groups implemented the innovations, while collectives "accommodated themselves to their environment [and] . . . transformed their goals, in practice if not in theory, from radical social change to ameliorative service projects" that were "politically innocuous" (Freeman 1975: 145). However, I found it was the more bureaucratically-oriented women whose approach to rape crisis work was more ameliorative and less political. The anti-rape movement originated in the collectivist strand, and it created a relatively new form of mobilization, the activist service project, without relying, as Freeman predicts, on an older, bureaucratic feminist organization to implement the innovation. Instead, it was institutions outside the movement that expanded implementation and tended to depoliticize the work.

Although resource mobilization theorists have held that analyzing the movement according to structure was more appropriate than by ideological distinctions, structure can be directly associated with ideology and values. Recent scholars studying the "new social movements" have emphasized the political relationship between structure and ideology, treating activists as intentional agents of social change (Dalton, Kuechler and Burklin 1990). Collectivist feminists did not just come upon that form of organization accidentally, but organized in that way because they were part of a larger cycle of protest, which engaged in creating a new frame of meaning that challenged the existing social paradigm (Tarrow 1989; Kriesi 1989; Dalton, Kuechler and Burklin 1990).

Thus, for collectivist feminists, as for activists in the environmental and peace movements (Klandermans 1990), organizational style was part of their radical critique; the means to achieving a goal were as important as the end itself. Feminists opposed bureaucratic organization because its rules conflicted with their values on equality and friendship norms as the standard for organizational relationships; hierarchy, impersonal rules, and differential rewards were seen as expressions of male power trips. Not all feminist activism fits easily into these characteristics of the new social movements, however. Many feminists in the U.S., operating within the dominant societal framework, did not make an issue of their structure. To them, conventional organization was a matter of convenience and effectiveness. In addition, many women also joined the movement who did not feel strongly about either form of organization. Looking at empirical cases reveals that structure and ideology were related, but also quickly undermines any rigid distinction between collectivist and bureaucratic feminism. As this story shows, women with various positions came together in the anti-rape movement, resulting in ambivalence and conflict as they sought to work out their differences.

My findings underscore the fluid nature of actual organizational practice. As Ferree and Hess suggested, the distinctiveness of the bureaucratic and collectivist strands rapidly diminished and U.S. feminism embraced "a spectrum of organizational modes" (Ferree and Hess 1985: 68), although the cultural critique embedded in collectivist feminism remained (*cf.* Taylor and Rupp 1993). It is misleading to think that collectivist groups simply became more bureaucratic or disappeared. The collectivist critique of organizational process and style has influenced groups that are no longer collectives. Even hotlines that were founded as collectives and became more conventional still retain non-bureaucratic practices after having become much more formal and professionalized.

Rather than give "excessive attention" to the bureaucratic–collective structural dimension, Martin (1990) argues for a more intricate analysis of the many dimensions on which feminist organizations vary, focusing more on outcomes for women, the movement, and society. Some of her organizational framework points in the same directions as political process and new social movement models (Tarrow 1989; Dalton and Kuechler 1990; Jenkins and Schock 1992). In addition to structure, we also need to ask how social movement organizations express ideologies, values, goals and outcomes which are positive for women and how they relate to external entities (Martin 1990). In this study I examine activism in the context of political processes and institutions, which allows for taking stock of the ambiguity and mixture of gains and losses that characterize activism in the real world (*cf.* Jenkins and Schock 1992; Dobash and Dobash 1992).

One source of confusion in talking about these strands and the changes in feminist organizations is that the two kinds of organization exist at two levels; they are both ideal types (Rothschild-Whitt 1979), to which no actual organization will ever conform, but the collectivist form of organization also became an ideal – a goal and standard some groups tried to enact. The passionate criticisms of and disappointment with collectivist groups arises from this level. Ferguson (1984) collapses these two levels, treating bureaucracy as discourse that is inherently anti-feminist. Alternatively, Eisenstein (1991) examines the ways in which feminists can use (state) bureaucracies for their ends. I want to problematize bureaucracy in a way that borrows from both these authors, treating it as actual practice – both (impure) organizational structure and ideological discourse. State organizations embody the extreme case of bureaucratic organizations at both these levels. Feminist organizations range along a continuum, with actual structure and ideology not necessarily being consistent. Taking collectivist and bureaucratic feminist organizations as ideal types, the question is not why did collectives fail or become bureaucratized, but to what extent do actual organizations adopt features associated with collectivist or bureaucratic ideal types, and how do those work out over the life of the organizations, what gets changed, and how? For example, do organizations become more bureaucratic gradually, inevitably, or as the result of a combination of external pressures and internal political processes? How are social relationships constituted in actual organizations structured according to either of these types?

My research shows that rape crisis work has been influenced by a more conservative social service approach that has threatened to submerge the radical feminist political analysis that inspired it. However, my study also demonstrates the extent to which activists have maintained their feminist political goals even after they have structurally adapted themselves for survival. A major theme in this story is the ongoing struggle between women in the movement and state agencies, to continue to raise consciousness about sexual assault and to locate its meaning in a political context of sexism. Whereas earlier this was accomplished in consciousness-raising groups, now it is done in workshops and presentations offered in the community and schools. Although the message may be presented in more conventional forums, it continues to make a profound difference. However slowly, our cultural understanding of the meaning of violence against women is changing.

THE STATE AND PROFESSIONALIZATION OF REFORM

Talking about "the state" is problematic, so before going further, I want to make explicit my use of the term. An extensive literature exists about the capitalist nature of "the state" (e.g., O'Connor 1973; Domhoff 1978; Alford and Friedland 1985), arguing whether the relationship between capital and the personnel, policies, and structure of political institutions is dependent or interdependent. A less well-developed dialogue has tried to do the same for gender relations, examining the masculinist or patriarchal underpinnings of "the state" (Hanmer 1978; Burstyn 1983; Walby 1986; Gordon 1988; Pateman 1988; MacKinnon 1989; Watson 1990). However, feminist attempts to theorize the gendered nature of the state have typically treated it as a coherent institution, taking some aspect of it to stand for the whole (e.g., MacKinnon's 1989 treatment of law). "The state" is composed of numerous institutions, agencies, and organizations that have different functions acquired through processes that are social, political, and historical. In other words, the current formation of the state is a product of struggles between specific social groups. As it is composed of different agencies, the state is not monolithic, and its various sectors may be at odds with each other or operating in concert at times. The extent to which there is regularity to the interests and actions of state agencies in relation to gender politics is an empirical question, which is only partly answered by past research.[1] I think the findings are sufficient to justify using "the state" as a shorthand reference, keeping in mind that the use of this term does not imply a monolith.

In my study I talk about specific state organizations: the city council, police departments, the state legislature, the Department of Social Services, the National Institute for Mental Health, the federal Law Enforcement Assistance Administration, the state Office of Criminal Justice Planning, and how they related to the anti-rape movement. Alford and Friedland's description of the dynamic nature of such relationships captures the approach to the state I use:

> Both fragmentation and centralization are dynamic properties of the state. . . . The political compromises between different groups inside and outside the state produce extremely ambiguous legislation but also give public agencies considerable leeway to define what the programs should in fact be. Once a political compromise is worked out . . . and an ambiguous piece of legislation is passed, the inconsistencies have to be dealt with by the administrative agencies. The resulting organizational conflicts between different agencies and

even within agencies reflect, we believe, the contradiction between the democratic and bureaucratic aspects of the state.

(Alford and Friedland 1985: 210)

Following from this view, I pay attention in this study to contention between state agencies and anti-rape organizations. Conflict often occurred over the efforts of state agencies to centralize control of the programs they oversaw. Routine bureaucratic practices were the means by which this was attempted and, especially in the context of the feminist critique of bureaucracy, sparked particular resistance. Rape crisis organizations have tried to guard their organizational autonomy and resist the information-gathering function of state bureaucracies, which has become a primary tool of managing society (cf. Giddens 1987).

The state as it appears in this study, reflects three significant features of modern Western states noted by Thomas and Meyer: the expansion of the state's jurisdiction, its rationalization, and bureaucratic expansion. State funding for the provision of rape crisis services may be seen as part of the trend toward "the redefinition and expansion, even in the poorest parts of the world, of human welfare rights and of at least nominal programs under state management to fulfill them" (Thomas and Meyer 1984: 478). Several people have linked the expansion of welfare to legitimation of the state (e.g., O'Connor 1973; Friedman 1981). The emergence of state compensation and treatment for victims of crime as a "right" is a recent phenomenon that illustrates this process. Through demands by collective actors, including the anti-rape movement, there is a new recognition that the state is not only responsible for controlling crime, but also for compensating its victims in order to remain legitimate. In addition to responding to collective demands, this development may signal that the experience of crime itself has become redefined in a more social context, like unemployment or old age, for which the state is viewed as having responsibility.

Scholarship on social movements, whether from the symbolic interactionist collective behavior tradition or the resource mobilization approach developed in the 1970s, has attended to internal movement dynamics and movement relations with the environment, and to the life-history of movements as they grow, decay, change course, or institutionalize (see, for example, Zald and Ash 1966; McCarthy and Zald 1973; Marx and Wood 1975; Turner and Killian 1987). The 1970s and 1980s have seen increased attention to two aspects of movement dynamics: professionalization within movements and authorities' responses to movements. Resources were the nexus of these concerns:

the material means to carry on work were both the *sine qua non* and the result of professionalized social movements. The state's ability to facilitate or repress movements by making collective action more or less costly made it a significant player, at least in cases where the state was the focus of demands by a movement (Tilly 1978; Tarrow 1989).

The feminist movement, along with others, has been affected by the trend toward professionalized social movements. The anti-rape movement in particular is a good example of this, only occasionally putting on the clothing of mass uprisings in demonstrations and other visible protests. Rape crisis centers as they evolved fit quite well the features by which McCarthy and Zald (1973) characterized professional movements: they have full-time leadership; a small mass membership base; a large proportion of their resources come from outside the aggrieved group; they attempt to speak for a potential constituency; and they try to affect policy on its behalf. The leaders of such movements become experts on the problems they are organized to change, which contributes to a related phenomenon, the professionalization of reform. That is, human service professionals become involved in movements to change society in relation to some social problem, of which they claim "ownership" as Gusfield (1989) puts it.

This brings us back to the relationship of a movement to the state. Movements often make specific demands on state agencies to change policy, and the resulting conflict is central to their stories. Some writers emphasize what the state does to movements, especially its tendency to coopt reform movements: for example, Wilson (1983) argued that "social movements are coopted by state agencies to preserve social control." But others point to professionals' tendency in reform organizations to "foster the notion that social problems are public responsibilities and in this sense orient demands toward the state" (Gusfield 1989). These are not mutually exclusive, but are two sides to a dynamic that sets and transforms the agenda of both the movement and the state. Even if social problems are successfully defined as public issues, they can still be reframed in ways a movement does not intend. Wilson argues that the state redefines demands and rights to fit its interests in quelling protest and maintaining legitimacy. As a consequence, problems addressed become defined more individualistically as medical, psychological, legal, and technical, and not as grounds for collective action. The state itself becomes "therapeutic" (Polsky 1991).

A simple cooptation model is inadequate to understand the relationship between the state and the anti-rape movement. In her study of the history of domestic violence, Gordon (1988) exposes a complex dynamic between women themselves seeking state intervention in a problem, and the ambiguous response of the state, in which social control functions of the state intertwine with its social welfare functions. Eisenstein's (1991: 35) model of feminists "finding niches and cracks in the system" and through that "contest[ing] the masculinist character of the state" is the optimistic account of the anti-rape movement's relationship with the state. That account is both true and incomplete: it is also important to note how what is taking place in those niches and cracks differs from what feminists might envision as their goals.

As the state became involved in the anti-rape movement, it recast the feminist definition of rape as a political issue into the problem of an individual victim. This translation of the feminist political analysis (rape as symptomatic of male domination) into an ameliorative concern was promoted by the state agencies that became involved.[2] I call this translation of the agenda as *managing rape*. I am not suggesting that the state imposed a completely alien framework onto a pristinely radical movement. The roots of a more therapeutically-oriented movement were present all along,[3] as I will elaborate further below, and were a source of ambivalence in the movement. But the state came down firmly on one side of that ambivalence, and had a significant effect on consolidating the more service-oriented framework. In order to participate in the state's grant economy (the most viable source of resources), centers had to play up the provision of services, constructing an individualistic "treatment" model of their work, in other words. The state's ideological preference was instituted by way of bureaucratic definitions and requirements imposed as a condition of funding, which affected the rape crisis organizations' structure. Thus, both the ideological changes and structural changes in the movement were produced partly by interaction with the state. Despite the state's attempts to absorb rape crisis services into its service/information bureaucracy, a strong social movement orientation in the rape crisis centers resists this trend.

Chapter 2

The national context

The Los Angeles anti-rape movement was part of a national wave of activism by women. Rape was only one of the many issues the new feminist movement of the late 1960s tackled. Two strands emerged in the broader women's movement (Hole and Levine 1971; Freeman 1975; Ferree and Hess 1985). The older, bureaucratic strand was exemplified by the National Organization for Women, founded in 1966 by Betty Friedan and other women who were already involved in mainstream politics. The younger, collectivist strand, also known as "small group feminism" and the women's liberation movement, had roots in the movement politics of the period, and originated as a trend among women involved in the Civil Rights and New Left movements (Evans 1979; Echols 1989).

Women in the collectivist strand, particularly radical feminists, were the first to address violence against women through sharing experiences in consciousness-raising groups as early as 1970. The New York Radical Feminists held the first documented events addressing the problem: 300 people attended a Speak-Out held at St Clement's Episcopal Church on January 24, 1971 (Largen 1981). A conference on rape followed on April 17, 1971 (Brownmiller 1975). In the subsequent two years, early feminist theorizing about rape took off. Susan Brownmiller, a feminist participant in the conference "who changed her mind about rape" wrote *Against Our Will* (1975). As women began to connect their individual stories of rape and battering into a societal pattern the slogans "The personal is political" and "There are no individual solutions" reflected their emerging commitment to do something collectively about the conditions of their lives.

Bay Area Women Against Rape (BAWAR) organized in Berkeley, California in 1972. This group put together packets of information on hitchhiking safety suggestions, medical information for rape victims and advocates (detailing not only what to expect at a hospital, but additional information medical personnel might not provide on venereal diseases, pregnancy, abortion, and therapy), and samples of the materials they used (log sheets, solicitations for donations, memos from police and hospitals they were pressuring to change procedures). By March 1973 the *Los Angeles Times* (March 1, 1973) reported that BAWAR had requested $25,000 in city funds to set up a rape crisis center. The money would have been used to support an office, pay a part-time coordinator, maintain a 24-hour answering service, and provide counselors for rape and assault victims, according to Julia Schwendinger, then a PhD candidate in criminology at the University of California. A statement by the group said: "We have demonstrated the viability of our project on a strictly volunteer basis. We find that in order to continue and expand our services, we need financial aid." However, in an organizational letter dated April 13, 1973 there is no mention of having received such funding.

Early in 1972 a rape crisis center in Washington, D.C. also began operating. Receiving about 20 calls a day, the women offered medical and legal advice, and "sympathy." They accompanied women to the hospital and to the police and provided a place "where a raped woman could get immediate help and support as well as a place to stay if she needs it" (*Los Angeles Times* July 6, 1972). The rape crisis center was organized by about a dozen women out of discussion groups at the Washington Area Women's Center, a women's liberation group. By early 1973 the Washington, D.C. Rape Crisis Center was producing a nationally distributed newsletter which substantiates a burgeoning national anti-rape movement.[1]

BAWAR and the Washington D.C. Rape Crisis Center became national networking hubs for the growing movement. While some groups were national hubs, there was active communication among other groups, facilitated by the lively feminist press. This underscores the segmented, decentralized structure of the movement. For example, a hand-scrawled note to the Crenshaw Anti-Rape Squad in Los Angeles from the Roanoke Valley Women's Coalition, asking for information, captures the urgency women felt about the issue and emerging action:

Sisters
    Just read about your squad in *Spokeswoman*.
    As we are trying to get something similar going here – *please* send us immediately any information on what you are doing, how you are going about it etc., etc.

We are working on the counseling sort of thing but know this is inadequate.
Please help!

In archival copies of responses sent to other such inquiries the letters describe how the Anti-Rape Squad operated, some of the obstacles encountered, and provided a bibliography on rape. They also sent copies of their pamphlet "Rape: A Problem for All Women," materials on "Medical Information for Rape Victims and Counselor/Advocates" (probably modeled on the BAWAR booklet with a similar title), "Information for Rape Victims and Counselor/Advocates," and their "Sisters Give Rides to Sisters" bumper sticker.

INSTITUTIONAL TARGETS

Institutions that had traditionally dealt with rape victims quickly became the focus of action by activists, particularly the police and hospitals. Victims of rape often said that police questioning was as brutal and humiliating as the attack itself, with police asking questions like "Did you enjoy it? Are you a virgin? What were you wearing?" Feminists in the anti-rape movement called such treatment the "second rape." In response to their criticisms some changes began to appear in law enforcement. The New York City Police Department established an all-female investigation section in an attempt to make it easier for women to report rape. Quoted in a newspaper article, the head of the new section underscored that only 1 per cent of women who report rape are crying wolf and very few victims provoke the attack (*Los Angeles Times* February 11, 1973). The article records a shift in understanding, as it echoes feminist criticisms of police practices and quotes the investigator dispelling common rape myths and defending the integrity of rape victims.

Changing police behavior toward rape became an obvious plank in the anti-rape movement's program, but activists' relationship to the police was contradictory. Members of anti-rape groups met with varying degrees of welcome or hostility when they tried to raise consciousness among police about rape. For example, Dallas Women Against Rape members were encouraged by the invitation to address police cadets in training, while the Los Angeles representative who won that right found herself "ignored, baited, and branded" as hostile (*FAAR Newsletter* 1974). The relationship between activists and police was often based on more than just the police handling of rape. Anti-rape activists who came from the New Left and counterculture felt a general antagonism toward the police, based on police treatment of hippies, anti-war demonstrators, student activists, and so on, and the feeling was mutual. Young, anti-establishment women in the movement had neither the political savvy nor the power-base to develop more workable relationships with the police. Furthermore, they saw it as a dangerous sell-out to attempt to do so.

Hospitals were another target of anti-rape activists as they worked to change hospital policies and medical treatment given to rape victims. Bay Area Women Against Rape negotiated policies of better treatment for victims at the major county hospital (Herrick), but their pamphlets warned advocates that these new policies were not always followed. The policies included, for example, allowing an advocate to be with the victim in the examining area for support (except during the pelvic exam). Movement organizations also tried to provide medical information that the hospitals often neglected, such as about VD and pregnancy.

Working with hospitals seemed to carry particular risks of cooptation. Since these institutions already dealt with rape victims, they saw it in line with their traditional missions to add programs of treatment, but movement women were often edged out once hospitals got their programs going. In 1973 in Atlanta, a group that started as the Metropolitan Atlanta Rape Crisis Committee and later became the Multi-Area Rape Crisis Council (MARCC) brought together various people engaged in rape projects, initiated by a representative from Grady Hospital. The group established a speaker's bureau, developed and disseminated educational material, and collected statistical information about rape. In 1974 Grady Hospital established a rape crisis center, soliciting community input through MARCC during the proposal stage, only to relegate that group to an ambiguous advisory status once the center was set up. A rift developed because women in MARCC felt their "expertise and commitment to combating rape could not be so limited in scope" (*FAAR Newsletter* 1974: 6). Furthermore, several women from MARCC who applied for volunteer counselor positions at Grady's rape crisis center were turned down. In response, MARCC broadened its scope and began to try to set up another RCC. Meanwhile they were highly critical of the Grady center on two counts. One was that although over half of the rape victims the hospital treated were black, none of the initial 15 counselors were, despite the fact that three black women from MARCC had applied. Second was the quality of training received by the new counselors, which consisted of a two-hour orientation session. Rape crisis activists had established by then that intensive, specialized training was required for counselors to address adequately the psychological, medical, and legal needs of rape victims.

Also during this period, legal scholars were challenging the ways in which rape law and legal practice held the victim responsible and made prosecution exceedingly difficult. Pamela Lakes Wood (1973), Camille LeGrand (1973), and Thomas McDermott (1975), for example, wrote influential articles in law journals. Legislators were also beginning to pay attention. The September 1973 *Congressional Record* reports the introduction of Senate Bill 2422 by Senator Mathias of Maryland to establish a National Center for the Prevention and Control of Rape, which was established in 1975 after having been vetoed by President Ford, then successfully reintroduced (Largen 1985). In California, Assemblyman Alan Serioty, Chair of the Assembly Criminal Justice Committee, held hearings in October 1973 in preparation to revise the California rape laws. This responsiveness by lawmakers gave a boost to members of the early movement as they saw real effects of their work.

CULTURAL CHANGE

The overarching project of this movement was changing consciousness about rape. It attempted to redefine publicly the experience of rape from the victim's point of view, rather than from the perspective of the rapist or law enforcement officials.[2] Whether phrased in terms of sympathy and humanitarianism or resisting men's domination of women, the message was that women should be believed and the needs of the victim should take precedence over those of the rapist, police, and courts. This challenged the prevailing view of rape, which posed it as either the problem of a few misguided and perhaps sick men or as the result of suspect behavior on the part of women.

At first women in the movement worked on changing their own consciousness. They collected articles about rape cases in the news-papers and marked passages that demonstrated the kinds of attitudes they were determined to change. Letters to the media expressed their indignation at how rape was treated in articles and movies. Most import-antly in terms of the intellectual context of the movement, rape itself was being redefined and tied to gender relations. Rape was posed not just as a sex crime, but as a problem of male domination. As the *Washington Rape Crisis Center Newsletter* put it: "[Rape is] a political issue, where men violently exercise their power over women. It logically follows that rape will not end until men do not have power over women" (*Washington Rape Crisis Center Newsletter* 1973).

Developing a feminist theory of rape and a coherent political perspective about it occurred through discussion, argument, and critique among feminists of various stripes, a process that continues twenty years later. In early materials, even movement organizations sometimes expressed prevailing rape myths. For example, BAWAR distributed a leaflet listing cardinal rules for hitchhiking, including the admonishment: "Bear in mind that the way you are dressed may affect a man's behavior. Don't wear 'sexy' clothing when you are going to be hitching." Later activists would be more precise: old women at home in flannel nightgowns get raped, too, not just young women out in revealing clothes. As the self-defense movement developed within the anti-rape movement, advice on clothing would emphasize the ability to fight back and escape in particular clothes, rather than its presumed effect on men's propensity to rape. Women were cautioned instead about the effect wearing "sexy" clothes might have on how seriously their complaint would be taken by police and others.

In the effort to shift blame from victims of rape, activists emphasized the violence in rape and down-played the role of sexuality. This took place in the wake of radical feminists grappling with the nature of sexuality and its place in the liberation of women. Was sexual desire (heterosexual or lesbian) to be incorporated into revolutionary gender relations or was it all a product of false consciousness (Echols 1989)? The anti-rape movement removed itself from such troubling questions by promoting the idea that "Rape is violence, not sex." The controversial sex–violence nexus in rape resurfaced in the 1980s in feminist debates about pornography,[3] but during the 1970s the movement's message focused on violence.

Feminist activists used their new formations as springboards for creating new services. This demonstrates the reliance of the anti-rape movement on the broader context of feminist activism. Like the Washington, D.C. Rape Crisis Center, some groups organized out of autonomous women's centers. Many other groups were founded by women's coalitions or centers on university campuses. Answering the question why rape crisis centers were necessary when other institutions could address the needs of rape victims, Sandra Hollin Flowers of the Atlanta Multi-Area Rape Crisis Council pointed to the voids in the traditional concerns of hospitals and law enforcement agencies:

> Societal attitudes toward the rape victim have been nothing short of harsh and often run the gamut from brutal to indifferent. The legal definition of rape recognizes "forced vaginal penetration", but the psychic rape of the victim is discounted and the political nature of the crime goes unaddressed. With low self-esteem and little supportive reassurance from key people in her life, the rape victim becomes an outcast at a time when she is most in need of psychological uplifting.

The rape crisis center is the vehicle through which all these voids in society's handling of rape can be filled.

(*FAAR Newsletter* 1974: 7)

Thus the concerns of the early anti-rape movement included law enforcement behavior and legal changes, hospital practices and counseling, self-defense and community education. The national movement provided significant support for local organizations, although formal national coalitions were not formed until the late 1970s. Women in Washington D.C. formed the Feminist Alliance Against Rape (FAAR) in 1974 for the purpose of better communication and visibility of the movement. They acknowledged that they were not a true working coalition, and that such a body was needed. As in the larger women's movement, exchange of information, ideas, and analysis through letters, newsletters, and activists contributed to the development of a coherent movement, even though it was organizationally segmented. They inspired each other. Changes that began to occur in legislatures, courts, and police departments supported optimism; activists felt there was an opportunity to make a difference.

The Los Angeles anti-rape activists were part of this national network. They exchanged information with other groups, especially the Bay Area Women Against Rape and Santa Cruz Women Against Rape. The latter provided a model for the Los Angeles women who formed the first organizations there. Within a four-year period, 1972 to 1976, three hotlines were started in the large Los Angeles area: the Los Angeles Commission on Assaults Against Women (LACAAW) was the first, followed by the Pasadena YWCA Rape Crisis Center, and the East Los Angeles Rape Hotline.

Chapter 3

The birth of the Los Angeles anti-rape movement

When women begin training to volunteer for the rape hotline at the Los Angeles Commission on Assaults Against Women (LACAAW), they are told how, after a woman was raped on Sunset Boulevard, a group of her friends started organizing the first rape hotline in Los Angeles. This "origins myth" of the organization, however, leaves invisible the context in which this organizing took place. Among the friends were women already mobilized as feminist activists, involved in consciousness-raising, women's centers, and publishing. Organizing their Anti-Rape Squad was not simply a personal response to a friend's misfortune, but was grounded in the political work they were already doing. In June 1973, a year after the formation of an *ad hoc* Anti-Rape Squad out of the Crenshaw Women's Center, this group formed the Los Angeles Commission on Assaults Against Women. Within three years, two additional rape crisis organizations had joined them: the Pasadena YWCA Rape Crisis Center and the East Los Angeles Rape Hotline.

The growing national movement against rape that emerged in the early 1970s provided both context and examples for the founding of the earliest such groups in the Los Angeles area. Animated by a vigorous new feminism, organizations developed from divergent sources. Though they shared the spirit of the times, each group was shaped not only by an emerging redefinition of rape and gender relations, but by the micro-cultural context of the women who became involved, whether countercultural feminists or social workers, whites or Latinas.

What was the context that shaped the early anti-rape organizations? The new feminist movement, and the wider context of social and political activism in the late 1960s and early 1970s not only set the stage for the anti-rape movement's emergence, but also afforded it a base from which to start, including people, ideas, organizations, and models. Women in the anti-rape movement invented a new type of organization, the rape crisis center, and applied the critiques of existing institutions developed by the radical movements of the time. Rape crisis centers as envisioned by radical feminists were to be grassroots, run by women, non-hierarchical, empowering, do-it-yourself, and democratic.

LOCAL CONTEXT

In Los Angeles the women's liberation movement was in full swing in 1972. Small groups of women were running consciousness-raising groups, sharing the technique all across the county, a newspaper called *Sister* was being published in addition to coverage in the leftist *LA Free Press*, and an autonomous Women's Center on Crenshaw Boulevard was active. Women's groups of various sorts were organized on the university campuses.

This was a period of dynamic organizing – groups formed and changed rapidly; there seemed to be boundless energy for starting projects as women were exposed to and transformed by the ideas of women's liberation. It was not hard to be exposed to women's liberation; the media had adopted the movement as a hot topic and the coverage was abundant, if sometimes mocking. Women were making gains in many professions and new women journalists often gave sympathetic coverage. Many of the women drawn into the women's liberation movement were already activists, of anarchist, socialist, or New Left backgrounds, or counterculture participants generally: artists, people running food co-ops, peace activists, and environmentalists. The women's movement was predominantly white, but there were efforts to stay involved with the Black movement of the time, which had by then become more militant and separatist (e.g., the Black Panthers). Explicitly feminist organizations of Black women were still to come.[1]

The earliest expression of the local anti-rape movement arose directly from radical, collectivist feminists, but was soon joined by women activists with different approaches. The first years of anti-rape work in Los Angeles were characterized by the intertwining of the collectivist and bureaucratic strands Ferree and Hess describe (1985). This chapter details how three early hotlines began.

The earliest group, the Los Angeles Commission on Assaults Against Women (LACAAW), was founded between 1972 and 1973 and corresponded most closely with the ideal typical image of collectivist feminism. Many of the women who started it were countercultural white feminists involved in consciousness-raising. The organization's officious-sounding name is an ironic legacy of having flirted with becoming a city government program early in its history. This is only one indication of how complex and full of contradictions the actual story of this organization is. Begun by a group of radical feminists, over time LACAAW became the establishment in rape crisis centers, often criticized by other groups for being too mainstream, professionalized, and non-feminist.

The Pasadena Rape Hotline was founded in 1974 by women who were members of a network of human service professionals. They were more mainstream feminists of the time, also predominantly white, interested in seeing women get their share of rights and services. They were not working outside of the system, but tried to humanize the system of which they were a part. Begun on an *ad hoc* basis, their organization was so small as to not approach any form of bureaucracy. On the other hand, they lacked a strong ideological stand about working as a collective.

The East Los Angeles Rape Hotline was begun by Chicana feminists in 1976, but received part of its impetus directly from LACAAW. Unlike the countercultural feminists of the West Side, these women were professionals who had gained a foothold in the system. They did try a collectivist approach at first, but from the beginning had clear leadership, and early on adopted a more conventional structure. Their feminism was informed by racial politics, as many of them were involved in other Chicano organizations.

In the sections that follow I tell the stories of how each of these rape hotlines began. Participants' accounts of what they were trying to do and how they went about it reveal the goals and values they were trying to promote. Differences emerge along several dimensions, including the kinds of activists they had, how they approached training, their access to resources, and their relationships with outside authorities, especially the police. Despite the significant differences in their early roots, they converged in style in the years following their inception, which I examine in the following chapter.

THE FOUNDING OF THE LOS ANGELES COMMISSION ON ASSAULTS AGAINST WOMEN

What eventually became the Los Angeles Commission on Assaults Against Women (LACAAW), the earliest hotline, was officially founded in June 1973, but its inception was earlier. Two autonomous women's centers were active in Los Angeles in the early 1970s, run by radical feminists engaged in consciousness-raising. Educated, but not in the labor force full-time, a number of women devoted considerable time to movement work, a continuation of their involvement in various social and political movements of the 1960s. The organization of the hotline emerged from *ad hoc* discussion groups that formed as women began to talk to each other about rape. Several feminist groups were the precursors to the hotline.

The Crenshaw Women's Center

Rumblings of organizing for women's liberation were occurring by 1968, when two UCLA women attended the Chicago Women's Liberation Conference and returned to start a campus women's liberation group. Anti-war activism and the accompanying New Leftist intellectual movement were strong on campus. Recalling divisions between the "politicos" and "feminists" at the Chicago conference (Echols 1989), conflict ensued in Los Angeles between leftist women who wanted to have a study group to examine Hegel, Marx, and Lenin on the "Woman Question" and the women who had attended the Chicago conference and wanted to explore the new practice called "consciousness-raising." The leftists prevailed, but two women decided to start a consciousness-raising group on the east side of town, which they named "Women's Liberation 1."

One of the two, Joan Robins, worked part time for *The Free Press*, a political and counterculture publication in which they advertised the new group. They started meeting at the Haymarket, a leftist meeting place on Hoover Street that was used by various groups, but soon moved their meetings to a Methodist church near Crenshaw and Olympic. Robins recalls that the first group attracted about a dozen women, ten of whom were white and two Black. They experimented with consciousness-raising geared toward direct action. For example, in addition to weekly meetings, they demonstrated against CBS for being sexist, picketed a local "head shop" for displaying phallic candles in the window, protested against sexism in the movie M.A.S.H. in Westwood, and performed guerilla theater on Mother's Day in the Santa Monica Mall.

Attending a retreat organized by politically involved Catholic and Methodist women to discuss changing women's role in society was a watershed experience for some of these women. Robins recounts:

[F]or me it was the first time that I had been away from my husband . . . and [the] first time to have any idea about being independent. . . . [The women had] heard that there was a women's center up in

Berkeley or something like that, and that it was a place for women to meet free of men and to have groups to discuss women's role in society, just a meeting place and a drop-in place, where you could have coffee and things like that. So we were motivated, I think, by seeing [the film] "Salt of the Earth" where the women organized. We wanted to do something, so we discussed at that point starting a women's center. I don't even know how I got connected with this group, because I wasn't involved with any religious organization. Somebody told me about it and encouraged me to come.

One of the women involved in the retreat, Susan Rodman, had connections to UCLA and somehow was able to get the university to help fund a Los Angeles women's center. It was housed in one side of the duplex in which Rodman lived on Crenshaw Boulevard and was open for groups to have meetings and for individuals to come on a drop-in basis. Robins recalls:

[Rodman] had an answer-phone there and she would get the messages of people who called and the more leftist women [who] were involved – the Socialist Women's Organizing [Project] – I think that met there – SWOP . . . started to give a lot of time to the place so that it could be open more than just in the evenings when Sue got home from work.

Although a disagreement between leftist feminists and consciousness-raising oriented feminists among the UCLA women was one impetus to the founding of the Crenshaw Center, the fact that socialist women became actively involved in running the center suggests that this split was not as deep as in some places (*cf.* Echols 1989). Shared interests and resources and how they intersected with the geography of the city seem to have been equally important in facilitating the founding of the center. UCLA remained an active site of feminist organizing while the Crenshaw Women's Center drew women from parts of Los Angeles other than the West Side, and those who were not involved in the university. The networks of activists at this point were quite loose; women from various backgrounds and commitments were involved, which reflects the historical time. In the late 1960s–early 1970s period there was so much social–political activism that people often were hooked loosely into several networks through which they might have heard about women's liberation or the Center.

Rape became an issue to be dealt with collectively when one of the women involved in the Center was raped while hitchhiking. Robins recounts its genesis:

So what happened was, she was hitchhiking, this was probably the second time that she had been raped and we wanted to do something about it. We didn't know what to do, but we had been reading about an anti-rape squad, either in Berkeley or Santa Cruz, that would go after rapists and confront them. There wasn't any way to confront – I don't know, I think we were a little intimidated by the situation. She was white, and the rapists were Black, they had taken her to a home someplace, so I think possibly that she could have identified that, but she didn't want to make it a racial issue. I remember talking with the Black Panthers, or somebody somehow connected with the Black Panthers or other radical groups in the Black community, about whether there was any way of them dealing with the problem. And there didn't seem to be any solution that way. . . . I think we were feeling pretty powerless. We wanted to be supportive of her, and from there we started [making] "Sisters Give Rides to Sisters" bumper stickers, because she was raped hitchhiking. And so we printed them ourselves on a silkscreen that we made and we were distributing them at the women's center, and most of us – it was like five people involved: Z Budapest, Dixie Zouts, Sherry was the one who had been raped, and maybe a couple of other people. And all of us had been involved in working at the Women's Center, so we were staff, volunteer staff, and involved with some of the other organizations that met there. And so we just kind of let it be known that there was an anti-rape squad. We probably wrote something up for the newsletter, *Sister*. And the group did not do much else, other than respond when women called up that they had been raped. We'd sort of revitalize the anti-rape squad, and have a meeting, in our homes or something like that, where somebody could come and talk about how they had been raped and whether they would like to do something like go out and talk to the guy, get him busted for drugs, or something like that.

[Did you do confrontations with some of these people?]

No, most of the time the women didn't really want to confront them, and I think in Venice, later on, the Westside Women's Center had an anti-rape group there . . . that they did do at least one confrontation in Venice with somebody.

As this account shows, the Anti-Rape Squad based in the Crenshaw Center operated mainly on an *ad hoc* basis. Women got together around that issue when they felt something needed to be done. At this point there was no formal leader or division of labor in the work on rape; the style was informal and collective. A small group who were both volunteer workers and *de facto* staff of the center did the work. They did not have specific routine responses to rape yet. Rather, the primary value on being supportive and raising consciousness is apparent in how they got together and allowed the rape victim and other women to decide whether they wanted to do anything. This approach was a significant precursor of the importance the feminist anti-rape movement placed on empowering the victim.

It is also significant that none of the options for action that Robins mentions here include interacting with the establishment, such as the police. Instead, direct action targeted the rapist or attacker. This reflects the antagonistic relationship to the police that these women had. The police at this time were enemies of people who considered themselves radical. This was not paranoia, but was based on then current police activities, which included spying on and harassing radicals. (It is interesting that one of the ways to retaliate that Robins mentions, getting the culprit busted for drugs, is the same method of harassment that the police used against radicals.) Meanwhile, on the West Side of the city other women were also organizing around rape. The Crenshaw women exchanged ideas with them early on, and Joan Robins later joined with them in creating the more formal rape hotline after the Crenshaw Center closed in 1972.

The Thursday Night Group and the Westside Women's Center

A large house on Third Street in Santa Monica had gradually become a collective women's house in 1971. Weekly consciousness-raising meetings held there were attended by as many as 60 women. They would break down into smaller groups and use the many rooms in the house for sessions. When the residents were evicted at the end of 1971, the consciousness-raising groups continued to meet at the nearby church in Ocean Park, which lent its facilities to various community groups. Out of this group the Westside Women's Center formed.

Rape became an important concern for these women as they discovered, from analyzing their own experiences, how common it was. Patricia Hoffman, an early participant, explains:

> In consciousness-raising groups, it would turn out that there were a number of women who had been raped or were victims of incest . . . or were getting battered in their homes. With that information coming out, we realized that it was a societal problem rather than a problem that belonged to the individual women and so we formed our Anti-Rape Squad.

The women who began the Venice Anti-Rape Squad contacted the Crenshaw Women's Center and they shared information about what they were doing. As Robins, from Crenshaw, explained, they came from an anarchistic orientation and were willing to help anyone form a group. But this was also typical of the segmentation of collectivist feminism, in the sense that groups freely shared ideas and encouraged each other, without initially making efforts to coordinate and centralize their work.

The Venice group, tailoring their activities to the specific conditions in their area, became more organized than the Crenshaw group had been initially. Patricia Hoffman explained:

> We decided to provide a support network. One of the differences between the Crenshaw area and the Venice area is that we were more encapsulated. We had real boundaries to what was Venice and we had a higher density per block. It was almost as though there was someone you knew on every single street in Venice, because there just aren't that many streets, and so we could form things that resembled safe houses at that time, you know, where you could go in your neighborhood if you were being harassed or bothered.

Thus Venice's neighborhood character affected the way these women organized and did their work. The women involved in the Venice group were concentrated in a smaller geographical area than those involved in the Crenshaw Women's Center. In addition to being more self-contained, the beach area was heavily populated with countercultural types and had more of a walking culture than other, more spread out, parts of Los Angeles. These features of the area made a tactic like a safe house system more feasible.

In addition to creating a safe house system, these women also took direct action against known assailants of women. As a political method the point of their consciousness-raising was not just to develop an awareness of sexism, but to take action to end it. The process of sharing experiences in a group provided the organization with a basis from which to act, which was an integral part of validating women's perspective. Actions in their repertoire had a guerilla quality – they were dramatic and unmediated by the legal–bureaucratic system of redress. As a participant notes, in retrospect their actions seem outlandish, but at the time they were essential and fitting modes of protest:

> We also did some guerilla action of our own, following men who women said had physically or sexually abused them – these are not things that I would do at this time in my life, but at that time they seemed

really appropriate.... And they were necessary because the focus of the country and the understanding of what the crime of rape was all about was not there yet, and so we followed men who were threatening to women and put signs up on the beach of pictures of [them]. There was a man on the beach who was punching out women. Now when I look back at it, he may have been schizophrenic or ... [have] predated the current homeless crisis, and he had punched several different women who were affiliated with the Women's Center, and a woman took his picture anonymously and put it on a poster saying "THIS MAN ASSAULTS WOMEN" and he came to us and agreed not to do it. At the same time there was a man who had gonorrhea who wasn't getting treated and he was having sexual relationships with lots of women. He was threatened with the same action and agreed to go to the Venice Clinic to get his gonorrhea treated.

These actions were efforts to redefine social relations between men and women in which violence against women was ignored or taken for granted. The activists shifted the balance of shame and blame and attempted to make visible who was responsible for assaults. Targeting the immediate source of the problem, activists also bypassed the civil authorities. Like the Crenshaw women across town, their early forms of work were anti-establishment and like the illegal abortion collectives that operated during this period (Schlesinger and Bart 1981), they took matters into their own hands. These activists felt a real urgency about the problem of women being assaulted and felt empowered to do something collectively. Since the authorities appeared as part of the problem, they were not the ones to turn to.

Such direct action differentiated the collectivist, consciousness-raising oriented feminists from the more bureaucratic strand of the women's movement. Although these guerilla tactics were short-lived in the movement as other forms of action became routine, the tradition carried on in later years as anti-rape activists continued participating in marches and demonstrations. Later participation in visible, street-level political action was usually directed against authorities, such as the police, not individual assailants.

The relationship between the Anti-Rape Squad and Westside Women's Center was typical of the loose structure of collectivist organization. The Anti-Rape Squad eventually had a regular meeting time on the Women's Center calendar, but was not formally a project of the Women's Center, with the hierarchy of authority that implies. They were autonomous groups, that had overlapping members and shared time and space. The Squad was not quite a collective either, meaning a set group of people with an ongoing commitment to work together. While such a core group was emerging, there were also a lot of women who came and went during the early period.[2] The Westside Women's Center became a *de facto* hotline, as word spread that women could call there to talk to someone about rape.

Merging the two groups

As the Westside Women's Center became established, the Crenshaw Center folded. While the conditions for mobilizing on the West Side may have been more favorable, due to the concentration of activist women living there, the new center also drew energy and resources away from Crenshaw, which may have contributed to its demise. At least a few of the Crenshaw activists transferred their involvement to the Westside Center. Among them was Joan Robins, who later became the co-director of the formal hotline.

While still informal, anti-rape work on the West Side was more systematic than the *ad hoc* meetings of the Crenshaw group. The Anti-Rape Squad had a regular meeting time, which opened the door to more women getting involved. They also went beyond informal counseling with rape victims, and engaged in the direct actions described above.

In 1972 Hoffman and Robins went to speak to the Venice police about rape. Hoffman recounts how they got into the police station by attending a police–community meeting:

The Basic Car Plan was sort of like Neighborhood Watch, and it was a way of organizing a small part of the community to be aware of their neighbors. . . . [W]e had a Venice station at that time, which helped our orientation to the community in the anti-rape squad, and the captain of the Venice police came to a Basic Car Plan meeting at the Venice Pavilion and I kept raising my hand and saying, when are you going to teach your officers about rape as a crime of violence?. . . I did this about six times and then he said, why don't you come in and we'll talk about it?. . . I thought I was going to be talking to him and maybe someone else, and Joan came with me, because I was afraid of walking into a police station by myself . . . and then it turned out that what we were going to was the roll call, and Joan fortunately brought her tape recorder . . . and recorded a good portion of it. . . . And she just sat there, I kept looking over at her and saying help me, help me and she wouldn't. . . . There we were in this room, there were about 35 men who were armed and sitting in these rows in these blue uniforms. . . . I was about 23, wasn't a college graduate, didn't have any training, was really sort of flying by the seat of my pants, and had read everything that was available at the time, which wasn't that much, and was trying to tell these men how to do their jobs! It was real frightening.

The intimidation women felt at approaching the police makes their action all the more striking. Taking Joan Robins along was part of the feminist strategy of socializing new activists by pairing veterans with neophytes for confrontational actions:

The other thing that we did from the Women's Center in general and the Anti-Rape Squad also was that on any speaking engagement we'd send a veteran and a freshman, someone who was a little green at it, so we were expanding the network of people who were able to speak about various issues, and I think when we went to the police station, Joan may have been the veteran, and that this was my first chance to do something like this.

This strategy helped Hoffman follow through on the opportunity she had gained by challenging the police captain as a citizen at a public meeting.

This event marked a shift for the early movement. Their guerrilla tactics had limited effectiveness. Despite their hostility toward the police, as the women became more involved, the extent and gravity of the problem led them to take on members of the law enforcement establishment, rather than continuing to bypass them. The earliest attempts to change law enforcement's view of rape were grassroots efforts. Going to speak to the police roll call is an example of their early focus on direct, street-level concerns. Before organizing to change legislation, they began trying to reach the people at the bottom who could make an immediate difference rather than going through "channels." This approach reflected feminists' concern with women's immediate, every-day encounters with sexism and also who these activists were: young women without developed ties to higher political authorities.

As some of the participants became more politically savvy, developments in conventional politics also provided opportunities for action during this period, as female public officials who were sympathetic to women's issues won elective office. A new City Councilwoman, Pat Russell, was trying to establish forums for citizen participation. The Venice Town Council was one of these. Hoffman recalls:

I was one of the members of the original Venice Town Council . . . [which] was Pat Russell's idea of how to bring her office to the people. It was a wonderful idea and she realized by about the second or third month of it that it had really become a bottom-heavy organization, and it wasn't going to do as she directed it to do. . . . Because of my being a member of the Town Council I had some very direct access to her, and I talked to her about what was going on in hospitals, and what was going on in the police station, and she was sensitive to those issues, and put her money where her mouth was by giving us at the Women's Center $600, which was $50 a month to run the first rape crisis hotline. It was staffed by us, and we were at that time still our own trainers, and we were sensitive people who wanted to listen, who would go with women to the police station or to the hospital or to trial if it got that far.

Russell's interest and support led to the first money to run the rape hotline. The name of the now formalized organization, the Los Angeles Commission on Assaults Against Women, was created during a brief period when it seemed that the group might actually become a city commission, but that idea faltered. Thus, a local politician's efforts to build legitimacy among her constituents created an opening for the nascent hotline to take off.

Hoffman's account also demonstrates the closely intertwined connection between values and resources that enabled the first real hotline to start. Outrage at violence had already led a group to start acting, but sensitivity to the women was their main value commitment. The work of listening and accompanying women reflects the same values as consciousness-raising, which at its best was intended to validate women's experience and then lead to direct action for social change. Just as consciousness-raising was supposed to start from individual experience and lead to generalizations and theory, the work planned by the anti-rape organization started from individual experience and included plans to change how rape is handled in our society, and ultimately to stop violence against women.

In addition to feminism, these activists held other values that shaped their style of organizing. Many of them were influenced by the New Left's commitment to participatory democracy. This was recast as *feminist process*, a model that featured non-hierarchical organizational structure and consensus decision-making.

The networks of women committed to exploring these processes and values was indispensable to the founding of the hotline. From the loose networks, actual organizations had emerged, which shared material resources in the form of a physical location and phone number, as well as the publicity media of flyers and the center newsletter, all of which advanced the emerging anti-rape group's mobilization. The movement's rise at a time when social activism was legitimate and normative provided a pool of politicized volunteers who helped stimulate the political analysis of rape being incorporated into the work, so that it was not just a humanistic impulse to help the victim. The connection to Councilwoman Russell was there because participants were politicized about the issue. When the Los Angeles Commission on Assaults Against Women was officially kicked off as a hotline at a conference in 1973, Russell helped give it legitimacy as well as the small but crucial funding.

FOUNDING OF THE PASADENA YWCA RAPE HOTLINE

The second rape hotline in the Los Angeles area was started only slightly later, but out of a quite different social milieu. The women who founded what became the Pasadena YWCA rape hotline were part of a professional network involved in human service work. The initial group in Pasadena and the San Gabriel Valley area were organizational activists who incorporated the rape hotline into their paid jobs. As with the counterculture feminists at the Crenshaw Women's Center, an individual's experience was the catalyst for mobilization – not just any individual, but one who was connected to an existing network of people. Nancy Ward, a member of the Pasadena Human Relations Commission, organized discussions about the lack of services for rape victims in 1973 after a friend was raped. Among those invited was Grace Hardgrove, a social worker who eventually became the director of the new service. As Hardgrove recalls:

> I was there as a "concerned citizen" partly because as a woman I wanted to learn more about this, as a professional I sure as heck wanted to learn more about this, and I was fascinated by the idea of this networking effort to bring people from the sheriff's department, from police departments, from mental health, from the health department, from community agencies, all together to deal with a problem that nobody wanted to deal with before.

Out of the initial discussions, Hardgrove participated on the Mental Health Subcommittee of the Los Angeles County Ad Hoc Committee on Rape, which produced a draft of recommendations in April 1974. Other members of the subcommittee were mostly representatives of county mental health centers and hospitals; there was also a representative from the Los Angeles Commission on Assaults Against Women. In contrast to materials generated by the women's liberation anti-rape organizations, the tone of these recommendations was decidedly pro-establishment. The actual suggestions were not that different, including reforms in law enforcement approaches and hospital treatment, the provision of courses in "self-protection and self-defense," and counseling. The overlay of institutional language is striking, however, as these proposals were discussed in the context of developing interdepartmental services, with an emphasis on training "qualified" personnel from police departments, emergency rooms, and mental health facilities.

Not all participants were equally enthusiastic. According to Hardgrove, some were resistant, but because the group was sponsored by a legitimate county commission, they reluctantly cooperated. In spite of the overlay of institutionalized social service concerns and the absence of explicit political analysis, the influence of the more enthusiastic participants is evident. For them it was a great learning experience. It prompted Hardgrove to read what little material had been published on sexual assault at the time, including the earlier feminist writings that linked violence against women with women's subordination generally. As they studied and shared information, they pioneered in the area, especially in meshing the feminist analysis with a social welfare perspective.

Hardgrove describes the group's main proposal, which was to organize

cross-training with different departments – getting the expertise, for instance, in evidence collection combined with what mental health folks should know if they didn't already [in order to provide] sensitive services so you weren't treating somebody like an object on the examination table, but were dealing with her as a whole person.

During this time, Hardgrove was working for the Pasadena YWCA in a Big Sister program and a 13-year-old girl was raped.

As we, the staff, looked around Pasadena, which has always been a real good community for resources, we found that people weren't really hostile to the idea of providing services for this youngster, but nobody knew anything about how to do it. Nobody was educated, not mental health, not the health department, the school basically was uncomfortable having her there, because she might, you know, have a bad influence on the other kids if she got upset or something. They figured it was probably best if she stayed home. So we saw the process happening of this kid being isolated, nobody dealing with her on a one to one basis, nobody trying to help her.

Out of this incident and the lack of services it revealed, Hardgrove began talking to women she knew in other agencies with the idea of going beyond the discussions and cross-training that previously had been done.

> I had a very good friend who . . . was running the patient services department at Huntington Hospital. I spoke with another friend who was at Pasadena Planned Parenthood. Another person that I met through these other people . . . was at Foothill Family Services Mental Health Agency. I knew the woman who was at that time doing the sexual assault investigations at the Pasadena Police Department, and . . . gradually . . . we got this idea that we could have, without anybody coming up with any money because nobody had any money, an interagency network in Pasadena to provide services for women who were raped. I mean, we hadn't even thought about incest or anything like that at that point. And it was great because we started doing the cross-training, and drew even more agencies into it. But [it] . . . was the Y, that agreed, in my spare time(!); no money, we were just going to have a little hotline! [laughs]. . . . Pasadena Planned Parenthood was paying the bill for the answering service that we finally got. Actually our first hotline was through LARFP – Los Angeles Regional Family Planning Council – because Pasadena Planned Parenthood arranged that and said use the LARFP after hours line, and there won't be that many calls, right? And Huntington Hospital was in on it, and Foothill Family Services agreed to send their counselors to all these training sessions we set up, so that they would be aware of rape trauma syndrome and sensitive to helping people through the crisis of sexual assault. And there we were, suddenly we had a rape hotline.

Clearly this mobilization differed from the counterculture, radical feminist impetus behind LACAAW. Established social service agencies, rather than grassroots radical activists, were the foundation of the new service, including a hospital, a mental health agency, the police department, as well as community service organizations like the YWCA and Planned Parenthood. The individuals representing these agencies may have been mavericks and innovative, but they were still primarily oriented to correcting flaws in the service-provision system, rather than operating out of a feminist political analysis of rape.

With the basic framework for a hotline and related services in place, they began recruiting volunteers. A few women who had been involved in the previous year with LACAAW joined them, including two who were also involved in the related self-defense movement, Cathy Barber and Marie Wood. They managed to recruit some Spanish-speaking women, but generally found it difficult to attract women of color, especially African Americans. They listed the opportunity with the Volunteer Bureau, and placed flyers in the YWCA lobby and at some of the other participating agencies, such as Planned Parenthood, potentially drawing volunteers from a broader community base than LACAAW. The first group trained was large, including about 40 women and one man, although not all of them stayed on.

The cross-training model developed by the earlier network provided the framework for the new hotline's training. The police were invited in to talk about their part of the problem. When the subject was the medical examination and hospital accompaniment the session was held at Huntington Hospital where they tried to get the advocates familiar with the emergency room people and procedures. Hardgrove tried to arrange things so that volunteers being trained "had a real sense that they belonged to a system."

Few materials on sexual assault were available in the beginning, but within the first year Diana Russell's (1974) *The Politics of Rape* was published and used, as was Susan Griffin's "Rape: The All-American Crime" (1971). Material on crisis intervention from the social work and psychotherapy literature was also included. As time went on, the increasing availability of published, feminist anti-rape information was a boon to the movement, providing ready materials for training, including guidelines from previous experience (for example, Russell's book reproduces, as an appendix, some of the BAWAR guidelines on hitch-hiking). Thus, although the path the Pasadena hotline took represents a divergence from the political motivations of previous groups, it was educated by and incorporated many of those concerns.

Eventually the new hotline settled into being a program of the Pasadena YWCA. One of the largest YWCAs in the United States, it has a substantial endowment donated partly by the Gamble family (of Proctor and Gamble) early in the century. The city itself has large amounts of "liberal" money that can be tapped by the right organizations, and the rape hotline became that kind of project. A major benefit of its location within the YWCA was that the Y's fundraising staff began to work on behalf of the hotline. Thus, unlike LACAAW and East Los Angeles Rape Hotline, who were like emancipated minors having to fend for themselves financially while trying to get off the ground, the Pasadena hotline had an organizational safety net.

The Pasadena hotline's location, from its inception in a social service agency, influenced not only its ideological stance and access to resources, but also its organizational style. The founder was able to use her professional status and network to draw on material resources from several agencies, and was able to incorporate this work into her paid job. A consequence of this arrangement was an organizational structure with a stronger leader than the collectivist style of LACAAW. The YWCA was not a highly bureaucratized context, but was a "mini-bureaucracy" (Martin 1990) and other important members of the service-providing network were large bureaucracies. But it is important to note that the network of social workers and others who contributed to this rape crisis service worked with each other face-to-face to create an innovation, mitigating bureaucratic features of the organization. Thus, as Martin cautions, bureaucracies are no more purely bureaucratic than collectives are collectivist.

FOUNDING THE EAST LOS ANGELES RAPE HOTLINE

Women working in social services were also crucial for a third anti-rape organization, the East Los Angeles Rape Hotline founded in 1976. In 1975 Irene Mendez was manager of a County Community Services Center and president of the Comisión Feminil, a new Chicana feminist organization. She was called upon to represent the Latino community in sanctioning LACAAW's still relatively new rape hotline. As she recalls:

[S]ome women from the Los Angeles rape hotline . . . called me, they needed a letter of support for funds they were going for and they wanted to get a cross section of minority ethnic groups. I didn't know anything about rape, I didn't care anything about rape, so when they asked me for a signature I wanted to find out what I was signing. I said, why don't you come and talk to my staff about rape, and that'll get rid of my responsibilities for one month – I had the responsibility for bringing in speakers . . . training for staff; I had about 30 people. So they did, and I got so interested in it, and so did some of my staff, and they got interested in us because they saw that the majority of the staff were Spanish-speaking and that was the one group that they hadn't been able to recruit and they needed help with.

Thus LACAAW's pursuit of legitimacy produced a serendipitous opportunity to recruit volunteers from a different and important community in the city. Finding this group of interested women in the Spanish-speaking community must have seemed like an organizer's prize to LACAAW, and their approach was simply to absorb them into the organization. As often happened when a few "minority" women were recruited into predominantly white organizations without any real change in structure or strategy, this response had severe drawbacks LACAAW did not address successfully, leading to the genesis of a new organization.

Mendez recounts the change in her consciousness about sexual assault that occurred as she was trained and began working on LACAAW's hotline:

> As it turned out, they had a lot of Spanish-speaking rape victims, or "survivors," as they're called now. And it was funny because I really didn't believe them. Not that I didn't believe them, but I didn't believe that Spanish-speaking people were really raped. And the reason was that at that time I thought that women who were raped were the ones that hung out in bars, that run around half-naked, parading, and that kind of thing. Shows you how dumb everyone was.

Several women from the Community Services Center managed by Mendez got interested enough to start the training, but Mendez was the only one who became an active hotline worker. She quickly found herself overextended by the demand for her bilingual services.

> They trained maybe about 4 or 5 of us. We got trained. Then the others eventually dropped out, and I ended up being the only one who was taking calls. Pretty soon, within a month or two months, I was getting so many per day . . . it was interrupting my work life, my home life. You know, I had two young kids at home, [and was] the sole responsibility.

A hospital social worker in East Los Angeles was glad to find her. Mendez recalls how Connie Destito underscored the importance of the work she was doing:

> After a month or two, another woman called, and this was Connie, and she worked at the Women's Hospital and they were setting up the first rape trauma center in this area at the hospital. And she said, oh I'm so glad we have a Chicana who's a rape counselor, because we really need someone. And I said, what? I'm already drowning in this stuff. So she started referring victims to me, and it was just . . . I mean within the three months, I was ready to crack up . . . you know, it was too much. . . . [A]round December, I said, Connie, I've got to talk to you. And we had never met, it was funny, we had just talked on the phone, but we got along so well. So she had a feeling it was something like this, so she said let's meet. We met, that was the mistake or the good point, because we liked each other so much. I told her, it's

too much, I just gotta quit. And she said, no, no, you can't! You know, one of those things. And so we said, the need is there, what are we going to do? We both felt so guilty, you know, because she was the only one also. So we said, hell, if they can do it, let's do it. We didn't know what the hell we were doing. So what happened is, luckily we knew a lot of women, so we trained them.

Destito and Mendez's collaboration in starting a new hotline, oriented to the needs of Spanish-speaking, Latina and Chicana rape victims was driven by two commitments: First, having recognized the need for rape crisis services, they wanted to see quality services provided in their communities. Token multicultural participation in a predominantly white organization was a failure as far as providing services, as the one Latina at LACAAW was stretched beyond her limit. One of the structural problems of tokenism is that having *someone* in the organization relieves the group from facing deeper problems of becoming truly integrated and addressing different communities.

Second, Mendez and Destito were interested in building *Latina* strength, and saw the value of having a separate organization, both in terms of the number of women they could recruit and the quality of service they could provide from within the Latina/Chicana culture. A separate hotline gave them the opportunity to determine the most effective ways of reaching women in those communities without having to justify their different approaches to white women. Latina and Chicana women were flexing their political muscles in a new way.

Destito and Mendez recruited among the women they knew and gathered about 20 women interested in working with rape victims. Drawing on what Mendez had learned through the LACAAW training and Destito's social work background, their first act was to train the group of volunteers. At the end of the training they announced to the participants that the hotline was not set up yet. But by this point the group was committed. They pooled their resources, each of them donating $25 to send a representative up to Sacramento, where they had a contact who would walk the papers through the state process to incorporate the group as a non-profit corporation. They held a cake sale[3] to raise funds to get started. Teresa Contreras, an early recruit, recalls:

They did a lot of car washes and bake sales and established the hotline. Because some of the people that were supporting them knew about incorporation and so on, they continued in the organization of the hotline and applied for non-profit status in order for them to be able to generate more funds. They were able to get a grant from the

Presbyterian Church for $1,000. That was the biggest contribution that we'd gotten at that point, and that $1,000 paid for the phone. Actually, [they] didn't have the money for staff or anything. Irene, through her position with the county, provided space for an office.

Contreras recalls that by the time the second group of volunteers, of which she was a member, was recruited, the East Los Angeles Rape Hotline was incorporating as a non-profit organization and establishing by-laws:

[O]ne of the volunteers was assistant manager at a bank. So she knew that in order to generate funds you need to have non-profit status, and then . . . Irene, through her connections, knew people in the county and legislator's offices and city council offices, and there was a gentleman who she got in touch with who said OK I'll help you with the articles of incorporation, and at that time [Los Angeles city] Councilman Allatorre, was an Assemblyman in Sacramento, and Senator Torres was an Assemblyman then, and both agreed to help us, walk the papers through up here in Sacramento, through the Franchise Tax Board, for us to get our non-profit status.

This story highlights the contrasting modes of organization available to these women. The leaders and volunteers were professional women. They were informed and sophisticated enough to know that being incorporated as a non-profit organization would benefit their cause and they were able to use their connections in the community to help them accomplish this. By contrast, their early fundraising efforts, taking up collections from their own resources and having bake sales, were very grassroots and traditionally feminine.

As they got started, Mendez's position at the County Community Service Center was very helpful:

We didn't have an office, but . . . we got a little cubby hole [at the community center]. There was a couple, a pregnant woman and somebody else on welfare, and that kind of thing, who were able to work during the day. And again because I was the director I was able to get some student workers, college students working during the summer and after school. We got them hired, paid by the county, so we had a staff, and that was it, that was the beginning.

Like LACAAW, which drew on the people power of pre-existing organizations, the East Los Angeles Rape Hotline was able to consolidate a group out of a network of women already in place. But the networks were very different. While LACAAW grew out of counterculture feminists, the *Raza* movement for Chicano and Latino identity and self-determination was crucial for the East LA women. They were Chicana professionals and students at California State University, Los Angeles, where the *Raza* movement was strong. Like the Pasadena women, the founders were inside the service-providing establishment. Mendez was a manager for the county; Destito, the cofounder, was a social worker employed by a county hospital; together they recruited among women who worked in social service agencies and offices.

Ideologically there were differences among the Chicanas who became involved and between them and white feminists. Mendez was an early leader in creating a Chicana feminism, but not all of the women saw themselves in that light. Contreras recalls:

I think one of the other things that we learned in that process was who we were as Chicanas and who we were as feminists. Getting involved in the women's movement *as* Chicanas, understanding what our role was within the women's movement, understanding who we were as feminists, that we had a different philosophy. We were the first hotline that had male board members, and most of the hotlines at that time were adamant at not having men involved in the organization, but we knew from the very beginning when we started this organization that in order for us to be successful in our community we needed to have male support. We couldn't take the radical feminist position of not involving men in the organization. And we were criticized for that, we felt that we were criticized for that by some of the feminists. You know quote unquote feminists, whoever we are [laughing].

Involvement in anti-rape work contributed to the development of a feminist perspective among these activists who were initially motivated by the need for services, but only as they gained confidence to define "feminist" on their own terms. Conflict emerged between East Los Angeles and white feminist anti-rape groups. Although they shared important practices, such as not allowing men to work on the hotline, some of these were based on different cultural premises, and the ideologically-oriented white feminist anti-rape activists tried to impose their view on the Chicanas. Contreras articulates the tensions:

[T]here was an assumption that, if you got involved, you were a feminist and you knew, you understood feminist philosophy, and I don't think that that was the case. I don't think that that was the case for everybody; it certainly wasn't for East LA. You know, the reason why East LA got involved was because they knew that there was a need. There were women, Chicanas, Latinas out there getting raped and they needed a service and I think it was established more on that premise and basis than it was on a feminist philosophy that says that women should be providing services for women. . . . [F]rom a cultural perspective we knew that the services had to be provided by women, that Latinas were not going to discuss sexual abuse or sexual assault with men.

Women from the different hotlines met at meetings of the Southern California Rape Hotline Alliance. In addition to disagreements about practices, some of the tension arose from differences in style:

I think that when we first got involved we didn't understand a lot of the feminist philosophy. In fact, I'm fairly sure that some of us felt threatened by the jargon . . . the feminist politics, and the . . . assertiveness of the women involved in the rape crisis movement. Their confrontational style was totally contrary to the Chicana style. So that was hard to deal with initially. I remember our first director was the one that went to the Alliance meetings and she used to come back really upset because of things that were said or implied as far as the different approach that our hotline was taking. And in fact some of the women in our group didn't want to be involved with that really strong feminist approach . . . We finally started identifying other Chicanas who were working in other areas of the women's movement who were saying . . . Chicanas can be feminists and . . . it doesn't have to be totally contrary to your cultural traditions or teachings. So we started identifying ourselves as feminists. That we didn't need to be, that we didn't want to be against our feminist sisters who were also working as diligently in promoting the rape crisis movement, and that we wanted to find ways that we could work within that and stay within our cultural – the things that we knew we needed to maintain in order to be accepted and be supported by the culture and by our community.

LACAAW's serendipitous recruitment of a Chicana, and the burden of her being caught in the position of token were important events that led to the founding of a new organization. But those events could just as easily have led to Mendez dropping out and the consolidation of an all-white anti-rape movement. Fortunately, the confluence of several historic contextual factors prevented that. First, Mendez was a leader and politically experienced. She had been involved in the Chicano movement in Texas, was a leader in the Comisión Feminil, and was a professional. Second, Mendez's County Center which provided such crucial resources for the fledgling hotline, was a product of the times. It was funded by federal block grants, a branch of the War on Poverty. When the hotline got started, the community center provided material support: an office and phones, staff time, and an established base in the community. Even as an unofficial project, the hotline's identification with the center gave it a head start in mobilizing. Third, the fact that there was a network of Chicanas who were educated and in the professional work force, and had organizational skills was very important. This, too, was an historic development; the gains of the civil rights movement had opened some doors that earlier had been closed to Chicana women.

CONCLUSION

An important focus of the new feminist movement was the effort to create alternative forms of organization. The collective became the normative form of organization, with its egalitarian, non-hierarchical structure and commitment to inclusive, consensus decision-making. In contrast, bureaucratic and parliamentary styles with more or less elaborate divisions of labor and clear lines of authority were criticized for reinforcing traditionally masculine interest in power and exclusiveness. Collectivist feminists not only challenged this pervasive feature of modern society, but also the sociological belief in its inevitability.

Feminist scholars have been interested in exploring whether, given their ideological commitment to creating new kinds of structure, women's organizations are in fact any different from the male dominated ones on which past theory has been based. Recent studies have contrasted the two forms of organization and found that problems inhere in the collectivist form as much as in the bureaucratic form (e.g., Freeman 1975, Rothschild-Whitt 1979) and have noted a meshing of the two strands in the feminist movement. Specific organizations seldom exist in ideal typical form, because movement organizations adapt as a result of their changing context and internal dynamics. These organizations can be located on a continuum between collectivism and bureaucracy, along which they move in both directions at different points in time. However, some important features of the groups are not captured by analyzing them according to that dimension.

Reviewing the founding of the first three hotlines in Los Angeles, it is clear that different strands appeared very early in the local movement.

From the beginning each of these organizations had different structures and perspectives on the work they did. Activists with different backgrounds set up different kinds of organizations. LACAAW inherited the most collectivist form of organization from its founding milieu in small group countercultural feminism. East Los Angeles Rape Hotline was somewhat more formalized early on because its founders were professional women who were investing themselves in succeeding within the system, while working to change it. The Pasadena group was a product of progressive people working within the system also, but was even more firmly located within that system than the East Los Angeles women.

This differentiation among the early organizations by the mid-1970s indicates how quickly the bifurcation of second wave feminism into two strands was mitigated in actual organizing, as Ferree and Hess (1985) suggested. The perspectives represented by the collectivist and bureaucratic strands can still be applied to understanding later tensions as the movement developed, but they do not capture the entire picture. Two aspects of the emergent movement modify the analysis.

First, the humanistic, as opposed to bureaucratic, impulse of the social workers who were involved offers one challenge to viewing the differences simply in terms of collectivist versus bureaucratic feminism. The social workers did tend to be more oriented toward establishment agencies in planning and developing rape crisis work than were women whose activism was cast in the counterculture's mode. But as Hardgrove's (Pasadena) pursuit of more feminist self-education illustrates, this was not a unilinear process. Feminist influences entered the establishment via women whose consciousness was being raised while working within the system. Thus, women working with the authorities that the movement criticized were a significant vehicle for importing feminist views into state and state-related agencies.

Second, the collectivist versus bureaucratic dichotomy ignores the different experiences and interests of women of color. Latina women were not only alienated by the style of radical women in the movement, but also were unwilling to sacrifice their own strategies in order to meet white feminists' standards of radical action. So, women in the East Los Angeles hotline chose to adopt a more conventional structure and to struggle with men involved in the organization rather than completely excluding them. While to many feminist analysts, this would automatically categorize them as liberal or bureaucratic, such a view fails to encompass the cross-cutting influence of ethnic concerns that shaped the Latinas' feminism.

In the next chapter I examine the consequences of their differing origins on the three hotlines' development. Although their roots in feminist politics and social service continued to play a role, the organizations began to converge in style, prompted by the demands of actually operating the hotlines.

Chapter 4

Surviving the early years

Despite their origins in different communities and organizing styles, the rape crisis centers founded between 1973 and 1976 all faced similar challenges as they struggled to survive their early years of operation. The drama and excitement of starting new projects gave way to the hard work of sustaining the work they had invented. While their divergent origins and ideological and structural foundations continued significantly to shape their development, LACAAW, Pasadena, and East LA also began to converge in style from 1976 to 1979. Internal dynamics varied with the style of leadership and decision-making practices each had developed. But all had to promote their organizations' survival by recruiting new members, a process that was similar for the three groups. Their approaches to funding and relationships with other agencies, such as hospitals and the police, were influenced by ideology, the social position of the members, and particular opportunities that arose outside the groups. Their growing similarity resulted from the requirements of the work itself, an emerging process of working together in coalition, and their relationships to external agencies.

Different origins were most significant in resolving leadership and decision-making dilemmas and in how each group approached funding, but these resolutions were temporary. The groups were more similar in recruitment and training, largely because they all influenced and patterned themselves after each other in this area. Differing relationships with outside agencies were shaped not only by the group's origins but by the particular political connections they were able to establish. The geographical differences between the small city milieu of Pasadena, the less permeable institutions of central Los Angeles, and the mixture of small cities and unincorporated county areas of East Los Angeles played a role in the kind of access the hotlines had to insiders in these institutions.

All three of the hotlines became more formalized, but this posed different dilemmas for each. LACAAW's grassroots feminist origins set the stage for tumultuous conflicts over decision-making processes and policies that at times threatened to tear the organization apart. The Pasadena hotline, begun as a prototypical example of the professional network organization, experienced a period of changing and confused leadership, but was not divided to the same extent as LACAAW. Its location in the YWCA provided stability which LACAAW lacked. East LA, having emerged from a mixture of professionals and activists, benefited from the professional cast, but experienced "combat fatigue" that nearly finished the group. It worked to create an identity within the Chicano community and cooperate with the other hotlines. The beginnings of a loosely organized Southern California Rape Hotline Alliance facilitated interaction among the groups.

Once founded, constant work was required to keep the hotlines functioning. Ongoing workable relationships had to be established among the activists. Leaders emerged and decision-making processes were tried and debated. New volunteers had to be recruited on a regular basis and integrated into the organization. Relationships to agencies in the community had to be worked out, and money had to be found to keep the work going. This chapter examines four issues that confronted each group during these years: leadership and decision-making; recruitment and training; funding; and relationships to outside agencies, especially the police and hospitals. Decisions and events in each of these areas affected the possibilities and developments in the others. I discuss the differences among the three in how they tackled these issues, and the incipient transformations that occurred as a result.

LEADERSHIP AND DECISION-MAKING

At first leadership was carried on primarily by the women who had been instrumental in founding the organizations, corresponding with Turner and Killian's observation that movement leadership is "typically self-appointed on the basis of willingness and determination, with unformalized cooperation from movement adherents as the continuing unofficial referendum" (Turner and Killian 1987: 229–30). The original leadership is by the people who are ideologically committed to the movement, who are charismatic enough to get others involved, and have the personal resources (such as time, contacts, money, stamina) to mobilize other usable resources (such as members, money, publicity, elite support). Once the hotlines were established, willingness and determination were in high demand, for operating the hotlines was literally a 24 hour a day job. As enough volunteers were recruited and trained, they were assigned shifts to work the telephone hotline, but leaders were commonly on call all the time, to fill in time slots that were not covered, to help handle crises, and to referee incipient conflicts over decision-making.

Leadership in social movements takes various forms: those who symbolize the wrong that the movement addresses, those who articulate its message to outsiders, those who mobilize potential and actual participants, and those who are decision-makers (Turner and Killian 1987). The women in the forefront of the anti-rape movement tended to be less symbolic and more decision-makers, articulators, and mobilizers. The movement had a powerful symbol in the imagery of *all* women living with the threat of rape, which was used to appeal to constituents. Although many of the early leaders are legendary within the movement for their dedication, none of them became known outside the movement along the lines of a Cesar Chavez or Martin Luther King, Jr. Concepts for analyzing leadership tend to focus on the individual, but collectivist feminists had a strong antipathy to glorifying individual leaders and some radical feminist groups (e.g., The Feminists and Redstockings collectives in New York City) had well-developed strategies for avoiding the creation of media stars. While too often women who were successful articulators were "trashed" for trying to be in the limelight (Echols 1989), the positive side of this stance was a commitment to democratize leadership skills. LACAAW, like many feminist groups, practiced a "buddy system" for speaking engagements in which a less experienced volunteer would accompany and help someone who was an old hand, in order to acquire the skill and confidence to do such tasks. The Pasadena hotline created a speakers' bureau that operated in a similar way.

The collectivist style in LACAAW

While the group was still located in the Westside Women's Center, LACAAW was coordinated informally by Barrie Levy, a social worker who got involved while doing an internship in community organizing, and then by Barbara Allen, one of the original Anti-Rape Squad members. Valerie Nordstrom, a costume maker who worked from her home, then took on the job, devoting extraordinary amounts of volunteer time to the work. Joan Robins recalls:

[T]he person who [was] coordinator . . . at that time ended up with all the [hotline] shifts. Whenever there was nobody to cover the line, they would cover the line. And whenever the counselors had a problem, they would call them. It was an enormous job.

Within a year, Joan Robins, who had been involved from the earliest anti-rape squad organizing, joined Valerie Nordstrom as co-director of LACAAW. This came about after they applied for and received a small grant for innovative crisis intervention programs from the California Department of Mental Health. Robins was to be the director of education and Nordstrom would direct the hotline. The selection of these two women as co-directors was practically automatic, since they had been working hard for free. Also, both women were basically self-employed, which made them available to do the work.

These decisions illuminate a series of contradictions which had been brewing in the organization. The untenable condition of having over-worked, uncompensated leaders led them to seek what they saw as a relatively benign form of state funding, in spite of being basically antagonistic to the state. Funding from mental health did not carry the same ideological baggage as law enforcement money. While having paid staff was a large step toward formalization, the manner in which the staff was chosen still reflected their informal, collectivist mode of operation. Furthermore, these women were available largely because they were not in the full-time traditional labor market, but working in a sort of alternative economy of self-employment and freelance work. This would change. Having grants would move the organization and its employees more into the economic mainstream. The worsening economy in the 1970s made surviving on very little income increasingly difficult. Also, the waning of the countercultural era and the aging of the activists meant that they were less willing to live on a pittance.

Robins and Nordstrom were a sympathetic pair who worked very well together. As in many collectives, the norms of friendship guided the development of work styles as much as any planned program. LACAAW's basic program outlines fell into place: one directed the hotline and the other directed education work, then the two figured out ways to fill in the details. The easy relationship between Joan and Valerie was productive in the early stages. However, the style of decision-making and leadership they developed became problematic as LACAAW grew, especially in 1976, when a large pool of funding increased the complexity of organizational structure.

In 1976 LACAAW dramatically expanded. Joining with a community mental health center, the group got a grant from the newly established National Center for the Prevention and Control of Rape, a new program of the National Institute for Mental Health (NIMH).[1] The $150,000 grant for community-based rape prevention education led to more structured work among a larger staff. Barrie Levy explains:

We really got structured, because it was a research and demonstration center . . . we had an obligation in terms of products that we had to develop, training manual, educational manual, and we had to evaluate, do an assessment and develop the programs and then evaluate them. So we went through kind of a formal process of development, using the expertise of the people at the Commission, building on what they were already doing in the way of educational presentations, testing what we were already doing, changing it, revising it, and developed a manual of educational presentations for adults and children.

The grassroots work LACAAW members had been doing was now cast as "expertise" and staff people were paid to share it. This was a new role for women who had aversions to authority and were suspicious of pretensions to expertise. In addition, the increase in staff numbers complicated the familiar informal work processes.

All of a sudden there were five new staff people at the Commission. You know Valerie and Joan had just been working it out on their own. They did as much work over phone calls in the middle of the night as they did anywhere else, and all of a sudden there was money for rent and there was an office to relate to, to take care of, to staff. . . . Everybody went into a major crisis. You know it's the kind of thing where you expect to be happy when you get your money and everybody's totally depressed, because the change was very hard.

The organization tried to maintain its commitment to being an egalitarian, participatory community, but faced the difficult process of integrating new members into a group (cf. Freeman 1975: 125ff) and fitting decision-making into a more complex matrix of relationships. They evolved a compromise that distinguished between minor day-to-day decisions and larger ones of policy and principle. Still, their experience echoes findings on the time-consuming and emotionally demanding decision-making process that is typical of collectives (Mansbridge 1973; Rothschild-Whitt 1979). As Barrie Levy recounts:

Well, we set ourselves up as a collective. Everybody made the same salary, everybody made decisions together, there were people who were not salaried people, but who were volunteers, who were actively involved. There was a whole process of trying to develop a decision-making process which included hotline volunteers as well as staff. It meant that every decision was agonizing. The major decisions had to be discussed at meetings of hotline volunteers as well as staff. So I think that eventually we did conduct a good portion of the business of running the hotline at staff meetings which we had every week, for the people who were on staff, and there all the time. And the major policies, the very major changes taking place in the Commission happened at membership meetings, or hotline volunteer meetings.

These years were rough ones, as the organization struggled through balancing a commitment to a collectivist structure and process with new requirements imposed by the other agencies with which it had chosen to work. The friendship ethic, with its assumption of shared values and concern for interpersonal ties, lost effectiveness. As a result, unexpected dilemmas that were not easily resolved through consensus-building and the tradition of informal decision-making began to create rifts in the organization. These came to a head later, when the structural and material circumstances changed again at the end of the NIMH grant. I will return to this later, but now turn to the contrasting styles of leadership and decision-making in Pasadena and East LA.

The professional network style in Pasadena

The Pasadena Rape Crisis Center-Hotline began in 1974 as a network of social service professionals in separate agencies coordinating their services, then evolved into a distinct organization with its own identity, located under the umbrella of the Pasadena YWCA. None of the other agencies had provided organized, direct services to rape victims before, so none had a particular claim on the project. Grace Hardgrove's determination to see the hotline succeed created a leadership role for her and led to the hotline being based at the YWCA under her directorship. Although the YWCA is an entirely appropriate setting for such a project (rape crisis services sponsored by YWCAs are common across the US), housing the Pasadena hotline there was not inevitable. Hospitals were by this time getting involved in providing rape crisis services and a major hospital was part of the network. But even in the context of established agencies, leadership was again largely voluntary, based on who was most motivated, determined, and willing to add to her workload. (At the time Hardgrove was also directing the YWCA's Big Sister Program and was acting as the resident clinical social worker.)

The women who formed the network that became the Pasadena hotline approached the work from a very different perspective than LACAAW members. Since they were not members of a close-knit organization, they did not have the same investment in creating new process, just a new service in a slightly different framework from the human service agencies in which they already worked. Many of them were social workers. Their political concerns were not so much with recasting rape as a form of oppression against women, but more conventional ones of keeping pressures on the right agencies to participate and provide good services to women who needed them. This was not a permanent situation; in later years the Pasadena hotline became more politicized in its definition of anti-rape work, but the early years were informed by a less critical social service outlook.

Working for the YWCA, Hardgrove was surrounded by women who were already working for women's causes. The women who ran the YWCA were what might be called "regular feminists." Many of the leaders at the YWCA were lesbians, although closeted, and clearly were sympathetic to many of the goals of women's liberation. I hesitate to label them in the terms that have since gained currency (e.g., radical, socialist, liberal, cultural) because these terms were not used by many women to identify themselves in an everyday sense, and it is thus misleading to apply them to women's activity at that time (cf. Jaggar 1983; Cott 1987). They may not have been in the forefront of developing new analyses of women's oppression, but working from the YWCA's woman-centered tradition, they were responsive to the spirit of the times. As a consequence of this environment at the YWCA, Hardgrove could break new ground and experienced few constraints from higher up. Answerable to both the executive director of the YWCA and to its board of directors, she was able to proceed with various actions without great hindrance, as long as it did not reflect badly on the YWCA:

> They have consistently agreed to have women in there who are only going to make waves, you know, but waves that wind up being very positive in the community. . . . And that's neat, but it could have gone the other way, so I think it has a lot to do with an organization, if there is an organization behind the program, and the stands that they choose.

Although she was formally answerable not only to the YWCA executive director, but also to its board of directors, Hardgrove also suggests that the way in which the hotline got started may have created more space for innovation and less supervision by the sponsor:

Because it was one of those things that just happened, it wasn't a planned program . . . they pretty much just left me to do what I wanted to do with it. And I think anything would have been okay, as long as they weren't getting flack from the community and I wasn't getting arrested or anything. Right? . . . But, I think I got away with a whole lot more than might have happened if it had been a very planned thing, where I was getting a lot of supervision. I think they might have been a lot more nervous about some of what we were doing.

Although she has the sense that the *ad hoc* nature of her work gave her surprising freedom, she reflects further, that the YWCA leadership were apparently genuinely interested in the program and made personal investments in it.

Although, I have to tell you that in the beginning, we had Y board members who wanted to go through that training. They sat through hour after hour of that grueling, terrifying, painful stuff that you go through in the training, because they wanted to know what we were doing – that was fine, but they just really wanted to know – and they wanted it for themselves, and that was neat. So I guess I can only say, whether it was from lack of knowledge, and in part probably it was in the beginning, or whether it was maybe not wanting to be as intimately involved as some of the rest of us were, but believing it was important to do, I had no complaint about that.

Hardgrove, being the only staff member in the early years, and without the encumbrance of a prior collectivist group, had a relatively easier time than LACAAW working out a style of leadership that suited her personally. She invested herself heavily in the project, sacrificing a great deal of personal freedom to run the hotline. For example, she did not delegate carrying the "beeper" to others, but was on call 24 hours a day for several years. This made her style of leadership an impossible model to follow.

Not having been actively involved in collectivist or much other organized feminism, Hardgrove's political consciousness was incipient during her early years as the hotline director. Her basic framework, out of her own background and structural position at the YWCA, was a social welfare model.

Cross-cutting styles in East Los Angeles

Like Pasadena, in its formative stage the East Los Angeles group drew on a network of professional women. The operation of the hotline became integrated into the founders' paid employment. However, while the Pasadena YWCA adopted the hotline as a program, the East Los Angeles Rape Hotline (East LA) had a more ambiguous relationship to the agency in which it was initially housed. Although dependent on resources such as office space and staff time from the County Center that Irene Mendez managed, it remained an independent organization with roots in community activism as well.

LACAAW had been a significant model for East Los Angeles, and many of the women who joined the hotline were also involved in Chicano or Chicana movement politics. So while they shared some of the professional characteristics and outlook of the women running the Pasadena service, they also had a strong social–political movement orientation. Because they were connected to the Chicano movement, their political concerns revolved around serving that ethnic community. In order to do that, they needed legitimacy with male Chicano leaders. The social work model was less threatening and divisive than the feminist political analysis of rape, so the East LA women leaned toward that, but it was combined with a strong current of political consciousness. Over time, some of the women there reconciled their Chicana ethnic politics with their views on gender issues to define a uniquely Chicana feminism.

After briefly operating as a collective, the organization adopted a more conventional structure in order to meet the legal requirements for non-profit status. Specifically, a board of directors had to be formed separately from the volunteers. As a result of their adopted structure, women who joined the East LA Rape Hotline were quickly catapulted into leadership positions. As an early leader recalls:

> [We] continued and became more sophisticated in recruitment of board members and trying to identify people who were going to have the skills that we needed to help the organization grow, and got to the point where we had a good 30 volunteers and about 15 board members, and they were two separate groups.

But, having adopted a more bureaucratic structure, the tension between participatory values and the authority of a board led to a rift between counselors and board members:

> The group really progressed pretty rapidly and began, in its organizational growth, to experience problems that are common, but again, we were not experienced enough in organizations to know that those are the kinds of things that we should have expected. There was a bit of a rift between the counselors and the board members, because

counselors, having started out as counselors and supporters of the organization, didn't understand the difference between the role of counselor and the role of a board member. . . . Counselors felt like they wanted to have a complete vote as individuals on the board . . . a big group of counselors dropped out of the organization. Primarily it was because, as the organization grew and the board changed from a collective perspective to the more traditional type of board, people had a real hard time accepting that and giving that much power to the board, and not having as much control or decision-making power as they had originally. You know, not being able to influence, or feeling like their views weren't being heard.

Their resolution was to have two counselor representatives serve on the board of directors in an attempt to manage that tension.

In addition to contention over the decision-making process, there were disagreements over organizational philosophy and policy, especially as they related to funding.

People had differences in philosophy about who you shouldn't accept funding from, for example Coors [Brewery]. That time was when the Chicano community was really active in boycotting a lot of companies. I think at that time, Coors had already offered the hotline money; Playboy Foundation offered the hotline money. . . . [T]he organization decided not to accept the funding from those groups, but there were some people who thought we should accept the money because you know, the intent was to support the organization.

In spite of having a formal structure, the work required to arrive at such decisions took a toll on the participants' energy. Indeed, though bureaucratic structure is supposed to alleviate some of the most inefficient aspects of collectivist process, the East LA group had a real mixture of these organizational styles: formal bureaucratic structure was mitigated by a membership with a short but powerful history of active participation in decision-making. Contreras points out that both culture and the political context favored participatory styles of decision-making:

Some of [East LA's early structure comes from] the cultural perspective. The culture operates more on a community philosophy . . . that people have a right to speak and to be heard, and a sense of community and working together toward a goal. . . . And the other thing that was happening in LA was people were real influenced by Saul Alinsky's style. We had the community service organization that was organized in East Los Angeles which was part of Saul

Alinsky's and Raza's approach to organizing [the] Latino community. A lot of organization was being done with the migrant workers, the farmworkers' union was organizing, and Chicanos were real conscious of supporting that.

Nevertheless, East LA reached a period of stalemate after the first several years of rapid growth. Differences in philosophy, and the continual need to address funding and personnel issues made some participants feel that the organization was not making progress. Contreras attributes the problems that arose to lack of new leadership on the board. [T]here was not enough of a rotation in the board members, so the original people who had been on the board obviously were going to have a real strong sense of ownership with the organization, and had some real problems because of old history . . . and not allowing the organization to move forward.

Contreras' perceptive analysis suggests that an oligarchical tendency led the group to a stalemate. The "sense of ownership" of the organization by long-term members combined with recurrent, unresolvable issues contributed to a crisis developing after the first several years of operation. I will come back to this event, which led to Contreras' return to the organization, in the next chapter.

Leadership and decision-making patterns thus varied among the organizations. Where leadership and organizational structure grew out of an egalitarian, activist relationship among participants, more conflict seemed to develop. Internal friction characterized both LACAAW and East LA, in spite of their differing structures. The East LA history points out that formal structures do not necessarily preclude conflict and even crises of leadership. Pasadena's relatively harmonious history stemmed from the fact that its arrangement from the beginning was more hierarchical and less political. Pasadena's founders were members of a professional network, but the volunteers they recruited were not, thus rank and file members in that organization were more socially removed from the leadership. In East LA many of the volunteers were professional women and activists, and thus were more assertive and concerned with participation.

In addition, Hardgrove's overall approach to organizing the inter-agency network, was oriented more toward *articulating* movement concerns to a larger community. The women of LACAAW and East LA were more oriented toward *mobilizing* active participants in the movement. This orientation, combined with the struggle to create a different style of organizational decision-making, while under the daily pressures of providing services, led to more friction.

RECRUITMENT AND TRAINING

Operating the hotlines was labor intensive work that required a large cast of highly committed activists. That fact exerted a profound influence over decisions within the organizations and set the stage for recruitment and training to occupy an important position in all three of the hotlines' ongoing work. New volunteers had to be recruited on a regular basis because, while many of the core group stayed involved and active for several years, there was turnover among the less involved advocates. By 1975 LACAAW was recruiting volunteers every few months through promotional radio spots and newspaper announcements, as well as through the feminist network of the Westside Women's Center. The East Los Angeles and Pasadena hotlines enlisted women by speaking to community groups and leaving flyers at the agencies where women did human service work.

Volunteering for the hotline involved extensive training from the beginning. Training sessions covered information on rape collected by the movement, pointers on dealing with the police and hospitals, and training to sensitize the prospective counselor/advocate to the needs of the caller. Early members who were social workers brought in models of crisis intervention from their field. Activists adapted and expanded upon materials from the Washington, D.C. and Bay Area anti-rape groups that addressed many of these issues, including a feminist analysis of rape. This excerpt from early LACAAW training material on "Counseling Guidelines" illustrates the way that political analysis was combined with counseling suggestions:

> The recognition that rape is a violent and vindictive attack on a woman by a man is necessary to having empathy and understanding in working with rape victims. It is important to realize that the victim has two equally important needs: access to factual information and concrete resources [and] access to someone who can help her deal with her intense and usually normal feelings about her experience.

This material goes on to list some of the feelings commonly experienced by rape victims, including anger, helplessness, guilt, uncleanliness, worthlessness, and isolation. Counselors were advised that active listening and focusing on her experience and feelings would be the most helpful. The emphasis was on acceptance, support, and giving the woman back control of her life:

> Give any specific information or referrals that are appropriate for the caller's needs, i.e. medical or legal aspects on which she can act

immediately. The woman has just been through an experience in which she was stripped of consent and control, so it is important that the counselor enable her to make her own decisions. Making the decisions can be an important step in reestablishing her self-esteem, taking control of her life again, and dispelling the feelings of helplessness. It is important that you, a counselor, let her know that you believe in her ability to make her own decisions about her life.

(LACAAW Counseling Guidelines)

Given the inherently disempowering experience of rape, training stressed the need to put women in control of their experience. This was at the core of the *empowerment* model of counseling that feminists consciously adopted, a practical reflection of the political roots of the project.

Training was intensive and incorporated the kind of consciousness-raising process that had become integral to the women's movement. A member of the East LA group describes the attention given to women's personal transformation as they went through the training process and the effects it had on their lives outside the movement:

[W]e went to training two times a week for about 4 or 5 weeks and [it] involved a lot of sensitivity training. We did a lot of dyads, a lot of role playing, a lot of information sharing, I guess you would call them consciousness-raising kinds of things about what rape really was. . . . The thing that I remember most about the training that I liked and that I have continued to use throughout the time that I've ever done training is giving people an opportunity to feedback. The sessions always opened with where a person was at, a kind of a check in . . . what they had done in processing the information that had been given to them in the previous session. What was the response of people that were involved with them, their significant others, their spouses, their boyfriends, their friends, males and females involved in their lives? You know, were they getting support, what kind of reactions were they getting, what kind of negative reactions were they getting, and how were they feeling about all this information that they were getting? We did a lot of role playing, and I think that was it basically, just information about what rape is, that societal impact, the historical kinds of things.

Not all of the women who became interested in working for the rape hotline were feminists. The training was designed as a form of political education, intended to build a common understanding of rape as a product of patriarchal society among women who came in with widely differing views. Some were already feminists looking for a place to act on that commitment, while others were interested in doing good for victims of a heinous crime. And many were somewhere in between, combining an interest in women's issues with a desire to do constructive volunteer work. The rigorous training that developed over the first few years of the hotlines provided the grounds for these women to work together, both drawing on some participants' previous beliefs and structuring a "conversion" experience for others (cf. Ferree and Miller 1985).

Training functioned in three ways for the organization:

1 It built membership commitment, screening out those who were not dedicated enough to make it through several weeks of training and who, by extension, might not meet their responsibilities for covering hotline shifts.
2 It created a solidary incentive for participation by providing a situation in which intense emotions were shared, that joined trainers and trainees in a common experience.
3 It produced, among those who participated, greater homogeneity of values, viewpoints, and skills necessary for being able to count on individual members to do their part.

Creating homogeneity was particularly important for LACAAW, which retained a collectivist form of organization. Collectives depend for stability upon their members working and thinking in a similar way, in order to provide the shared meanings that enable them to reach consensus (Rothschild-Whitt 1979). But the fact that this was important for the other organizations that were less collectivistic in structure suggests that it was also a function of the distinctive demands of the hotline work itself. These movement participants could not be just "paper members," as is often the case in professionalized social movements. They were committed to pulling their weight in the organization by taking their assigned shifts on the hotline and meeting the needs of callers in ways that required emotional work as well as just the dissemination of information. Although they could be more or less involved in the solidary life of the organization, the minimum level of participation was fairly high.

Expansion creates a contradiction for collectives. If they take on work that requires more than a small number of people, which the hotlines did, they need to recruit more people. People drawn in through friendship networks may be socially homogeneous, but may not be as ideologically committed as the founders of the movement are; others, recruited through mass publicity, may be outsiders on both accounts.

Thus the small numbers and homogeneity that make collective operation possible are lost. Extended training mitigates the problem of non-
homogeneous recruits. Since their beginning the hotlines have had fairly
long training compared to many groups – two months or more. A high
level of commitment was required in order to participate, and groups
also screened people out during this period. The extended training not
only gets people prepared to do the work (its ostensible purpose), but
also fosters commitment to the movement and creates the common
ground that might not naturally be there when drawing people into the
movement from diverse backgrounds. It does not just provide substantive expertise, but socializes members to organizational process and
ideology. Even the groups that had moved further away from a collective model were vulnerable to these problems; all of them needed
committed members in order to survive. After training, volunteers continued to meet in support groups and educational meetings, which
helped maintain that commitment.

"Burnout" is a common reaction among dedicated activists in any
movement, but in the anti-rape movement its onset appears to be acute
and rapid. Women who have experienced or observed burnout talk
about the weighty burden of doing the work, feeling like they are just
"putting a Bandaid on the problem" that is pervasive and insurmount-
able (Cashion, Pasadena Hotline). Many women stop being hotline
volunteers because they find it too frustrating. Hotlines tried to take
positive steps to manage burnout by providing opportunities to
volunteers to debrief regularly in small groups and occasionally having
more structured programs to address just that issue. Most of the hotlines
operated by asking for a minimum time period of commitment after
training (e.g., six months of service), but in addition to the natural
turnover in volunteers in a movement organization, the intensity of the
work led to women dropping out.

Though anti-rape work is meant to empower women, one unintended
consequence of work on hotlines appears to be a heightened fear of
sexual assault. The succession of crisis calls increases volunteers'
awareness of their own vulnerability. The anti-rape movement articulates a profound reality of women's lives in that women constantly
live with the fear of being raped. The movement was the first to point
out the myriad ways in which women rearrange their everyday lives in
order to avoid sexual assault. It provided additional safety suggestions
while also claiming women's right to be free of this fear. But being
confronted on a regular basis with the reality of women's vulnerability
is not empowering; instead it reminds many activists just how realistic

their fears are and heightens awareness to a level that can interfere with daily life. Another function of the regular meetings and support groups was to provide a place to address those fears. But several women told of periods during which they withdrew from the movement in order to get the distance and perspective they needed.

FUNDING

The five years between 1974 and 1979 were crucial ones in which the rape hotlines formalized their programs considerably. Finding resources to continue doing the work was a major impetus to formalization. At LACAAW, concern with meeting women's needs for a sympathetic space outside the system, and with pressuring the system to change, gave way to more organizational concerns. As the hotline became a routine service to be provided, there was more need for regular co-ordination. The leaders in the organization began to look for ways to pay someone to do this as a regular job. Each of the three organizations resolved the funding problem in different ways in the early years. Pasadena and East LA faced some of the same issues about funding as LACAAW did, but their different arrangments enabled them to resolve these issues more easily. The Pasadena hotline had a paid staff person who took primary responsibility for running it. Although she worked as hard as the volunteer leaders at LACAAW, the Pasadena hotline's founder was able to integrate supervising the hotline into her paid employment at the YWCA. In East LA Mendez worked out a variation on this approach. Her position as manager of a county-funded community center enabled her to locate the hotline there and supervise it from her workplace. LACAAW, on the other hand, did not have such an option available.

This raises a knotty problem about the character of women's unpaid work in social service organizations. Where does paid work end and voluntary activism begin? For both Hardgrove and Mendez there was a blurred line between their paid jobs and volunteer work. They certainly ended up working more than full-time for the same pay. The difference between them is that for Hardgrove, the extra work formally became part of her job, whereas for Mendez the situation was more ambiguous. Thus, what amounted to extraction of additional labor from these individuals benefited the movement. This became and remains a contradiction for people doing activist work. At the same time, the ability of professional women in these organizations to mobilize institutional resources for activist political projects signals an important aspect of women's social service work.

Rape had become a legitimate topic not only in the grassroots movement, but was being discussed at all levels of government. Feminist attention to rape coincided with increased concern about violent crime generally. "Law and order" anti-crime rhetoric focused on conviction rates, while feminists on many local fronts raised additional questions about getting cases into the system at all, and about help for victims of crime. It is not clear how conscious anti-rape feminists were of coopting the anti-crime rhetoric for their own ends, but funding services became a particular nexus for state involvement in the movement. Locally, the city had contributed funds to the movement in its embryonic days, but had not made a commitment of public resources to sustain the ongoing work. In 1978 and 1979 the California Department of Social Services provided limited funding under the rubric of crisis intervention. The establishment of the National Center for the Prevention and Control of Rape (NCPCR) as part of NIMH in 1975 brought a stream of money into movement-related projects. In addition, the federal Law Enforcement Assistance Administration began offering grants for rape crisis services in 1974.

Public funding, however, changed the terms of work for these organizations. East LA, for example, applied for the Department of Social Services grants available in 1978 and 1979. However, increasingly stringent demands on the organization accompanied the funding, as Contreras explains. Whereas ELA had previously provided whatever services they could, at their own discretion,

> When we started providing those services under the state funding, then we had to provide a whole lot of service for very little money. The first grant that we got was for $5,000 from the Department of Social Services, and then that went up to $10,000, but for the $5,000 we had to provide the 24 hour hotline coverage. . . . We were expected to provide advocacy, you know going out and meeting clients at the hospital or the police station and providing the crisis intervention. That was kind of implied and later on it became an actual requirement. And not only having to provide those services 24 hours a day, but also having to do community education. . . . A lot was expected for the very little money that we received. And we thought we were doing great to get a $5,000 grant, because all of our efforts to keep the hotline going were primarily small fundraising efforts, we never really did any major fundraising.

Although the small fundraising events East LA held in the community were well received, it did not go after major corporate funding. Like other groups, it turned down some corporate funding on political grounds; for example, it upheld the boycott of the Coors Company by the Chicano community.

The Playboy Foundation was the most visible aspiring corporate donor for women's groups during these years. Despite the need for money, the Los Angeles groups staunchly refused its offers. Some people felt that they could take the money and do good work with it, while others felt that the anti-rape movement would lose credibility and lend legitimacy to the Playboy Foundation by giving it the opportunity to boast about its alliances with feminist groups. Furthermore, many saw the exploitation of women in *Playboy* magazine as promoting the very violence that rape crisis groups were trying to eliminate. This became an official position of the Southern California Rape Hotline Alliance by 1979. The close relationship between the anti-rape and feminist anti-pornography movements, epitomized by Women Against Violence Against Women (WAVAW), bolstered support for this position.

The Law Enforcement Assistance Administration (LEAA), the funding branch of the Justice Department, began to sponsor research and reports that were critical of how the criminal justice system handled rape. As early as 1974 LEAA was offering funding to rape-related programs (Schecter 1982). However, the prevailing stance on the criminal justice system within the feminist anti-rape movement remained hostile. Politically oriented feminists had a theory of the state; they viewed law enforcement in particular as repressive. Because law enforcement and the courts had been an early target of feminist criticism, taking money from them was seen as cooptive, potentially tainting the anti-rape movement. Specifically, LEAA requirements conflicted with their approach to rape crisis work. As Schecter notes:

> Grassroots feminist groups provide the data and analyses to LEAA consultants but their work is neither acknowledged nor compensated; funding is given to criminal justice bureaucracies, not the anti-rape or battered women's movement groups who provide caring service and competent advocacy. The criminal justice bureaucracies, with a large funding base, gain legitimacy and take over "victims" services in their local areas, often providing victims with minimal service and no understanding of why they were raped or battered.
>
> (Schecter 1982: 185–6)

The LEAA's main purpose was to improve prosecution rates, and in offering funding to rape crisis groups, ignored the fact that that goal was not always compatible with rape crisis goals of helping the victim (Schecter 1982: 187).

In LACAAW the question of applying for LEAA funding led to the first split in the organization, as Barrie Levy recalls:

[T]he line [had been] going for about a year on a hand to mouth kind of basis, looking for and writing proposals to whoever we could find to write them to. We tried the city, and we tried foundations, but when it came to submitting a proposal to the Law Enforcement Assistance Administration, which was a very likely source of funds for us, the membership of the Commission divided right down the middle. . . . [W]e never did apply for that money, so the people who left must have been those who wanted to, and those who stayed were the ones who refused . . . [W]e saw ourselves as . . . an alternative to criminal justice system involvement for rape victims, because the criminal justice system was doing so badly, and . . . the issue was that if we took money from the criminal justice system then we would have to participate in that system. And in fact, most of the LEAA money had with it, as a requirement, the necessity that whatever victim uses the services make a report, a police report. And at that time we were advising women not to.

The critical stance feminist anti-rape activists held toward law enforcement was an obstacle to an "easy" source of money, and for many groups all over the country, taking this stand meant a more hand-to-mouth existence for years to come. Those groups that did accept LEAA funds gained considerable budgets.[2]

While LEAA money was controversial, in general government agencies were the most likely source of funding, so the issue of getting money to support the organization immediately began to turn on how they would relate to the state. Clear lines were drawn in the anti-rape movement about relating to the law enforcement and criminal justice systems. Most groups saw themselves as a feminist alternative to these systems. Less controversial was funding from apparently more benign sectors of the state, such as the mental health or social service agencies. Cooptation from this direction was more subtle, involving the imposition of bureaucratic requirements and promotion of a perspective requiring social service agency intervention rather than political action.

The story of LACAAW's search for funding and the changes it wrought in the organization provide insight into the dynamic between participants' beliefs about how things should be done, the need for resources to do the work, and unforeseen consequences of choices made in managing these tensions. Although these processes occurred in a different way in the other two organizations, LACAAW's transformation warrants extra attention because it eventually became the most powerful of the hotlines in the area, and because it represents an unusual case of long-term endurance for an originally collectivist group.

LACAAW's funding saga

In 1975 LACAAW succeeded in getting a small grant from the state Department of Social Services for innovative crisis intervention. Two members of the group became paid staff members for the first time, as described above. Meanwhile, Vivian Brown, director of the Didi Hirsch Community Mental Health Center (CMHC), had received a request for proposals from the newly established NIMH program in rape prevention, the National Center for the Prevention and Control of Rape (NCPCR), and contacted Barrie Levy, who had devoted considerable work to getting the hotline off the ground as part of a community organization internship for her M.S.W. degree in 1973. LACAAW and Didi Hirsch CMHC won a grant during the NCPCR's first funding cycle in 1976 for a jointly sponsored two-year project as a research and demonstration center on rape prevention education. Although the grant was earmarked for community education, in fact it ensured the survival of the hotline, since the same people were running both projects.

The $150,000 NIMH grant lasted from 1976 to 1978 and enabled LACAAW to increase the salaries of the two co-directors and hire additional staff, which led to dramatic changes in its internal organization and decision-making process. In addition to the transformation of work relations and decision-making processes, there were other new tasks that had to be undertaken. Having been incorporated into the social service grant economy the activists had to meet its requirements for accountability and conduct systematic assessments of need and impact. These requirements put pressure on the organization to formalize its basic approach to work, which proved to be a source of tension for the members. Counterculture activists who never thought they would be working "within the system" found themselves doing all kinds of routine bureaucratic chores in order to continue their activist work.

A further source of funding that exacerbated the structural and procedural changes in the organization was from the federal Comprehensive Education and Training Act (CETA) program. Many non-profit organizations gained workers they otherwise could not afford to pay, through CETA positions during this period. However, they did have to meet certain standards in order to qualify for the positions. Once LACAAW had become a formal entity with a budget from the NIMH grant, it was able to pursue CETA slots. Barrie Levy describes the disorientation that ensued.

> So here comes inexperienced people who are looking for a work experience and, under the requirements of the program, they [CETA] had a certain way of defining "work." It didn't match what we did as a grassroots organization. . . . [W]e were having to structure an employment experience for people who . . . got these jobs mostly, theoretically, because they needed that training. And that training was supposed to lead them into some mainstream of employment. And neither did most of the applicants that we got for these CETA positions have any notion of what this feminist business was all about. So we had to find someone who was eligible for the CETA funding who would work within this collective process and still comply with the requirements of the employment system the way CETA related to it, in other words, somebody had to be a supervisor, there *had* to be a boss. Somebody had to do the paperwork and sign off on this person's work, okay. Everybody who had been there before was doing it out of the dedication and commitment that comes out of being a feminist and wanting this service to take place.

This process graphically points up the contradiction between a collectivist and activist orientation to work and a bureaucratic one. Working as an activist collective required a basic shared commitment to the project. The inclusion of women who had no activist inclination and further were untrained workers, created chaos in the organization. Furthermore, the necessity of supervision, a hierarchical relationship, pressed the organization toward a more bureaucratic structure that conflicted with its previously collectivist process. Doing rape crisis work at this point lacked the routinized, predictable work patterns recognized by bureaucracies. Without routinized work, as Levy put it: "It was a given that you were going to work 'til you were dead! Didn't matter how many hours you got paid for, right?" This raises an underlying question that activist-workers continue to grapple with: What is the work? Is there a way to define the work that does not assume exhaustion and burnout are the measures of completion?

Identical resources can have different effects depending on how the organization receiving them is structured. The East LA hotline also used CETA workers, but they were brought in under the existing community center structure, and did not create such turmoil in the organization. Unlike LACAAW, the kind of environment required by CETA was in place at the community center: a bureaucratized structure with clearly delineated authority and expectations for work, as well as the necessary procedures for monitoring and keeping records of the work done.

After a series of CETA employees who did not stay, the LACAAW women finally found women who were interested in anti-rape work and could qualify as CETA workers. But this led to new problems; smoldering conflict erupted between the leaders from the grassroots days and newer paid staff who also had movement backgrounds. Leaders create not only a style, but also define their turf, and then protect it as the basis of their authority. A CETA-paid office worker who had anti-rape movement experience from another city began to encroach on the co-directors' turf.

Meanwhile, the NCPCR–NIMH grant, which by then served as the financial life-line for the hotline, was only for two years. Feminists in the movement were dissatisfied with the NCPCR's concentration on research and demonstration projects, and refusal to fund ongoing service provision. The grant foreshadowed that new money would have to be found to support the organization. LACAAW's directors began to look for other sources of funding, but nothing as substantial as the NIMH grant was available to support ongoing direct services.

Furthermore, tensions arose between the partners on the grant. The LACAAW women knew that the mental health center would go on whether the grant was renewed or not, whereas they were much more dependent on it for survival. Along with the apprehension over resources, there was a struggle over claims to expertise, with hotline staff feeling that their pioneering work would be coopted by more socially legitimate experts. As Barrie Levy put it:

> While we were all working very closely together, there was this kind of undercurrent of distrust between Didi Hirsch and LACAAW staff. It kept coming up in some of the same old ways that any grassroots movement experiences. The people on the Didi Hirsch staff were degreed people, the people at LACAAW were not . . . especially as the grant came close to ending, I think the people at LACAAW began to distrust that the people at Didi Hirsch would now be established and with their degree would go out into the world and do the work. . . . [The LACAAW women] using the term "para-professionals" as it was used in the mental health system would not have access to a livelihood doing this kind of work the way Didi Hirsch staff would. And who trained them, anyhow? Right? [There was] that anxiety about how you're going to get to keep doing the work that you're doing and going to be doing at the same time. So I

think that the volunteers and staff at LACAAW didn't trust that Didi
Hirsch wasn't just going to coopt LACAAW's efforts in developing
the program and go off and running with it and survive financially
and survive as an institution, and leave LACAAW in the dust.

In fact, these fears were justified, as the Didi Hirsch Community Mental
Health Center successfully applied for a new grant from the NCPCR the
year after their joint project with LACAAW, to establish a clearinghouse for information on rape that could be used by all of the hotlines in
Southern California.

In 1978 the second year of grant money ran out. Documents from the
organization's files suggest the story of the search for funds. There was
a proposal to the Domestic Violence Project, Inc. for a Regional Technical Assistance Center grant. For the first time an invitation to a
fundraising dinner at $100 a ticket appears – a fancy invitation clearly
aimed at an upper income constituency. But by December 1978 a flyer
appeared that was an "open letter to the women's community" pleading
for help. Part of the graphic contains the slogan: "To a rapist, there is no
such thing as separatism," hinting at sectarian, ideological conflict in the
movement. The letter states:

> We are the women of the LA Rape Hotline – we provide services
> to 400 women and kids in crisis every month. We support women
> during police and court procedures – we arrange medical care –
> we help women confront their attackers – we help women
> organize in their neighborhoods for protection – we teach self-
> defense – we talk to schools and community groups about sexism
> and violence towards women – we are available 24 hours a day,
> every day, to talk to any woman who needs a caring friend . . . but
> we may have to stop.
>
> For 3 years we have supported our services thru [sic] research
> projects but the grants have run out and there is no money available
> to pay for the services we provide. We need your support to stay open
> – we need $1,500 per month to pay our phone bill and rent.
>
> Please make a donation or a pledge right now – tell your friends
> about us – offer your time to raise money – *We need you* if we are
> to continue being here for women who need us.
>
> In loving struggle,
>
> the LA Rape Hotline

Conditions at the hotline rapidly deteriorated. The problems with money brought to the surface other dissension that had been plaguing the organization. Tensions between staff members erupted and a substantial turnover in leadership occurred for the first time since the organization's founding five and a half years earlier. Joan Robins had resigned earlier in 1978 after a painful confrontation with one of the new office staff members. In February 1979 Valerie Nordstrom also resigned in great bitterness. Almut Fleck Poole and Cathy Barber (who had been working with the Pasadena hotline) took on the work of directing the floundering organization. They sought media coverage to try to garner public support. A January 1979 newspaper article addresses why the funds were running out. One reason cited was the declining popularity of rape as an issue. Thus the organization faced one of the major contradictions of being funded by grants, whether state or otherwise: funders tend to seek out what is new and innovative. Seed money is more readily available than continuous funding for an ongoing service.

A crisis deepens

LACAAW's plight was not unique. Many of the rape crisis organizations found themselves in financial crises by 1979. The Southern California Rape Hotline Alliance, resurrected after a hiatus, increasingly focused its attention on the political fortunes of various state and federal bills that held the promise of future funding. The Pasadena YWCA announced that it no longer could support the rape crisis program, which would have to find other money or close down. East LA by then was funded by a modest Department of Social Services grant, but as noted above, it was not sufficient to support the services adequately. In the early months of 1979 the financial crisis was so severe that several groups in southern California announced that they could no longer afford their phone service, which was the focus of the hotline project. In March, the Southern California Rape Hotline Alliance held a press conference to inform the media and public about the crisis in funding:

> The message is that the Southern California area seems to be concerned about rape and providing services for victims and we are giving the service. But no one is providing funds for us to service and do a really competent job. We want everyone to begin to think about what it will be like if we all burn out, can't pay our phone bills, and can't provide the service.
>
> (Alliance Minutes March 10, 1979)

A local radio reporter from a popular station (KFWB) broadcast a very critical report, saying that the hotlines failed to give quality services. Members of the Alliance wrote numerous letters to her, and later to her supervisor, first trying to meet with her to correct her impressions of their work, then trying to acquire a copy of her broadcast so they could respond to specific errors they felt she had made.[3]

> Alliance members who have been able to reach you have advised you of the errors in your reports and the obvious disservice the repetition of those errors has done to the reputations of our agencies in the community. Since these attempts at clarification, we have observed no change in the tenor of your reporting, nor any good faith attempts to provide a balanced view of a many-sided situation.
>
> (Letter from C.J. Barber to Barbara Essensten July 17, 1979)

The materials in the Alliance files reflected important processes going on at that time. Many of the organizations were in the midst of a crisis, and struggling to survive. Their concern with how they were portrayed in the media was a matter both of protecting their reputation and maintaining their autonomy. Essensten's attacks occurred at a vulnerable time when the hotlines were trying to increase their legitimacy in the community and find reliable financial support. The appeal for public support thus backfired as a member of the media was able to use their weak position to argue against the grassroots provision of services.[4]

Several additional rape crisis centers located in hospitals were in operation in the city by this time. The Santa Monica Rape Treatment Center at Santa Monica Hospital was quickly gaining legitimacy for its professional "treatment" of rape victims, and was squeezing out some of the support for community-based programs.

Thus, 1979 was a turning point in the anti-rape movement. Survival on soft grant money had proven unreliable for the long haul. In LACAAW the collectivist spirit of running the organization had run aground on competition. The consensus about goals and strategies seemed to have evaporated for the time being. Somehow the work continued, but in a curtailed fashion. A flyer dated July 1979 proclaims: "reports of our death have been greatly exxagerated" (sic) and lists a new phone number. A list of counselors, dated November 1979, has 29 names on it. This crisis was a watershed event in the LACAAW's history, as it reconstituted itself with a different structure, and made the decision to apply for funding from the state law enforcement agency, the Office of Criminal Justice Planning. This new state funding quickly became the standard means of support for California rape crisis programs, a story I turn to in the next chapter.

RELATIONSHIPS WITH OTHER AGENCIES

While funding was essential for the movement to carry on its work, the heart of its project was to change society, something which takes place concretely not only through reaching individuals, but by building relationships with other agencies, organizations, and institutions that can help or hinder the changes sought. The anti-rape movement put pressure on a variety of institutions, including the mass media, corporations, government agencies, hospitals, and community groups. These relationships were important because the rape crisis centers' reputations affected whether they reached women and were able to intervene effectively on their behalf with other agencies that rape victims saw, whether they were listened to or taken seriously, and whether they were able to garner the legitimacy necessary to win funding (as is demonstrated by the problematic media coverage discussed above).

As Gornick, Burt, and Pittman point out, combining their social change goals with providing services puts rape crisis centers in an often precarious position:

> At the heart of the difficulty is the fact that the actual goals of centers, although often fluid and unstated, may include somewhat antithetical efforts. For instance, they may need to gain the cooperation of the hospitals, police and courts while criticizing the structures or procedures of these agencies. They also need to gain the trust of the community at large while challenging people's deeply held assumptions and beliefs concerning sexual assault and related issues.
>
> (Gornick, Burt and Pittman 1983: 1)

Relationships with the police and hospitals were important; the anti-rape movement saw itself as an alternative and supplement to the work of these institutions. Some activists were better at smooth relationships with these agencies than others. This was affected by centers' timing, ideology, the community, their institutional affiliation, and luck.

Police

The anti-rape movement's relationship with the police was ambiguous from the start. Women sought more effective intervention, while at the same time resisting the law enforcement definition of the problem of rape. Linda Gordon (1988) has pointed to a similar dynamic in the history of state intervention in family violence. From the beginning of the movement, the police represented the worst embodiment of the system women were trying to change. The memory of harsh police treatment of radical activists in the immediate past[5] and their notorious harassment and abuse of people of color meant that anti-rape activists saw the police as threats for reasons other than how they handled rape. Their mistreatment of women victims was only one more indication that they were the enemy.

Nevertheless, these were years of consciousness-raising among law enforcement officials. The Law Enforcement Assistance Administration was studying the problem of rape from the law enforcement perspective. For example, an LEAA study reported in the *Los Angeles Times* in 1978 focused on the difficulty of getting convictions in rape cases, which occurred in only one out of five cases. This consciousness may or may not have been trickling down to local officials, but the anti-rape movement was most concerned with how the cop on the street treated women who reported the crime.

Under pressure from RCCs, local police stations during these years began to offer training to officers, often provided by members of the hotlines, about rape and how to handle the victim sensitively. The East LA and Pasadena hotlines were fortunate to find members of the police force they could contact when rape victims calling the hotline reported mistreatment. Irene Mendez, founder of the East LA Rape Hotline, recalls:

> In the early days it wasn't too good. One person that helped us so much, in fact she's on our board, was a female police officer who was stationed at East LA. She used to do also our training session on police, . . . how it works and everything. We were just so lucky because she was so great. She helped us a *lot.*

Grace Hardgrove, founder of the Pasadena service, contrasts the situation there with LACAAW's experience in the city of Los Angeles:

> A lot of the organizations, agencies, people in Pasadena sure didn't want to hear what we had to say either, because they didn't want to deal with rape, you know. And they didn't want us fussing and they thought we were in the way a lot, you know, all the things that you run into in terms of resistance, but it wasn't the kind of thing that LACAAW experienced where they were literally seen as the enemy by the police department. So we had it a little easier.

Having an inside contact was helpful, but did not head off all problems. Cases of racist treatment were then and are now still common, especially in smaller jurisdictions of the county, as an East LA leader recounts:

There were some real obvious racist kinds of things happening where women weren't given due respect, weren't taken seriously when they tried to file a report, and that was due to racism, blatant racism. It was real interesting because a lot of times we didn't identify ourselves as volunteers or rape crisis counselors or advocates, and when we would first arrive at a police department we were ignored or treated rudely, and we'd let that happen, just to see how they would treat an ordinary citizen, and then when they'd find out who we were then we'd get a whole different treatment, you know. That only emphasized in our mind what kind of treatment people were getting if they went to law enforcement directly.

One tactic police used to intimidate Latinas was to question their immigration status, which created an additional obstacle for many of the women the hotline served. Adopting a different strategy from LACAAW, the East LA hotline tried to get women to exercise their rights by reporting the crime, as Mendez describes:

[O]ne of the important things, we could not get the undocumented to make a report. So, we had to make sure that if anybody did make a report, that they were not to be asked, we got that in writing, not to be asked about their status. It was illegal to do that, to ask anybody what their status was, but they were doing it anyway. You know, either they didn't want to make the report or it didn't sound like it was going to be a good one, so if you asked are you illegal, that would scare them away, and they would say, no, I don't want to do anything anyway. But we were trying to get them to make reports.

Because of the activism in East LA, racist treatment of Latina rape victims by police is better documented. The East Los Angeles hotline challenged the police practice of using Latina vulnerability to create obstacles to justice. Racism aimed at Black women was certainly also occurring, as it still does. The construction of Black women as strong, as sexual animals, and the related assumption, applied especially to poor Black women, that they are prostitutes, are sources of the skepticism which the police direct at Black women who attempt to bring sexual assault charges (*cf.* Hill Collins 1990; Frohmann 1991). During the period I am discussing here (1973–9), the predominantly Black communities of Los Angeles were the areas least served by rape crisis centers. Only in the mid 1980s did rape crisis centers rooted in South Central Los Angeles and other largely African-American communities appear. (See Chapter 7 for more discussion of this.)

In East Los Angeles the hotline had one sympathetic female contact in the police force. The Pasadena hotline established more formal access to the police. The multi-agency network out of which the hotline was founded included the police department. The monthly meetings of network representatives provided a forum in which the department could be held accountable for its shortcomings in front of other community agencies. Hardgrove explains Pasadena's situation:

[So you had a fairly positive relationship with the police, it sounds like, from the beginning?]
Yes and no. Well, okay. First of all it was neat to have a woman who was doing the sexual assault investigations . . . and to have a woman police officer who was sensitive, who hadn't been so hardened, you know, by being one of the few women in a police department, who felt she had to become a, you know, junior male or whatever, to be in the network, but was a really very caring, very sensitive woman who definitely was law enforcement all the way, but was very open to learning, to sharing, would go out of her way to come and do our training, and was certainly not adverse to calling in our advocates if she needed them. Unfortunately she didn't remain sexual assault investigator. They "promoted" her to something, forgery? I don't know! And we had a series of men in there as sexual assault investigators who probably knew the police part of it, but hadn't the faintest idea about anything else and were, you know, somewhat antagonistic. Would sort of: we'll give the girls a little, tongue in cheek, they would go along with us. . . . We were convinced we were going to continue to do this cross-training, right? Because maybe they'd get educated. Some of them were so bad, so bad, that I could see the volunteers getting ready to just slit their throats before they left because some of the attitudes were terrible.

Hardgrove felt, on the whole, that even those police who were resistant initially were forced to modify their thinking somewhat during these years of activism. She attributes this in part to the greater feeling of community that accompanies Pasadena's relatively small size, especially in comparison with Los Angeles. Therefore the Pasadena police felt more accountable to the community than the more anonymous and fragmented LAPD. The network the hotline worked through was politically powerful, including influential institutions such as Huntington Hospital, and this acted as an incentive to get the police to behave responsibly.

Police representatives did part of the volunteer training for the hotline and the hotline used their network arrangement to be able to get into the local police station:

We went to roll call, for two or three days straight, at like 5, 6, 7 in the morning, and we would all go. Haven House [the battered women's shelter] went, we went, Pasadena Mental Health went, this woman who knew about incest went. All we did was talk maybe three or four minutes apiece, but we got all the line officers to think "This is what we can do." And if you run into a situation like this, here's our phone number. At least give this card to somebody. And we had little crisis cards printed up with all the interlinking agencies' phone numbers on it. So the police department allowing us in to do that and really feeling that they wanted to cooperate in some way, you know, was pretty good.

Rape crisis centers remained concerned with reaching the officers on the street – the ones most likely to come into contact with women victims. The movement had won the right for rape victims to be able to speak to a female officer, but because there were so few women police officers, even this was not always feasible. Nor was the presence of a female officer a guarantee of sensitivity, according to East LA's Contreras. So it remained important for the advocates to know how to handle the situation, as Mendez put it:

So we got to teaching our volunteers, that if somebody complained or said a cross word or anything to any of our survivors . . . we had little sessions on how to talk to a desk captain, and don't talk to anybody else, and that kind of thing. . . .

During these years groups had to hammer out a relationship with an agency that was often hostile toward them and that they viewed with warranted suspicion. Contreras discussed the dilemma facing East LA:

One of the problems initially was . . . that we didn't know how to relate to the criminal justice system and how to deal with reporting and going through the system when we knew that the system was so bad and that women were going to get abused by the system. And yet wanting to encourage them . . . we wanted something to be done to the rapist in order to stop rape and kind of compromising and, you know, identifying women that we knew were going to be stronger, that were adamant that they wanted to prosecute, that they wanted to go through with that, and supporting them; and finding that even though there wasn't as great a conviction against the rapist as we would have liked, that just going through that process in a way was therapeutic for women. And even Chicana women, Latina women, who seemed to be so meek and so vulnerable and not very outspoken, were willing to go through that and that empowered them, to have gone through that system and to have said, well, I've done everything that I could do and I did right and I was right, and that even though there wasn't a conviction that people believed them, they believed them enough to go through that system.

LACAAW had a different experience during these years. They continued to try to influence police but did not have the kind of set-up the other groups had. During most of these years they continued to take a stand of not encouraging women to report rapes to the police. They saw themselves as an alternative structure, and since what the police did was seen as monumentally ineffective, if not harmful, they had no reason to encourage reporting.

The size and complexity of the Los Angeles Police Department may have contributed to the kind of relationship that developed. Many of the women felt that they were treated with contempt when they did encounter the police in the course of supporting a woman through the criminal justice process. In such a large system, even if inroads were made at some stations with some police staff, the overall atmosphere in the Los Angeles police force was less supportive of the anti-rape movement's work than in Pasadena.

Hospitals

Hospitals were the other major institution that rape victims typically encountered, and were another focus of the movement's efforts. Unlike the mixed stance against reporting rape to the police, anti-rape groups often encouraged victims to get medical attention, because the risk of disease or pregnancy or the presence of injuries needing treatment usually made it in the woman's interest to do so. Feminist groups were critical of hospital treatment of rape survivors, but coped with this by preparing volunteers to be advocates for the women when accompanying them to the hospital. In general, hospitals were less intransigent than the police in responding to the rape crisis movement.

LACAAW apparently had little to do directly with hospitals during its early years. In 1976 they had a Medical Task Force working on collecting information about various health facilities as part of a funded project. The data they collected are instructive about LACAAW's orientation toward alternative institutions: they focus primarily on women's clinics rather than hospitals. For at least an influential segment of this organization, part of their vision as a movement was building a whole network outside the dominant institutions.

The Pasadena hotline had a good working relationship with Hunting-ton Hospital, which was an important member of the founding network. However, this relationship relied heavily on Hardgrove's personal commitment to it, and faltered when she left.

Women professionals in some hospitals, both nurses and social workers, became involved from inside those institutions in changing procedures for treating rape victims. Connie Destito was part of one such effort at the County/USC Medical Center Women's Hospital, where she and the director of nursing, Barbara Fletcher, created a new protocol for dealing with rape victims in the emergency room. In the process of setting this up, Destito got to know Irene Mendez, and they founded the East Los Angeles hotline.

Some hospitals set up their own in-house rape crisis services, often a result of someone on staff spearheading the effort. These varied, but tended to have a more medical–psychological, professionalized approach, not only in terms of organizational structure, but also in counseling staff. They were much less connected to grassroots efforts than the other hotlines. Their location in medical institutions has given these services legitimacy that was harder for the other organizations to gain. This has resulted in competition between some of the groups at times. The Santa Monica Rape Treatment Center is a well known example of a very professionalized agency that has used its status to undermine grassroots hotlines at times. Gail Abarbanel, its founder and director, has criticized the peer counseling approach still used by most of the hotlines, which rely on trained volunteers, rather than paid human service professionals, to provide direct services to women. Not all hospital-based services take such a position, however. For example, the rape crisis center at Cedars-Sinai Hospital has been an active member of the Southern California Rape Hotline Alliance, suggesting that it shares more common ground with the goals of the grassroots groups.

In its relationship with hospitals the anti-rape movement has worked to improve the treatment of rape survivors and legitimize the kinds of services rape crisis counselors provide. Negotiating with hospital bureaucracies in order to influence the kind of training that hospital staff receive on the subject of violence against women and to gain access for rape crisis counselors to the emergency rooms were the main focus of early work.[6]

Thus, successful relationships with external agencies like the police and hospitals were often dependent on establishing personal ties with sympathetic individuals within those agencies. When this happened, as for Pasadena and East Los Angeles, it paved the way for hotline volunteers to do their work with less interference. When individual incidents of mistreatment of survivors did occur, these organizations had a responsible liaison to advocate on their behalf, thus increasing the likelihood that such behavior would be corrected. Overall, it resulted in more respectful treatment of rape victims who needed medical attention or chose to report their assaults to the police.

CONCLUSION

The issues that confronted these three hotlines during their early years continue as part of their stories in later years. Their different conditions of founding affected their approaches to the practical problems of leadership, recruitment, fundraising, and relating to relevant agencies. Despite different original styles and perspectives, by the end of this period the three organizations were more similar than when they began. What explains the dynamics between the ongoing influence of their different origins and their increasing convergence? I have argued that while their origins exercised a powerful influence on how they approached issues, the demands of the work they were doing caused them to become more similar.

The necessity of funding and the requirements that began to be imposed by funding agencies (e.g., NIMH on LACAAW; the Department of Social Services on East LA), promoted similarity among organizations, in the form of incipient bureaucratic structures. All of the organizations became more formally structured during these years. The Pasadena hotline, already situated in a formal organization, became more integrated into the YWCA as an official program. East LA and LACAAW had more internal struggle with the process of formalization. While East LA adopted a semblance of bureaucratic structure more readily, those conventions collided with the vision of the organization's early activists and was no vaccine against contention within the group. LACAAW's need to mobilize sufficient resources to carry out the work gradually pushed it toward a more conventional structure. For LACAAW, it meant facing a basic disjuncture with its founding ideology and a painful struggle among participants.

The hotlines' relationships with their environment, increasingly the state funders, but also police and the medical establishment, were shaped by the willingness of those institutions to respond to the movement and the willingness of the movement to acquiesce to conventional modes of operating. Bureaucratization is a pervasive discourse that organizes social relations and presents an ideology of rationality

(Ferguson 1984; Smith 1990; Diamond 1992).[7] Emulating conventional structure enabled anti-rape organizations to "plug in" to state bureaucracies, gain access to dominant institutions, and enabled them to be seen as their legitimate auxiliaries.

The bureaucracy adopted was to some extent merely a veneer over more informal organizational practice, but nevertheless had an impact on these groups. The changes LACAAW went through in order to have the NCPCR–NIMH grant illustrate this. Bureaucratic procedures they were compelled to adopt, such as work supervision, had structural consequences because they could not easily be accomplished within the collectivist structure. Thus the rather halting process of bureaucratization was apparent when formal structure was superimposed onto actual practice, giving rise to contradictions in the organization, especially over leadership and decision-making processes, the heart of the collectivist critique of bureaucracy.

This was a period of state responsiveness, although state agencies often had different interests from the rape crisis groups, as in the case of the LEAA. Many members of rape crisis organizations felt there was sufficient fit between their goals and those of certain agencies, especially social services and mental health, to warrant the compromises necessary to acquire much-needed financial support for their projects. Others felt compelled to make the compromises in order to survive. The hotlines began to carve out a niche in the area of service provision, but with considerable ambivalence toward the state.

Although rape crisis services became a popular cause among the major funding bureaucracies for a while, by the end of the decade only small amounts of money were allocated for ongoing services, through the California Department of Social Services. Some organizations, including LACAAW, were still unwilling to meet the terms of that agency. Others, like East LA, were in the precarious position of relying on insufficient support. This situation, combined with unresolved internal organizational disputes led the rape hotlines into a crisis at the end of the 1970s, which I examine in the next chapter.

Chapter 5

The politics of crisis and a crisis of politics

Different ideological orientations and organizational structures in the Los Angeles anti-rape movement influenced how the organizations approached particular tasks and dilemmas during the early years of the movement. These hybrid organizations sometimes uneasily combined political work and service provision. The demands of the work chosen, relationships with outside agencies, and funding needs produced a trend toward a social service framework. Nevertheless, activists whose starting point was feminist politics resisted and interrupted the accompanying bureaucratization and depoliticization of rape.

The years 1979 and 1980 were a watershed for the anti-rape movement in Los Angeles. After several years of growth, during which they carved out a niche for their organizations, many anti-rape groups were in danger of folding. What was the source of this crisis? How was it resolved? This period culminated in the establishment of regular funding for rape crisis work administered through the California Office of Criminal Justice Planning, but before that happened two of the three hotlines in Los Angeles went through major organizational overhauls.

Movements constantly confront internal and external contingencies which affect their course (Turner and Killian 1987). Some progress through stages leading toward institutionalization while others are impeded or altered by these contingencies. By 1979 the rape hotlines had defined a mission and achieved some legitimacy for their work, which gained them a small niche in the network of agencies their constituents encountered. Zald and Ash (1966) proposed that movements in such circumstances are most susceptible to the "iron law of oligarchy," the conservatizing influence of leaders who have a stake in maintaining their positions of power in organizations. This may indeed occur if there are resources leaders can control, but the rape hotlines in southern California had no material resources, which led to a deep crisis and the possibility of failure.

How then did organizations in the movement avoid complete collapse? Although all the organizations experienced a financial crunch, the prospect of new sources of funding on the horizon kept the faltering movement alive. Hope is a powerful mobilizer in social movements, especially when victory appears imminent, and influences organizational dynamics (*cf.* Turner and Killian 1987). The successful organizing of the first few years provided the grounding for members' optimism that they could go on, despite the current struggles. One indication of this was the reconstitution of the Southern California Rape Hotline Alliance in 1979.

How did the hotlines respond to the crisis? The severity of the problems varied among the organizations in this study; they were most severe in LACAAW and East Los Angeles, both of which came close to folding, and milder in Pasadena. In both the former groups new leadership stepped in during the crisis, in both cases women with strategic insider–outsider positions. Although the Pasadena situation was different, its leadership was significant regionally in reviving the Alliance. Accompanying the new leadership was a restructuring, and a process of redefining goals and ideology. The organizations tapped the social service agency framework more heavily in order to become viable again. Thus, it was not entrenched leaders that instituted more conservative goals, but new ones, motivated by their commitment that the movement's work should continue, who were willing to compromise in order to achieve that goal. Compromise entailed relating to the community in a different way, and significantly, establishing a new relationship to the state that transformed the movement.

A further event occurred that is emblematic of processes and tensions in the movement. In 1980 a new hotline was started, the San Fernando Valley Rape Crisis Service, which sprang from two sources, a group of radical feminists and a Community Mental Health Center. Thus, even in the midst of a crisis, new groups were being formed, this one initially funded by the Department of Social Services. The Valley group, however, became the strongest feminist voice of dissent; as other groups began to accommodate to the requirements of funding, they chose not to apply for state money and operated as a collective.

Tensions between ideologies of feminist politics and social service provision, and different organizational principles of collectivist versus bureaucratic structure continued to be significant features of the debates and decisions within organizations during this period of 1979 to 1981. This chapter follows the processes of internal and external dialogue through three interrelated sets of events. I begin with the re-establishment of the Southern California Rape Hotline Alliance, which occurred early in 1979. I then examine the crisis in individual hotlines and the founding of the new Valley hotline. These events set the stage for the next chapter, which covers the origins of the funding from the Office of Criminal Justice Planning and the effects it had on the anti-rape movement.

THE ALLIANCE

Despite their differing interpretations of anti-rape work, members of the various hotlines talked to each other. Zald and Ash (1966) proposed that coalitions are most likely to be formed when a goal seems within reach; when the costs of investing seem small compared to potential benefits. Although it seems ironic, therefore, that this coalition of anti-rape groups would come together in the midst of a general crisis in the movement, upon closer examination the Chinese ideogram that links crisis with opportunity seems pertinent.

The Southern California Rape Hotline Alliance, first organized in 1975, only became a solid vehicle for exchange of information, ideas, and support in 1979, when it was reorganized after a hiatus. Grace Hardgrove, the founder of the Pasadena hotline, had left the organization and then returned as director in early 1979. She was a prime mover in reconstituting the Alliance, as part of her work of rebuilding the networks that she felt were so valuable, which had been neglected in her absence. Besides bringing together over a dozen rape crisis centers in the southern California area, the Alliance was a vehicle for communicating with similar groups around the state and, to a lesser extent, nationally. Minutes of the Alliance meetings for this year document the pervasive problems facing various organizations. Funding was a central topic of every meeting. Fundraising for the Alliance itself was an unresolved issue brought up for months running and members shared information about various potential sources of funding for individual hotlines. They tracked legislative bills, both federal and state, that promised some potential source of money. They also explored raising funds by getting "consultation and education" grants from community mental health centers. They shared ideas and supported each other's fundraising efforts, from LACAAW's $100-a-plate dinner to a $2-a-head disco dance held by Women Against Sexual Assault (WASA, a small group operating in the South Bay area).

In 1979 the Didi Hirsch Community Mental Health Center received a three-year research and development grant to establish a clearinghouse on rape prevention and education. Some members of the Alliance were suspicious of the Didi Hirsch staff; they were perceived as having "ripped off" grassroots anti-rape activists in their previous relationship with LACAAW, which left lingering resentment of the established group. Despite this history, the clearinghouse became an active member of the Alliance, and some grassroots LACAAW activists worked closely with it. For example, Almut Fleck (Poole), a long-time LACAAW member, edited *The Delphi*, a newsletter published by the clearinghouse.

In addition to funding, issues of legitimacy dominated the Alliance. Members were concerned with formalizing the Alliance so that it could act as a credible, unified voice representing the movement. They worked at finding common stands on ideologically divisive issues, such as acceptable funding sources (e.g., refusing Playboy Foundation offers) and having men work on the hotlines, and on practical problems, such as a common fee schedule for speaking engagements so that groups would not "shop around" for the cheapest hotline to do a presentation. They began to discuss developing credentials for their members. This was an internal concern, but also prompted by legislation they were tracking that would have granted confidentiality privileges in court cases only to certified rape crisis counselors:

> Robbins SB 500 . . . currently stipulates 40 hours of training or on-job training for certification of counselors, with either the police department or the health department doing the certification. If we cannot demonstrate that we have our own standards for training, we may have them imposed on us if this part of the bill passes.
>
> (Alliance Minutes August 11, 1979)

The Alliance sponsored a statewide survey about hotline training standards, also collecting information about concerns such as retaining volunteers, changes in the types of volunteers attracted, and interest in a statewide conference.

Meanwhile, in northern California a rape crisis center in Yolo County began to think about holding a statewide conference, too. This conference took place in May 1980 under the auspices of the northern group, and led to the formation of the California State Coalition of Rape Crisis Centers (the Coalition). From this point on there were two parallel associations that Los Angeles area rape crisis centers participated in: the more local Southern California Rape Hotline Alliance (the Alliance) and the California State Coalition of Rape Crisis Centers (the Coalition). Although there was no formal relationship between the two groups, most of the Alliance were also members of the Coalition. The Coalition was initiated by political moderates in the anti-rape movement, which had consequences for the ways the Los Angeles groups related to it. Despite the trend away from radicalism in the Los Angeles movement, radical feminists were still sufficiently vocal to cause dissonance with the more moderate women of northern and central California. I will expand on this conflict in the next chapter, but here note its effect on the local Alliance: difficult contact and an uneasy coalition with more moderate women sparked a radical resistance against the conservatizing trend in the southern California anti-rape movement. In the contest over defining Coalition positions, feminists became outspoken, keeping that per- spective alive in the movement.

The Alliance addressed numerous other issues: mass media treatment of rape, the dissolution of training for district attorneys on sexual assault, support for related movement organizations (battered women, anti-pornography), and relating to the County Commission on the Status of Women, which revived a rape task force during this same period. The variety of issues and evident enthusiasm denote optimism about their ability as a group and as movement organizations to continue to make a difference. Nevertheless, several groups were simultaneously going through severe tests of their ability to survive through a becalmed period of scarce resources.

CRISIS IN THE MOVEMENT

A detailed account of the crisis and ensuing transformation in two of the hotlines, LACAAW and East Los Angeles, follows. The situations had several points in common: both organizations had to rethink their relationship with the communities in which they worked. For LACAAW this meant a complete restructuring; most significantly, forming an independent board of directors. East LA had to rebuild and use more effectively the structure they had, a board with political ties in the Chicano community. In both organizations new leaders emerged who were insiders because of having been involved in the hotline, but outsiders to the current conflict. This position, along with personal charisma, gave each of them a strategic advantage in pulling the organizations back together. Finally, the advent of Office of Criminal Justice Planning (OCJP) money in 1980 provided the material base for a successful revival of both groups, without which the other factors might have been insufficient.

LACAAW's crisis

After the NCPCR grant ran out in 1978, LACAAW spiralled downward within a matter of months. Part-time CETA funded positions kept a skeleton staff in place through the end of the year, but in the spring of 1979 the remaining volunteers were talking seriously about disbanding, as one participant describes:

> When that primary grant was up, and the organization saw that it wasn't going to get another one, there began to be a series of people that sort of came in with various lengths of success, because of philosophy and how much of a consensus model they were able to get from the group, and how organized they were. A lot of the issues came down to money – paying the rent, having materials run off, and paying for the phone – those were the three principle operating expenses of that time. And all the legalities of non-profit status at that time.

Although lack of money may have been the root of their problems, members of LACAAW continued to take a principled stand on where they would get funding. They objected to collecting crime statistics for state organizations: "Law enforcement continued to offer money, and Social Services also continued to offer, but then you'd have to have client statistics, so the group still decided even after all that, they'd rather disband than provide all that information."

In the face of a crisis, the already challenging process of decision-making by consensus became even more tortuous. The experience of consensus-model collectives suggests that such a process becomes most difficult when disputes arise that are unresolvable. Radical feminists adopted this style as a way of reclaiming a more feminine approach to dispute resolution that values communication over control, and concilia-tion over competition (*cf.* Gilligan 1982), although mixed gender groups have adopted the same principles (e.g., peace groups, Students for a Democratic Society) (Sale 1973). Its advantage is that it encourages more thorough examination of multi-faceted choices and more balanced participation by all members of a group. However, the advantages can be easily undermined by processes of alignment and power-broking in a small group. The consensus model provides little in the way of safety valves for making a decision when disagreements are intractable. It provides little room for respectful disagreement, much less unscrupu-lous pursuit of self-interest. Assuming that people always keep the best interests of the collective as their primary consideration, the only method for resolving disputes is to keep talking (*cf.* Rothschild-Whitt

1979 on time-consuming processes in collectives). The presence of friendship and its particular ethic in the group adds further weight to the political manipulation that develops in any group. Loyalties based on friendship get carried over into decision-making in the organization, subverting the goals of the process. In addition to alignments forming around particular issues or individuals, an individual's objections can prevent the entire group from taking action. In parliamentary terms it is as though each person has veto power.

Process often is taken for granted until something happens to disturb its smooth functioning. In LACAAW, there were fewer debates and discussions over process early in the organization's history than occurred later, as the process of making decisions and carrying out the organization's daily work broke down. Feminist process clearly became a focal point of energy during the period of great upheaval and infighting in 1978–9, made problematic because several of the organization's dilemmas were unresolvable through the normal consensus process.

Because of this, even the decision to disband was agonizing. During this process, Judy Ravitz, a volunteer who had deliberately avoided involvement in the group process (she took her hotline shift during the regular Monday night meetings), decided to become more involved because she felt that the service they provided was too important to let the organization flounder. In the summer of 1979 Ravitz made a proposal to the organization: she asked that she be allowed to become an unpaid director for six months, while she tried to restructure the organization. Her goal was to have a $50,000 operating budget within one year. If she was able to raise the money she was to be paid retroactively. The quotes in the remainder of this section are from Ravitz's account of the changes she instigated.

I wanted an external board of directors because it was impossible for one person to do it alone, there hadn't been a fulltime person since 1978.... Also ... I wanted to feel comfortable coming in as a person who had some credentials and might have to use those credentials to achieve the longevity of the organization. I didn't have a PhD, but I didn't want to feel apologetic because I had an MA or because I might have to write a grant in a little bit different style than was the traditional way of doing those grants, and I may have to go outside to get a professional typist so it looked a certain way, and I know I was saying things that hurt people, from the past, but I thought it was the only way I knew how to operate, and to achieve it. I mean I knew how to operate in that other style, but six months isn't a long time to take an organization that had $5,000 in debts and turn it around. And $5,000 wasn't a lot, but I also went to them with a projection that after the first year I wanted to have . . . a general operating [budget] of $50,000, and they thought I was crazy. How are you going to go from [where] you couldn't raise $5,000? I think they were raising annually, like $2,500 a year.

The remaining members agreed to Ravitz's proposal. Embedded in her proposal was a new direction for the organization. Frustrated by the problems of how process worked in the organization, Ravitz was also disturbed by the loose (and illegal) structure the organization employed, in which the board of directors needed for non-profit (and thus tax exempt) status was not an independent body as required by law, but instead was composed of volunteers.

Ravitz began work on five major goals:

1 to build an external board of directors;
2 to raise enough money to operate the organization with staff;
3 to improve the relationship of the Commission to law enforcement and hospitals;
4 to improve training;
5 to increase the prevention work they were doing.

LACAAW's transformation

As LACAAW entered its second period of rapid transformation, it became a more formalized and professionalized organization. The earlier encounter with pressures toward professionalization, when the organization received an NIMH grant jointly with a community mental health center, had certainly wrought changes, but those occurred in the context of resistance. It was handled by the original founding activists who held strongly anti-professional and egalitarian ideals. During this second transformation, many of those people had left the organization (some only temporarily). Ravitz aimed to maintain many of the egalitarian features of the organization – for example, her proposal stipulated that any additional staff hired would receive the same salary as her own. The thrust of the changes, however, was to help the organization survive by adopting the bureaucratic structure that would make it more attractive to conventional funding sources.

[A]sking for the external board of directors, that became the biggest stumbling block. It took the organization about two months to make the decision and, when they were all out of funds and half the people had left, the remaining people said yes. And so by the time I came in there were 17 volunteers left. With maybe 45 shifts a week, only 17 left. So what I thought I was coming into, I didn't really come into at all. I was counting on at least 30 shifts [being] picked up and people were doubling up and in some cases tripling, but I didn't think it would have the holes it did. When I came in, the first day, I spent the first six hours just taking shifts. That was the immediate need, just taking shifts, it wasn't a matter of organizing the Commission!

Again the demands of the hotline work shaped action. The nature of their work, this distinctive hybrid of politics and direct service provision, meant that, unlike other movement organizations, they could not stop to recoup and raise money.

In September 1979, a month after starting work, Ravitz held a breakfast meeting at a prestigious department store, Bullock's Wilshire, to recruit members for a board of directors. She had solicited help in compiling a guest list from the chair of a subcommittee on sexual assault set up by the Los Angeles County Commission on the Status of Women:

> I just went [from] one contact to another contact that I had in the academic world or friends, or just cold, and asked for available people that . . . they thought might serve on a board like this, but I wasn't looking for people with money . . . it was going to be a working board. . . . I saw it as a two step process. You get a working board to go out to get the money, the professionals, the right judge, the right religious person, the right education person. But I knew that it was going to take about a year to do it. . . . It was also a matter of trying to restructure, because I thought it was highly illegal that the treasurer and everybody was internal, and they were calling it a board and people weren't voting, but their names were being signed for non-profit status, and everything had lapsed in terms of forms, and all this county stuff. . . . So I wanted to get a group in who could sit down with me and make decisions that were fresh, they weren't a part of the old days, the old days were over in many ways. And that created some real early tension.

Ravitz was successful at the breakfast meeting, recruiting about 40 women who wanted to become involved (some, it turned out later, actually were more interested in becoming hotline counselors). The process of trying to align two dissonant frames is evident in Ravitz's account which follows.

[I]t was really wonderful, it was a group of very committed people, who were unlike anyone who had ever been on the Commission before. They were living in Brentwood, some of them had a lot of money, they had a lot of traditional ideas, and they were uncomfortable with the word feminism. Some of them had been assaulted besides, some of them had been significant others, some of them it was just they needed, they felt as women they needed to volunteer – a kind of United Way kind of thing. It was the most diverse group of people possible.

Ravitz proceeded to carry out a precarious juggling act, on the one hand raising the feminist consciousness of her new board, and on the other hand soothing the concerns of old volunteers, many of whom were uncomfortable with the kind of women who were on the board and their potential influence on the organization.

They needed training . . . quite different from everything that we were accustomed to, starting with feminism. Starting with why peer counseling, it was the "whys", real fundamental, it was also at the same time teaching us, because it was very much early on a we–them situation, because the board was so different from the rest of the volunteers. . . . Then it was "I don't know which side I'm on." I suddenly didn't have a side, I suddenly became the negotiator for two sides because I got to know the board members very well. My big thing was, you have a board member, you go out to lunch with them, the first week, I mean you get to know these people. And I certainly knew the other volunteers very well. Other volunteers felt uncomfortable with money, with clothing, with good cars and . . . the kind of aspirations that the board had for this other group. To have a place, an office, a real office, made a lot of people very uncomfortable. . . . It was a real hard juggling act.

Ravitz had the class background to be able to meet these new women on their ground. She came from an upper middle-class family and had taught at an exclusive international boarding school in Switzerland. Bringing her own cultural capital to the situation, the women she recruited for the board of directors were not alien to her, nor she to them. Nevertheless, accustomed to the political consciousness of hotline activists, she saw a great gap in the new board members' understanding of the feminist underpinnings of the rape crisis service they were preparing to oversee.

As diverse as the board was, I was so floored by the amount of what I thought of as primary education they needed – it wasn't issues, no one comes in knowing sexual assault, knowing the statistics, or what this whole idea was for a rape protocol, and all these new ideas for a revolutionary thing. No one knows that, but women were un-comfortable being in an all-women's place, and yet they liked it, but they didn't know quite how to say that to their husbands, so it was a lot of consciousness-raising for that group. And toning down a lot of what they wanted to superimpose on this other group, and they didn't mean to look at the volunteers as less than [they were], but in a way they couldn't help it because they . . . had never worked with volunteers, they had been very comfortable, most of them, on boards of directors before, and they had been treated a certain way in the past with all the other boards they had been on. But obviously something propelled them to be on this one.

Participation on the board was as demanding as working on the hotline, which is unusual for comparable philanthropic commitments. But Ravitz saw this as a way of legitimizing the board members to the long-time activists; in her words, "they had to prove themselves."

The anti-establishment legacy of the hotline activists contrasted with the sense of entitlement with which members of the board operated. The activists resisted embracing the system many of them had repudiated, as Ravitz explains:

You know how now you talk about "power breakfasts," and that was the kind of woman that was on that board, that was already familiar with those kinds of patterns, was ready to assume, so let's go talk to the chief of staff of this hospital. But I had another group that wasn't ready for those changes that quickly. So it was a lot educating and slowing one group down, and then going to another group and trying to get them to not be hostile to the changes in the organization, and to see that counseling was being improved, on a monthly basis. There were in-services [training] within the first three months I was there. I mandated, as much as this director was able to mandate, since nothing had ever been mandated to anybody ever before, that you had to have in-services, because what else are you going to do to bring up the level of training? So, counseling was improving, and it seemed like there was light at the end of the tunnel, but there were a lot of people that were still real uncomfortable with the direction that "they" were taking it. So there was a lot of time spent listening to how we could accommodate everybody, and whether it was even possible to accommodate everybody.
[Did the volunteers stay with their commitment?]

A lot of people I think developed personal loyalty to me, but they lost a lot of it along the way to the organization. They were used to making administrative decisions and now no longer needed to do that, because we had another group doing that, and also I was working fulltime and starting to do it, so they sort of became my council of elders. Because, again, my big thing is, don't lose anyone, just recycle them.

Ravitz's structural position was an advantage in piloting the organization in new directions. As both an insider and an outsider she was able to promote the values of the organization. As an experienced volunteer she had legitimacy with those who had also dedicated their time to the cause. But because she had avoided getting very involved in the internal politics of the organization, she was not associated strongly with any of the main factions.

Paradoxically the shift in loyalties Ravitz mentions involves more personalized relations in the context of increasing formalization. Usually we think of bureaucratization as involving less personalized relations among people working together, but during this transition it appears that members had to shift their loyalty from the group, which was changing and no longer fitted with their conception of what it was they were committed to, to an individual, who, while spearheading the changes, was also seen as working for a larger goal they still shared. Within several months she was able to draw back into the organization in some capacity about 50 of the volunteers who had left. Ravitz used some mixture of traditional authority, gained as a member of the collectivist group, and charismatic authority, exhibited through her extraordinary commitment to the organization during a crisis, to legitimize transition to more bureaucratic authority. This raises questions (unanswerable here) as to whether bureaucratization operates differently in women's organizations.

A small group of volunteers became a "council of elders" with whom Ravitz would hash out difficult questions before going to the volunteers or the board of directors, which eased the transition for the volunteers who were accustomed to having more power in the organization. Respecting the volunteers' process, she allowed for that in the timing of decision-making:

[S]o I would run things by the group, and then take it to the volunteers, part of it was just practical process. In fact I owed it to that group, it always took them longer to make decisions, because you know that whole model of process takes longer.

The volunteer group was thus able to maintain the format of consensus process, although the operation of the "council of elders" undermined one of the features of the ideal consensus model: that participants should have no hidden agendas. Ravitz in a sense took advantage of one of the hazards of collective structure – the tendency for behind-the-scenes alliances to form and influence process – and made it part of her leadership style. Transformation thus was managed gradually, without imposing a completely hierarchical, formalized process on the older members, who certainly would have resisted it.

Contentious issues which arose in the process of bringing the volunteers and board together reflected the process of formalization that was developing.

> When I first came in my title, I think, was coordinator, and then it became director because you had to have a director in order to get the grants, but it was supposed to be in name only. I remember going and saying I think we're going to have a problem. I don't feel like I'm an executive director, I don't like the title, I don't even want to become whatever that title means, but I think we're going to have to have it for a series of reasons. It probably took the group about two or three months to make a decision to use it in name only, before I even went to the board of directors to start a process that was like day and night different, in terms of motions and seconds and discussion and all of that.

Ravitz played the part of the reluctant professional with the hotline volunteers, hesitant to incorporate structures that would aggravate their sense of lost jurisdiction over the organization. The changes were made, however, and Ravitz became an executive director instead of a coordinator. Simultaneously she worked on teaching the more traditional board of directors a new approach, trying to narrow the gulf between the modes of operating used by the two groups: "[T]hat group was . . . learning too, in terms of how to reevaluate parliamentary procedure and do it along the lines that the women's movement was sort of outlining for a lot of organizations."

In the midst of juggling these factions, Ravitz also set about finding money for the Commission.

> The second month, the end of my 30 days, I'll never forget this, because we had no money, I wrote a letter to the [Department of Social Services] . . . outlining . . . why they needed to give us money . . . and I cc'ed [carbon copied] that letter to everyone I could think of in local and state government. . . . At that time the largest grant

that they were giving was $12,000. So you can imagine what they were expecting things to run on. . . . Basically that letter was just begging to get some money, and the Office of Criminal Justice Planning picked that letter up.

Ravitz's appeal for money to the state occurred at an opportune time. The California Department of Social Services had been giving small grants for rape crisis centers for two years. Law Enforcement Assistance Administration money that had been available was being phased out, but new legislation in the California Assembly had just created funding for rape crisis services and the agency assigned to administer the appropriation was the Office of Criminal Justice Planning.

The emergency grant, based merely on her letter, was for $25,000,which bailed LACAAW out and allowed them to develop regular trainings and an Advisory Board. Ravitz was "euphoric." She felt that:

If you really do have somebody working fulltime, this really will make a difference. And I felt that way for years within the organization. Things just kept rolling that way.

The process was not to remain so simple, as state money quickly presented the organization with dilemmas.

They gave another $25,000 6 months later, and there was a grant proposal for that one, but it was like I already knew we were going to get the money. But it was a hard one because that board . . . didn't really know anything about a grant process, they didn't know anything about accepting money. They also, for the first time, had to deal with, what are we going to do with statistics? Are we going to give them figures? How are we going to base our figures? It was a big process of negotiation.

Thus, after years of refusing to apply for federal law enforcement money, LACAAW was rescued by a new law enforcement source. I return to this later, but first turn to East LA's crisis.

Crisis and renewal in East Los Angeles

The East Los Angeles Rape Hotline also faced a major crisis in 1980, as Teresa Contreras describes below:

In 1980 the hotline was going to close. It had progressed rapidly the first three or four years and then after that it kind of stalemated and because of the differences in philosophy and not understanding organizational growth, not understanding that issues were going to surface again and again, because there're some things that are just never resolved – there are always going to be funding issues, personnel issues, philosophical differences. But some felt like we've been over this over and over, and we're not making any progress, and not really seeing that the organization really had made a lot of progress.

Unlike LACAAW, the East LA by then had funding from the Department of Social Services, the administration of which was transferred over to the Office of Criminal Justice Planning that year. However, these small grants barely paid for a director and phone bills, and so had to be supplemented with other fundraising efforts. Whereas LACAAW's crisis was precipitated partly by the loss of a large NIMH grant, the East LA hotline had never been able to secure such funding, despite its unique position as the only bilingual hotline in the country. As Contreras explains:

> [E]ssentially the hotline had operated on its own fundraising efforts. We applied for funding from the National Institute for Mental Health, but we didn't have the research background . . . to qualify for the funding. We had a good proposal, we had support from NIMH, and they encouraged us, but we didn't have the support of a research organization. If we would have connected with somebody at UCLA or USC to do some kind of research with the women that we were serving. . . . So in that way we lacked sophistication in connecting with that in order for us to get the funding.

Their orientation toward the Chicano community gave them a populist approach to fundraising, which prevented them from pursuing potential corporate donors.

> We had the support, which was real interesting, because when we did fundraisers, we had a lot of community support, and a lot of corporations that bought tickets for our fundraisers. But we never hit them up for larger contributions or ongoing contributions. . . . Like the gas company, ARCO, Bank of America, corporations that, at that time, were putting money into the community, and taking it out!

Burnout played a central part in bringing the organization to the brink of closing. Debating the same issues repeatedly, combined with the constant struggle to survive financially, took a toll. In addition, Contreras attributes the problem to entrenched leadership:

What happened is that there was not enough of a rotation in the board members, so the original people who had been on the board had a real strong sense of ownership with the organization, and had some real problems because of old history . . . and not allowing the organization to move forward. Some people wanted to keep the focus strictly on sexual assault, some people wanted to expand the organization.

Teresa Contreras had been an early volunteer with the hotline. Although not a member of the founding group, she had rapidly become a leader, president of the board of directors, within the first year of the hotline's existence. But she had left the organization in 1978, burnt out and moving on to other issues. But in 1980 she was in a position to take the necessary cut in pay and return to the faltering organization, as she recalls:

I heard that the hotline was ready to close and that they were looking for a director to try to see if they could revive it because there were enough people in the community who didn't want to see it die. So I decided, oh well, I'll try it, I'll go on and I'll try to work as the director and see what we can do to get through more support. We did at that point have funding from the Office of Criminal Justice Planning. . . . Prior to that it was funded through the state Department of Social Services and it was a $10,000 grant, and basically paid for the director . . . which is not a whole lot of money! But that was basically all the funding that we had.

Like Judy Ravitz in LACAAW, Contreras presided over a dying organization. With the small group of volunteers remaining, she began the process of rebuilding the organization:

[W]hen I went to work for the organization in 1980 we had the $16,000 grant from the OCJP and we were down to 8 volunteers, and I think we had about 3 or 4 board members that were kind of hanging in there. So we had to redevelop the board and recruit for volunteers and as the director of the hotline, I did it all. . . . I did everything, and I'm not trying to give myself any credit for that, but that's what it took, is that somebody was going to put all their time into re-developing the organization.

In addition to recruiting new volunteers and board members, Contreras tackled the long-term process of strengthening the organization's support base. She employed two basic strategies: learning to be more "political," and diversifying the organization's programs. Being political meant forging better relationships with other community leaders. Perhaps a legacy of the distinctive feminist approach that these women had developed was that they had remained on the margins of the Chicano community. While men were more involved in East LA than in other anti-rape groups, the women were protective of their organizational autonomy, as Destito explained:

> The whole issue is like, we want this to be our program, we want to run it, we started it. It was during the time of the movement, so there were a lot of things going on. . . . There was a whole range of feelings about it. There were some of us who were pretty open-minded, but still pretty territorial, and if you knew somebody, it was easier to make it okay than if you didn't know them and you just voted on a blanket rule.

As a result of their ambivalence about how involved to allow men to become in the organization, they had not pursued strong linkages with male Chicano community leaders. Consequently, they had support in the community, but it was mostly latent. As Contreras elaborates:

> [O]ne of the things that occurred with the organization was that nobody wanted to have to kiss up to people, nobody wanted to have to go and shake the hands of the politicians, nobody wanted to have to be involved in other organizations, nobody wanted to have to go to other fundraisers, other organizational events, and we found out that that's what you had to do, you had to make yourselves visible and you had to get out there and support what they were doing in order to get their support when you needed them. We had the support of our legislators, in the sense that if we applied for funding, they would always write letters of support for us, if there was a bill that we were wanting to get some support on, we would call them up. . . . You know, we had that much credibility with them, but we didn't recognize what that meant; we didn't recognize that as power for the organization, and I think that that was all part of a learning process.

Contreras set about to activate the support more effectively, especially to generate funding for the hotline.

The second change instituted was to diversify the kinds of services and programs the organization would operate. Zald and Ash (1966) suggest that successful movement organizations sometimes look for new work to do in order to preserve the organization, but this situation suggests something different. Diversification is a survival strategy for movement organizations working in a grant economy. This strategy was effective in the context of new funding being targeted for innovative programs or "hot" social issues. As Contreras explains:

By the time that I came on as the director we had learned that through trial and error and a lot of pain and loss for the organization. But the support was always still there. . . . So . . . we went around and went back to the people that had supported the organization and started trying to utilize their skills and their connections to generate support and funding for the organization again.

The ELA activists learned to apply for multiple grants by treating the components of their program separately:

We broke up our program into components . . . crisis intervention, prevention, and child services. And we applied for funding for the crisis intervention, the advocacy and . . . going to the hospitals to assist the victim, and to provide the immediate crisis telephone counseling, and some face to face counseling, and the prevention program, going out and doing education in the community and teaching people, teaching women self defense, and then the children's program, going out and doing education in the schools and in the high schools, regarding prevention of child abuse, child sexual abuse, and rape.

LACAAW and Pasadena also used the strategy of branching out to work on additional kinds of victimization, in order to survive. The rapid expansion into new areas of service provision is an effect of entry into what Grossman and Kramer (1985) call the "grants economy" in which service-providing non-profit organizations rely on external funding sources, largely the government (De Silva 1987). The scramble for funds shapes the kind of work organizations do as they try to anticipate funding agencies' interests and policies. Diversification gives organizations a broader base from which to keep their initial programs going; they can unofficially move resources around among programs if necessary. It also lends them increased visibility in their communities. But organizations dependent on these sources of funds also become necessarily more attuned to the bureaucratic and political system from which they emanate. This both politicizes and depoliticizes them. They are politicized in the liberal politics sense of becoming more aware and involved in the political process that governs where money goes. As Thomas and Meyer state, "The expansion of state jurisdiction – often through the establishment of citizen rights – *politicizes* society, including the educational system, the family, medical arrangements, religious ritual and ceremony, as well as economic exchange and technological expansion" (Thomas and Meyer 1984: 469, emphasis added). They are depoliticized in the radical sense of becoming "chiefly oriented to the provision of services" (Wilson 1983: 66). Two different uses of the term "politicization" are at work here, both applicable to the rape crisis movement. The movement became the subject of politics and lost its distinctive oppositional political stance through the state funding relationship.

In her study of rape crisis centers in California, De Silva (1987) found that state funding had little effect on the political ideology of rape crisis centers, but she did not consider professionalization and bureaucratization as elements of a more subtle ideological shift from an oppositional frame to a more accommodating one. It was the early collectivist feminists, working out of New Left roots, who were most concerned with process and structure as political issues. The fact that these processes are seen as political by a diminishing number of women in the movement represents a shift in the discourse about power.

While the broader women's movement critique of bureaucratic culture became less salient in the 1980s, some women clung to the commitment to create alternative organizations as an inseparable aspect of their work. The Valley rape hotline was founded by such women during the midst of other rape crisis groups' move away from these commitments.

FOUNDING OF THE VALLEY HOTLINE

Many of the grassroots anti-rape groups were in crisis in 1979 and 1980. Nevertheless, new groups continued to form. In Los Angeles the San Fernando Valley Rape Crisis Service was organized during 1979 and began operation in 1980. Its founding exemplifies the new conditions of the movement. It was jointly initiated by a grassroots group of radical feminists and a Community Mental Health Center, which got a Department of Social Services grant to run a hotline. Despite this genesis with state funding, the Valley hotline embodied the conflict between feminism and the state's definition of rape crisis work. Soon after it began, when funding administration transferred from the DSS to the OCJP, the Valley set itself apart from most other groups by choosing not to apply for funding. This decision had consequences not only for that group, but for the movement locally and statewide, because these women became a dissenting voice regarding demands the OCJP made of rape crisis centers. In both the Southern California Rape Hotline Alliance and the State Coalition of Rape Crisis Centers, women from the Valley hotline were vocal critics of OCJP and kept the feminist agenda of the movement visible.

The circumstances facing this new group differed markedly from those of earlier groups. Eight years of organizing had brought recognition to rape crisis work among mainstream social institutions, which provided a more hospitable environment. Previous work by anti-rape groups furnished a model for what had to be done, so that starting and running the service was not as experimental. The feminism that had been the guiding force behind the earliest efforts had changed significantly as well. The collectivist form of organization had declined in feminism and groups that adopted it became anachronistic.

Efforts from several quarters merged to form the new hotline. In the summer of 1979 a group of women attended a week-long retreat offered by Califia, a feminist educational collective. During the retreat women met in geographical groups to form networks that might go beyond the week of "feminist summer camp." Carol Nelson participated in a group from the San Fernando Valley:

> [T]here were maybe 10 or 11 women who were at Califia who lived in the Valley, who were meeting there each day during that week, and we wanted to continue to meet. In fact that was part of the goal of Califia, to have women go out from that experience, a real intense week of all kinds of political stuff, coming back to their own communities, their own geographic locations and continuing to meet together and spreading out what they did.

The Valley group accomplished this goal, meeting again later. Wanting an activist project to keep them together, a rape hotline was proposed. Carol Nelson knew from volunteering with the Suicide Prevention Hotline that the San Fernando Valley was an unserved area of Los Angeles and offered to investigate whether any other efforts were being made to start a rape hotline:

> I wasn't working outside my house at that time, my son was like two, and I said, well, I have some time, I'd be willing to do some of that investigation. And so that's what I did. And I started by calling a couple of hospitals.

A notable clue to the changes that had occurred during the previous decade is the fact that hospitals were the first place Nelson checked to see what was happening. A few hospitals by this time had become involved in sponsoring rape crisis services of their own, such as the Santa Monica Rape Treatment Center and the Cedars-Sinai service. The movement had gained enough legitimacy to be incorporated into the services of large institutions in some places, although these were not numerous. This was a change from the earlier era in which hospitals saw rape crisis workers as an interference in their procedures and the movement saw the medical establishment as a focal point for change in the treatment of rape victims.

Indeed Nelson discovered a pending rape crisis project through Northridge Hospital:

[T]here was a woman in the administration department who said that . . . somebody . . . had approached the hospital and the hospital might be willing to give a room or do something, but she knew that nothing was happening at that time, and she wasn't sure who that person was, and she said I'll have to get back to you, and this whole thing started happening. And she gave me the name of this woman . . . [who] had come from Tennessee . . . and she had worked for two years all by herself garnering support for getting a rape crisis center started, had talked to politicians and done all of that stuff, and after two years had burned herself to pieces. But in the meantime [she] had made a connection with the San Fernando Valley Community Mental Health Centers.

When Nelson contacted the Community Mental Health Centers (CMHC), she met Janeen Carlo, who had begun to pursue a grant from the Department of Social Services, which was then providing grants for rape crisis work. This application was pending when Nelson contacted them.

Although the Califia women bore some resemblance to the founders of LACAAW in being a group of activist feminists, the circumstances of their involvement in rape crisis work were very different. When the Califia women came onto the scene, a project was already in the works and, significantly, was being handled by an established social service agency. The project was already in the bureaucratic pipeline, having an agency sponsor and the possibility of state funding. The Califia women decided to wait and see what happened.

After several months a Department of Social Services grant for $5,267 came through to staff and run a 24-hour rape hotline. Carlo, knowing that the project would need volunteer staff to actually run it, called on the Califia group and other feminists to take it on. She welcomed the participation of the Califia group, in particular because their feminism provided the grounding for understanding the issue. Nelson recalls:

[S]he said, one of the things I know, because you are feminists, is that I'm not going to have to teach you about sexual assault, and, how many women do you think you could have come to a meeting and get this started in some way? I said, oh, I don't know, but let's try it out.

Carlo also recruited women from a feminist course taught by Marilyn Murphy, a feminist community activist, which overlapped with the Califia group. A group of about a dozen formed to start the hotline.

Part of the context of the early 1980s was the massive push by federal and state governments toward privatizing social services. In keeping with this trend, the county-run community mental health centers were sponsoring grassroots projects that were expected to become auto-nomous. The practice was to provide the start-up funding and staff support and then hand the project over to the volunteers. This Reaganesque philosophy ironically suited these feminists well because, although they were willing to work with the CMHC, the women who took on the rape hotline project saw themselves as an autonomous group with different goals from the mental health institution.

These women shared a radical feminist analysis of their project. Lynn Magnan-Donovan, a founding member of the group, poses their commitment in contrast to other feminist groups of the time:

> We wanted to service it in a way that was consistent with what some of us would call radical feminism, a much more critical approach than just kind of being bourgeois, liberal, egalitarian procedurally, because I think we realized there were hotlines that were, quote unquote, feminist oriented that were not as visionary as we like to think that we could be.

They saw doing anti-rape work as political activism, and this notion was central to their existence as a group. Their political orientation to the work might have created problems if the CMHC had wanted to maintain more control over the project. Carlo, however, acted as a bridge between the mental health bureaucracy and the group. As Nelson put it,

> We were talking "feminese" and they were talking agency mental health. . . . One time it took me half an hour just to debrief a meeting with those people, with Janeen [Carlo]. And fortunately she was, you know, she spoke both languages real well and could really act as intermediary sometimes, because that was needed.

The two languages Nelson refers to represent distinct cultures present in rape crisis work: mainstream organizations that process rape victims and feminist activists (Martin 1993). Bilingual women, such as Carlo, were important in linking these two cultures (Eisenstein 1991). Although it began with an apparently routine relationship to the social service agencies, not an oppositional one, the Valley hotline became an organization that crusaded for recapturing the radical roots of anti-rape work. Their imminent refusal of OCJP funding was a radical act of resistance at a time when most of the other groups were capitulating to the temptation of a stable source of financial support.

Surviving in a changed context

The Valley hotline had to work out the same issues that had confronted its predecessors in the anti-rape movement, but how it resolved them was affected by its timing. Organizing in the 1980s differed from the 1970s. First, feminism as a theoretical framework had changed. The perspectives that had been experimental and fluctuating in the 1970s had become more standardized and codified in the 1980s. The outlines of different feminist perspectives were more clearly visible, based on world views or theories of women's oppression, not just on style and structure (cf. Freeman 1975; Ferree and Hess 1985). Whereas the women of LACAAW's early days could be termed "collectivist" feminists, the women who founded the Valley hotline defined themselves as "radical" feminists (cf. Jaggar 1983).[1] That is, their brand of feminism could be defined not only in relation to structure, but ideologically, because the various theoretical and ideological points of view had been thought out, debated, and more clearly formulated. The group was more ideologically defined from its inception than the rape hotlines founded in the 1970s. They came together because of a common commitment to feminist activism, and then adopted anti-rape work as its vehicle. Having a clear ideological sense of their mission gave a certain coherence to the project, but it also meant that they were less flexible about practical issues that took precedence for other groups. Second, the Valley group built on the preceding decade of anti-rape organizing. How they handled training, their political analysis of rape, and their relationships with other agencies in the community were modeled on, or, just as importantly, formulated in contrast to, the ways older groups had worked out these tasks. This group did not have to invent a completely new kind of organization. Third, this group arrived on a volatile scene. The social service agency framework was ascendant and other groups were adapting to the crisis brought on by working with few material resources. With their fresh energy, the Valley women revived the feminist and collectivist orientation in the movement, even if only on the margins.

The Valley operated as a collective. The group was set up with no formal hierarchy, it was initially small (about a dozen), and made decisions by consensus. Thus, it swam against the tide, operating in a fashion other organizations, notably LACAAW, were abandoning. In this sense, the Valley hotline can be seen as a reaction to the trends in the rest of the local movement. Their disapproval of the direction in which they saw it going bolstered their commitment to collectivist, radical feminist approaches.

Leadership within a collective is problematic. The egalitarian principles that are the backbone of the structure mitigate against formal division of labor. The preference is for rotating tasks, but leadership emerges nevertheless. Nelson, who was at the center of the Valley hotline for its six years of existence, posits that leadership emerges around doing work. Some people are more involved in doing the work that has to get done, and doing work gives you power. In the Valley, Nelson gained initial power, whether intentionally or not, because she was more available to do important work for the organization than were other activists. Reminiscent of Robins and Nordstrom during LACAAW's early days, she was not employed and later was self-employed in a business she ran from her home. Thus she had the flexibility as well as the motivation to give a large portion of her time to getting the service set up and later to coordinating it. As Nelson explains:

[In] the original group . . . people were either in school or working fulltime, and for a while I was the only person who had that kind of time to devote to those kinds of things. And really, I was like totally committed from the minute I started. And was very excited about that work. You know, it was just so important to me, I couldn't believe it. When I look back on it now I understand more about what that was about, but I think I probably spent a good 6 or 8 hours a day, every day. It was like that was my job. And you know I didn't get paid anything. . . . I wasn't doing paid work here [at home] as I am now. . . . So I'd just go out and I'd do it, and I would meet with Janeen once a week to talk about, you know, where the service stood, and I just sort of, it just sort of happened. When it became clear that we were going to become an autonomous group, that we were not going to be under the aegis of the Community Mental Health Center, we began to have a group meeting where we would talk about what was happening, and all along we had, on a monthly basis, we'd had what we called staff meetings, just everybody coming to somebody's house, usually it was here, sometimes it was other places, most of the time it was here and that was because I had a little kid and it was real convenient for me not to have to deal with childcare or taking him somewhere else, because the meetings were always at night. And sometimes we called this place Nelson Hall, because it seemed like a lot of things happened here.

In many ways, Nelson acted in the same capacity that other hotlines were calling "director," but without that title. Eventually she was paid a small stipend for doing the paperwork involved ($100 per month). But most significantly, her position and experience gave her a lot of informal power within the organization. She was the only person who was involved in all of the trainings, which gave her disproportionate influence over how they were run and who was accepted into the organization. In later years factions developed around Nelson and other leaders who challenged her. The fact that no one else wanted to or could afford to take over the work that she did, and it was not an elected position, is a further example of the oligarchical tendencies that plague collectives (Freeman 1975).

The Valley did have a board of directors, because it helped in fundraising to be registered as a non-profit corporation, but this body had no real meaning within the organization. The board was selected by drawing names from among volunteers, but after the papers were filed, the "board" had no more significance. In contrast, at the same time LACAAW was working on making its board fit the legal criteria of being an independent and active section of the organization.

As the group grew during its first several years, problems began to emerge. The process that worked well among a dozen women did not function as effectively with 60. Not everyone wanted, or was able, to commit the time required for a true collective process. Discrepancies in the amount of work volunteers put in led to power differences. A core group emerged who ran the organization, but factions developed within it. Volunteer training was a central place where their political disagreements were played out.

The founding group shared a common grounding in feminist political education, since most of them had gone through Califia. The first training series focused on crisis intervention skills. Several women had useful backgrounds for training volunteers. Carlo was a mental health professional, Nelson had years of peer counseling experience, and Lynn Magnan-Donovan had clinical psychology training. Nelson recalls:

Our first training was four weeks and it was basically how to work with people in crisis. I already knew that from my work at Suicide Prevention Center and so there was some translating my experience, the clinical aspects of it, to the other people, and Janeen and I kind of worked as a team. . . . She had already got together a lot of resources and referrals and had done some of that kind of stuff.

The Valley training was similar to the other hotlines in covering basic peer counseling and crisis intervention. In designing their training they were able to draw on the resources and materials that the movement had been producing for nearly 10 years.

As the Valley hotline developed, its training came to focus more heavily on political consciousness-raising. While other hotlines, notably LACAAW, moved in the direction of improving the counseling skills of volunteers (this was one of Ravitz's main concerns as she took on the directorship), the Valley women focused on challenging the beliefs of trainees, as Magnan-Donovan explains:

> [O]ur agenda was not to give people a lot of clinical skills, which clearly was what a lot of other rape crisis services have focused on. . . . [E]verybody got what is the difference between open-ended questions and closed-ended questions, because I did all that, but I ran through that very quickly because . . . it's very easy to give that information in a very short period of time, the other stuff is more difficult. . . . There were women who came from a place of being well-intentioned, but also from a place of being male-identified, being system-identified, being do-gooder identified, being charitably oriented, volunteerism-identified, and all these things we were talking about were very uncomfortable for them. I mean, to talk about sexual intercourse as an oppressive modality in this society was very threatening obviously for a lot of heterosexual women who had never really thought about it at all.

A distinctive issue that became contentious in the Valley was having an inclusive versus exclusive orientation to new members. As I have argued in earlier chapters, the fact that an extended period of training is required for participation makes the anti-rape movement somewhat exclusive to begin with. But most of the other organizations used the training itself to do the main work of weeding out undesirable people. At the end of training, the volunteers were evaluated. All of the hotlines reserved the right to exclude trainees from working on the hotline, but it was used only in exceptional cases. In the Valley group this process became contentious. Some members felt that anyone who made it through the "feminist fire" of training (Magnan-Donovan) should be able to join, while others felt that exclusion on the basis of political consciousness was appropriate. A struggle between these factions developed over what the legitimate grounds were. As the group got larger, these problems were all the more difficult to solve, as Nelson explained:

We started out as a group of like 12 or 13 women and then grew to a group, on our roster at least, that was more than 60. And you can't do the same kind of dialoguing, you can't do the same kind of problem solving, you can't do the same kind of anything with that kind of a group. It was like, it just was impossible. It was impossible for us.
[Can I ask, in that process of growth, how were new members recruited?]
We didn't do any active recruiting. Towards the end, I'd say the last couple of years, we would put like little announcements in the paper. Where we'd put most of our announcements was in the *Lesbian News* ... we got a different kind of people. Like you put an announcement in the *Daily News* or the *L.A. Times*, and you get a certain kind of person, and I think again, retrospectively, I think a whole lot of things were happening at the same time, but that one of the splits that came up in the group was about what kind of people should be involved with the group. And there was a basic philosophy that this should be an open group for any woman that wants to do this work, and if she comes to the training and sticks it all out, she should be included in the group. There was another group of people who said, just because you come to the training doesn't mean that you are qualified to work with survivors, nor does it mean that you are politically aware enough, you know, whatever all of that means, to do this work and to be with this particular group of people. I was a member of that second group. I don't think that rape crisis work is for everybody, I don't think being involved with a feminist group is for everybody.

The reference "politically aware enough, you know, whatever that means" is a linguistic clue to the problem. The criteria for political consciousness cannot be easily articulated, and yet were considered germane by many for admission to the group. Such disagreements, added to the demanding nature of the work itself, took a toll. Burnout reduced the ranks of hotline members, which made the contentious process of recruitment and training constantly necessary. Eventually a stratified membership developed, with a hierarchy of active hotline volunteers and a second tier of "support people" who could no longer commit the amount of energy necessary for full participation.

As a result of its timing and the conditions under which it was started, the Valley hotline had immediate access to a network of agencies which, by the 1980s, had become more supportive of rape crisis services. The hospitals were already primed for their existence. In fact, Northridge Hospital in the San Fernando Valley had offered material support during the effort to organize a hotline before the Califia group arrived on the scene. There was not as much institutional resistance to the advocates accompanying rape survivors through the emergency room procedures as in the previous decade.

Nevertheless, relating to personnel in the hospitals was still difficult. Magnan-Donovan believes this is because medical staff, like others, go into denial in the face of another woman's trauma because it reminds them of their own vulnerability. As she explains: "The most critical element is . . . that woman is you. And some place you know that . . . in the back of their mind . . . This could be you! This *is* you!"

While this activist understood the problem as basically psychological, studies of routinized care, such as Diamond's (1992) study of nursing homes, offer other explanations. Depersonalization of services is part of the process of defining a client in such bureaucratically organized settings (Ferguson 1984).

Unlike many of the other groups, who by 1980 had established some liaison with the police, the Valley did not regard relations with the police as a priority. Their determined neutrality about whether women reported to the police was reminiscent of the firm political stand taken by the earliest feminist anti-rape groups a decade before. Nelson recounts:

[A] really fundamental thing to our group . . . that really reflected our politics, [was] that we would not encourage women to participate in the criminal justice system, that we did not see law enforcement as a viable system for women. That we didn't discourage women from participating in it, but neither did we encourage. And for women who did not want to participate in that system, *vis-à-vis* reporting and all of that, we would offer strong alternatives, and strong support. Which is really oftentimes what survivors need in the immediate and then ongoing for some time. Like all they hear about is the police and reporting and the courts and what they should have done, and why it wasn't okay what they did, which was not report. . . . You're doing what's right for you. Other people can't mandate for you, other people can't dictate to you, and really trying to underscore that decision, because it's strongly felt by every woman in that group that women had a right to do what they wanted to do. . . . That we're trying to come from as value-free a place as possible, so if she wanted to deal with the system, we were there for her. You know, we went all the way through the system with a woman, and didn't say boo about it. We would be there very strongly for her. Go to court, go to lineup, go to the D.A.'s office, whatever she needed, and never say "you shouldn't do this," none of that. Just absolutely be there.

They were also critical of rape crisis centers which had bought into the system and encouraged women to report rapes. In keeping with their critical stance toward all mainstream institutions, including psychotherapy, they were particularly disdainful of suggestions that reporting the crime was emotionally beneficial to the rape survivor.

So that from that perspective we were real different. I mean there are centers today who still say you need to report this, if you don't report it you're responsible – like all those old lines that you know, you're responsible for the next woman that he rapes. . . . And they really say that today, centers say that. . . . [S]ome . . . couch it in this wonderful therapeutic garbage, you know, like it will be good for you, it will give you closure.

The comparison and critique of other rape crisis centers was a frequent theme among the Valley women interviewed. Living up to their vision of what anti-rape work was about and how to do it was a central motivation for their activism. Willingness to do the work as unpaid volunteers was a litmus test for commitment. "Why are we here? What are we doing?" was a refrain Carol Nelson used to get back to the fundamental issue of changing women's lives, in contrast to those she saw making a career out of providing services. However, this poses a contradiction for feminists who are concerned about women's unpaid and underpaid labor. Feminist ideology becomes an unwitting ally of the state's push toward privatization, relying on women's nurturing work to take up the slack as it defunds social services. It plays into the hands of the state in whose interests it is to keep down costs of meeting social needs – suspicion of women who are paid for doing the work stops them from demanding higher pay, which then enables the state to pay low wages. In its effort to disengage from dominant culture and power relations, this view denies that rape crisis work is economically valuable work done by women.

The Valley group provided a service to the movement in being a dissenting voice, but also created conflict. In their zealous stand on funding, which I will discuss further in the next chapter, they treated the decisions made by other groups as a failure of will, not a product of their material conditions. In the end, the Valley group succumbed to their own crisis, closing down in 1986. They reached a period of crisis after about five years of operation, similar to the older groups. This suggests that there might be an internal rhythm to social movement organizations. Fresh energy is essential for a movement organization to grow. Factors that affect whether such an infusion occurs are related to broader social and historical processes that movement organizations cannot control, such as changes in the economy, the aging of an activist cohort, and the decline of broader societal support for radical ideas. Thus, the Valley's critique of the compromises made by other organizations were ideologically justifiable, but were not grounded in recognition of the broader processes at work.

When LACAAW and East LA reached a crisis point in which the organizations were collapsing under old leadership, new leaders who had strategic relationships to the organizations stepped in and took them in a new direction. As "social movement entrepreneurs" (Staggenborg 1988), Ravitz and Contreras took on some of the tasks previously performed by the group, and were able to do that effectively because they were not new to the organizations. Pasadena got a similar infusion of fresh energy when its old director returned after an absence. All of these leaders were pragmatic, while understanding the importance of the movement's ideology. Unlike the three older hotlines, the Valley hotline's ideological stance precluded the kind of transformation in structure and willingness to bend principle in order to survive, to which the other groups acceded.

The changes wrought by new leaders prepared the organizations for better integration into the established system of service provision and fundraising through government grants. They began to orient organizational changes toward the potential new sources of funding that were on the horizon. When the new funding appeared, it was from an unexpected source, the Office of Criminal Justice Planning, but the organizations were compelled by their dire situation and commitment to continue providing services to accept it.

These events and the movement decisions taken in response to them suggest that the possible danger of the crisis was not so much in losing rape crisis services, as a struggle over who would define and provide the services, and how they would be funded. As Ferree and Miller (1985: 48) put it, "Movements direct their efforts toward strengthening their position along *both* dimensions: achieving control over resources and over the way in which the issue is defined." Thus the resolution of the crisis hinged on the interaction between ideology, leadership, and material resources, all of which underwent change. A significant development during this period was the OCJP funding that came to be the financial life-blood of rape crisis services in California. In the next chapter I turn to the story of how this source of money came about.

Chapter 6

Politics and bureaucracy
OCJP funding

In 1979 the funding base of the anti-rape movement in California changed dramatically when new legislation created a regular source of funding for rape crisis centers through the California Office of Criminal Justice Planning (OCJP). Small grants had been available through the Department of Social Services a year before, but until this legislation there had been no commitment to ongoing funding. The new appropriation propelled many centers from shoestring operations to full-fledged social service agencies.

State funding for social movement organizations is inherently problematic if part of the movement's agenda is to change social and political relations. Many of the early politically-oriented, feminist anti-rape activists were cognizant of this, as they had an analysis of the state which focused on its repressive character, and were therefore dubious of funding from certain government agencies. Out of the movement itself, with its hybrid of politics and service, grew an increasingly prominent social service or therapeutic perspective, which often lacked this critical stance toward the state. Social welfare professionals involved in the movement contributed to this trend, as did the service nature of the work. The consequence of regular state funding was to consolidate this trend and institutionalize its definition of rape crisis work. The expansion of state jurisdiction is a taken-for-granted aspect of contemporary life (Thomas and Meyer 1984). In a period of less grassroots activism and more professionalized social movements (Tarrow 1988), activists became less concerned with the possibility of cooptation. The crisis in the movement also contributed to a redrawing of boundaries around how the issue was defined and with whom to cooperate (*cf.* Snow *et al.* 1986).

Gusfield (1982) and Wilson (1983) note the influence of social service professionals in orienting social problems to the state. "[T]he demands, the benefits, the rights, and even the 'minorities' being catered to all undergo redefinition. They are taken out of the political arena altogether and become medical, sociological, psychological, legal, or purely technical issues" (Wilson 1983: 64). Wilson analyzed how collective labor demands have been reframed as safer, individual claims by the state. The OCJP engaged in a comparable translation of the feminist understanding of rape as a collective social problem into an individual mental health problem to be ameliorated. Agents of the state, in the form of program directors, monitors and law enforcement officials, shifted from the traditional law enforcement view of the rape victim as a suspect/witness, to recognizing her "right" to services as a victim. Her plight was individual, however, not a symptom of a larger social problem, and certainly not "political," as feminists had argued. Thus, the radical edge of the movement's ideology was blunted through the subtle imposition of a new frame, often by way of routine bureaucratic practices, and only occasionally through open contention over political issues of control.

State funding for rape crisis services became institutionalized in a paradoxical context. California's tax revolt movement, Reagan's election, and the recession of the early 1980s all contributed to the contraction of social services. But this period saw the expansion of particular services for victims of crime. Quite divergent political streams have merged to support funding for rape crisis services. Begun under a liberal Democratic administration, rape crisis funding continued and expanded under the subsequent Republican ones, until California's deepening fiscal crisis of the early 1990s.

In this chapter I review earlier sources of government support that preceded OCJP funding and discuss the politics of the legislation that created the new program. I show how a contentious relationship grew between the OCJP and rape crisis centers in Los Angeles and discuss the sources of ongoing conflict. I highlight those conflicts that resulted in increased control over the definition of rape crisis work by the OCJP because these are evidence of the contradictory effects of a movement's success in winning state support. The State Coalition of Rape Crisis Centers was the forum in which many of the conflicts were played out.

PRIOR GOVERNMENT FUNDING OF RAPE CRISIS WORK

In their search for financial assistance, early rape crisis groups often approached local government first. When successful, these grants were usually small. LACAAW's genesis, for example, was aided by City Councilwoman Pat Russell, who engineered a $600 grant from the city.

The Washington, D.C. Rape Crisis Newsletter records this as a common practice. When the Bay Area Women Against Rape (BAWAR) group approached the city council there for a grant of $25,000 they were unsuccessful.

At the federal level, two kinds of agencies, mental health and law enforcement, were potential funding sources. In 1973 Congress passed a bill to establish a National Center for the Prevention and Control of Rape (NCPCR), which became part of the National Institute for Mental Health. The materials inserted into the Congressional Record in support of the bill, which was introduced by Senator Mathias of Maryland, include extensive findings based on work by a Maryland anti-rape group, suggesting that he was responding to an organized constituency in that state. In line with its mission and organizational location, the NCPCR acted primarily as a clearinghouse and grantor for research on addressing rape. This funding source had local significance because NCPCR supported LACAAW for two years, from 1976 to 1978, through the joint research and demonstration grant with the Didi Hirsch Community Mental Health Center. NCPCR also funded the clearing-house subsequently established at the Didi Hirsch CMHC from 1979 to 1982. From the point of view of the rape crisis centers, the most notable thing about federal mental health funding was that it did not generally provide ongoing funding for direct services to rape victims, focusing instead on research and education.

The second source of federal money was the Law Enforcement Assistance Administration. The LEAA provided block grants to state agencies, starting in the late 1960s. Early money was used primarily to fund law enforcement resources such as Special Weapons and Tactics (SWAT) teams, but in 1977 the federal agency shifted to funding more social programs related to crime, including rape crisis work. LEAA funding was so controversial in the anti-rape movement, that many organizations refused to apply for it, especially those with strong roots in feminist activism. LACAAW, for example, debated and rejected the prospect of being funded by a law enforcement agency. Like other politically-oriented groups, they viewed the state in general, and law enforcement in particular, as repressive and therefore an anathema to their goals. However, other organizations accepted LEAA funding, which gave them quite substantial budgets. For example, the rape crisis center in Yolo County (Davis) received $48,000 from the LEAA in 1978, the same year that LACAAW began its financial crisis.

The California Department of Social Services made small grants to rape crisis services for two years. In 1978 the agency granted a total of

$100,000 to 20 centers in the state, each receiving $5,000 and in 1979 that amount was doubled, so that each center received $10,000. With this funding spread so thinly across the state it did not contribute significantly to centers becoming institutionalized. It could make a difference to a basically all-volunteer organization by paying rent or phone bills, or a part-time staff person, but in itself was not sufficient to transform it into a professionally staffed agency. Nevertheless, groups still had to meet numerous requirements in order to obtain the grants. The funding was significant, however, in setting the political stage for involving the state government directly in funding rape crisis services.

THE OCJP SEXUAL ASSAULT PROGRAM

In 1979 State Senator Alan Robbins and Assemblywoman Maxine Waters, from Los Angeles, sponsored legislation (SB 862) that substantially increased the funding for rape crisis services and mandated ongoing support. The bill, which passed in 1980, created a three-branch program including support for direct services to rape victims through rape crisis centers; training for District Attorneys about rape, and training for law enforcement. The bill was accompanied by an appropriation from the state's General Fund of $412,000 and the $200,000 previously granted to the Department of Social Services was added to it, making a total rape crisis budget of $612,000. The new program was to be administered by the Office of Criminal Justice Planning.

The Office of Criminal Justice Planning was founded in 1968 to administer federal LEAA block grants, which were for improving the criminal justice system and providing victim services. The OCJP was to "identify local and statewide criminal justice problems and potential solutions, establish funding priorities, select grant recipients, disburse funds, and monitor grant projects" (OCJP *Sexual Assault Program Guidelines*: 1). After the LEAA funding was phased out in 1980, state legislation directed the OCJP to continue developing criminal justice programs. Many of these are replications of successful programs initially funded by LEAA (OCJP *Guidelines*: 1). The Sexual Assault Branch was created by the Waters legislation under Democratic Governor Jerry Brown, but programs proliferated during the Deukmejian administration, which came into office in 1983 (*California Legislature History* 1985–6). These programs relate to victim and witness services, child abuse, crime watch, battered women's shelters, as well as rape crisis. Some of these programs originated under the aegis of other departments, such as Health or Social Services, and were transferred to the OCJP during the 1980s (rape crisis centers in 1980, domestic violence centers in 1986).

The legislation establishing the OCJP's Sexual Assault Branch directed the formation of a State Advisory Committee (SAC) to advise the agency on developing and implementing its program. The bill mandated two significant features of the committee affecting its composition and jurisdiction.

First, six of the eleven members of the committee are chosen by the State Commission on the Status of Women, while the other five are chosen by the OCJP. The commission's appointments include a medical professional and a representative of a rape crisis center (OCJP *Guidelines*: 5). Maxine Waters, an African-American state assemblywoman from Los Angeles, co-sponsored the legislation. She also sat on the State Commission on the Status of Women and clearly influenced how the program was set up. The commission represents an officially sanctioned and therefore moderate feminism, and is subject to the political appointments system. Nevertheless, it represents the achievement of some recognition of women as members of the polity. Thus, having them select the majority of the SAC was a gesture toward affording feminist oversight of the OCJP program. It insured that women as an organized group had input. The OCJP-appointed members are drawn from the criminal justice system, including District Attorneys, public defenders, and law enforcement officials.

Second, in addition to its composition favoring representation of women, the State Advisory Committee was given unusual authority to make decisions on the grants OCJP was to administer. Marilyn (Strachan) Peterson, who became branch chief of the Sexual Assault Program at OCJP, explained how it worked:

> That particular advisory committee had more authority than most . . . at the OCJP, because the statute specifically said that they had the authority to select grants. . . . [M]ost advisory committees . . . can only recommend to the executive director of OCJP that something be funded and he can either follow that or not, you know. But they had the actual selection power.

This stipulation made the Sexual Assault Program significantly independent of the preferences of the director of OCJP, although it did not insulate it from political pressures. Its relative autonomy, combined with the directive about the composition of the SAC, however, insured that there would be broader representation in the funding decisions.

These arrangements suggest that feminism was beginning to have some impact in the traditional political arena, as sympathetic state leaders treated feminists as legitimate constituents. The movement's moderate representatives were elevated from the position of challengers to become members of the polity. But by coopting some of the demands and representatives of the movement, i.e., the State Commission on the Status of Women, other more radical elements of the feminist movement were marginalized. Their continuing criticisms and suspicions of the state then appeared to be unreasonable in light of the concessions made.

Early work of the OCJP's sexual assault branch

When the new program got underway in 1980 the OCJP recruited a former rape crisis center director to be the branch chief. Significantly, this person was from the more mainstream side of the movement, which by this time was geographically widespread, somewhat fragmented, and differentiated in terms of style and ideology. In some places, like Los Angeles, radical RCCs were going through major transformations. In other places more liberal feminist RCCs, funded by LEAA and Social Service Department grants, were already guided by a mainstream social service agency orientation. Peterson, the branch chief of the Sexual Assault Program at OCJP, came from the latter strand. She had been director of the Yolo County Rape Crisis Center for four years, coming to that from a background in social work and as a probation officer.

Yolo County includes the state capital, Sacramento, and the city of Davis, where there is a University of California campus, as well as smaller farming towns and rural areas. Peterson explains how she got the job at the rape crisis center and what drew her into it:

I had also worked in Colorado as a volunteer at a rape crisis center for about 6 months, so I think at that stage, in 1976, I was one of the few applicants that had some previous volunteer experience and they just seemed to think, as they put it, that I could "pull it off," and it was to establish a rape crisis center that would be accepted by, you know, the police department in that jurisdiction and so they were looking for someone that had specific skills. So it was a combination of some experience and some social work background, and I believe, as it was put to me, that I could "pull it off." And I was just interested in the subject area. That's what drew me to it.
[From your social work background or your political perspective or . . . ?]
No, it was more from the social work background. Well, I had generally become aware of women's issues when I was a probation

officer in the District of Columbia, because we worked with battered women and we were rotated once a month into what was called the Citizen's Complaint Center and that was where battered women came to file their complaints.

Once she became head of the OCJP's Sexual Assault Program, Peterson's social service orientation to the issue of rape became a source of friction in the movement. Her hiring seemed to represent the state's legitimation of that ideological position. Later, as conflicts arose between politically oriented feminists and social service proponents, her move and those of other women from rape crisis centers to the OCJP came to signify to the radical women in the movement the dangers of cooptation. Over the years, the fact that the OCJP tended to hire women who came from the politically moderate social service framework reinforced the perception that the state was trying to silence radicals. This magnified the schism between these strands in the movement, which was compounded in practice by the increasingly direct competition among rape crisis centers for funds from the state.

Initially Peterson's work involved identifying the rape crisis centers across the state. She had done much of the legwork for this during the previous year while trying to organize a statewide coalition of rape crisis centers.

[In] 1979, we had done so well at fundraising in Yolo County Rape Crisis Center that we had about $1,500 extra, which seemed like a lot in those days. . . . I had been to the first NCASA conference in 1979 in Wisconsin. NCASA is the National Coalition Against Sexual Assault, and they'd talked at that time about the importance of having statewide coalitions, so I talked to the staff . . . and said . . . why don't we use this $1,500, which was unrestricted funds, and have a state-wide meeting and see if people would be willing to participate and have a statewide organization. I learned later that there had been an attempt to do that some years prior, but it hadn't succeeded and I really don't know who was involved in that.

Proceeding cautiously, she found and contacted rape crisis centers around the state and solicited opinions about the idea of holding a conference and organizing a coalition. The Southern California Alliance of Rape Hotlines, many of whose Los Angeles members were trying to rebuild their organizations and survive, was also contemplating organizing such a conference, but were not in a position to get such a large undertaking off the ground. Minutes of an Alliance meeting indicate some friction over their lack of input into the conference Peterson organized. The meeting was held in Sacramento in May 1980 with Diana Russell,[1] as the keynote speaker. A formal statewide coalition structure was created there, with a board of directors representing five regions of the state, and a chair and vice-chair. Eventually members organized various caucuses, the most active of which included the Third World Women's Caucus and the Lesbian Caucus. The Los Angeles rape crisis groups were now members of two overlapping associations.

Division in the Coalition

Although the California State Coalition of Rape Crisis Centers is technically an independent organization, its historical relationship to the Office of Criminal Justice Planning Sexual Assault Program shaped its politics and role in the movement from the beginning. If funding has mediated the relationship between the OCJP and individual organizations, the Coalition has been the vehicle through which the OCJP has related to the movement as a whole. In turn, the movement has used the Coalition as a forum for strategizing about its own relationship to the OCJP and battling out ideological conflict within the movement, increasingly related to OCJP policies.

Coming together in the Coalition made visible the different strands that had emerged in the anti-rape movement in its first decade. Involvement of the state, with its power over funding, made those divisions volatile. The differences echoed the same struggles that individual organizations dealt with, either in disagreements between members, or in the transformations initiated by organizational crisis, as in LACAAW, but these were magnified at the state level. Ideological questions immediately arose: how strident and radically feminist should the Coalition or the movement be? How central is the feminist analysis of rape to actual rape crisis work? Should rape be seen as one symptom of a broader oppression of women? If so, how should that affect service provision? What were the most effective ways to promote the cause? Ideological differences confounded this question because the participants did not necessarily agree on what their cause was. Differences in ideology overlapped with differences in style, which affected everything from how to dress to how to promote rape crisis work in the community. Peterson, a self-described moderate, characterized the divisions:

> [S]ome people are more assertive, well, they're more feminist in their philosophy, they're more left-leaning feminists, in terms of what they think should be achieved and the methods that should be used to

achieve that. And they think that they are politically correct in how they feel about it and they don't think other people are politically correct if they don't hold those same views. . . . [T]here were certain centers that seem to demonstrate that more than others, like BAWAR in Berkeley, the Pasadena program in particular, which probably evidenced that more than others, maybe Project Sister. But they were never really a player, I would say that BAWAR and Pasadena were more the players.

What happened then is that if you had set up a rape crisis center that worked in the [San Joaquin] Valley, a rape crisis center that would work in Merced, or . . . Fresno, it was more moderate in terms of its philosophy and its approach. . . . [T]hey knew they had to be moderate to work in that community, otherwise they wouldn't be tolerated . . . and the women that were in those centers, they had very similar kinds of approaches and styles. . . . I felt that . . . we knew state of the art information . . . but we were willing to present it in different ways, do a lot of training, do a lot of talking, you know, dress according to community standards, you know, in terms of working with law enforcement. . . . See, when you're trying to espouse a different point of view, that can be threatening to people, and so what you want to avoid is allowing them to put you in some kind of box, and labeling you, put you up on the shelf, so they don't have to pay attention to you. Because if they can label you in some kind of way which is easily derogatory, then they don't have to pay attention to you any more. And so if you can avoid that phenomena, if you can be just kind of moderate in approaching it, eventually they come around to your point of view.

This pragmatic and "moderate" approach contrasted with the anti-establishment style of leaders who identified more strongly with radical feminism and whose approach was considered unnecessarily abrasive and alienating by the moderate women. Peterson and other moderates felt they could be more effective by working within the system, and saw the "left-leaning feminists" as undermining their own desire for change.

The moderates also felt under attack by the vigor with which the radicals would descend upon women with whom they disagreed. Peterson was very conscious and cautious about *how* she approached issues, not out of a commitment to feminist process, but because she had observed the consequences of defying its protocol:

Knowing the nature of rape crisis centers, you have to be very careful in how you organize things, because there gets to be power issues, they get kind of strange sometimes. . . . I didn't even want to make those basic assumptions that people would want to do [the Coalition conference]. Because, I don't know, it just seems like people in rape crisis centers are very, I don't know, unless your process is absolutely perfect, there's always going to be someone that really criticizes what you're doing, that there's something fundamentally wrong and then it's like you get off on the wrong track. So I wanted to make sure the process was good.

Concern with process was only one manifestation of the pressure to be "politically correct" that became a code word for maintaining ideological purity in the movement. It arose in other debates, such as how rape crisis centers should relate to law enforcement. To the moderate women who were not necessarily drawn to anti-rape work by profound feminist sentiments, being sanctioned for their differing opinions appeared incredibly hypocritical and intolerant, and caused some groups to withdraw from being active in the Coalition.

Disagreements rooted in ideology and style often manifested themselves as conflict between lesbians (and women who identified politically with them) and heterosexual women, to such an extent that the issues were inextricably linked. Many of the women leading the more radical organizations were "out" lesbians[2] who saw the issue of violence against women and suppression of lesbians as interrelated aspects of the problem of male domination. Peterson explained:

As I understood it, what the lesbians [were] trying to achieve was saying, "Look, you have to have a broader philosophical analysis or political analysis in terms of what's going on in our society, and you have to realize that rape is one form of oppression, and then there's oppression against lesbians and oppression against minorities, and so when we're trying to advance this cause, you know, we're supposed to be addressing all aspects of what's going on, because rape is just one symptom of this larger oppression, and so we should be addressing it all." And not everybody felt comfortable with that point of view, because a lot of people were there because they wanted to do something about rape *per se*, and they didn't like the idea of . . . the social problem of rape being used as a shield, so to speak, or a piece of armor to advance these other causes, and I think that was kind of the heart of it. Because then what was happening, the people who were lesbians then felt . . . they have different interpretations of the other women's attitudes. I think their interpretation was maybe they were homophobic. . . . [it] was that kind of intolerance that if you don't believe my way, there's something politically incorrect about you. I think there were dynamics that would go with the lesbians, and then they would feel their own sisters, as they would put it, were homophobic.

In a sense, Peterson's analysis that lesbians have "used" violence against women as a vehicle for political activism is accurate. However, the fact that she sees this as covert or manipulative only highlights the fundamental differences at work in political perspectives. From the radical standpoint that many of these women held, such work made complete sense. For politicized lesbians, violence against women is a concrete manifestation of the larger problem of male control of women's sexuality; it represents the extreme case of what Adrienne Rich (1980) has called "compulsory heterosexuality." Working in the anti-rape movement is a way of doing something concrete about these problematic gender relations. Like women of color who are often torn between organizing along lines of race or gender, lesbians often choose between broader gay issues or those that affect them as women. Lesbians also have found political mobilization difficult to accomplish on the issue of lesbian sexuality, so they often become active in causes related to more general issues of women's sexuality, such as pornography and teenage pregnancy (Nestle 1989).

Lesbians and other marginalized groups in the anti-rape movement formed internal caucuses in the Coalition. This organizing strategy occurs in the wider feminist and progressive movements where the problem of multiple identities and conflicting allegiances has arisen (cf. Leidner 1991). Caucuses serve as a power base for advancing the group's concerns with the larger movement, and equally important, they insure members the opportunity to discuss topics among themselves without the critical eye of outsiders upon them. Caucuses proliferated during the 1980s as feminists became more conscious of differences among women, based on race and ethnicity, sexual preference, disability, religion, and class. Their formation also plays a consciousness-raising role in a larger group, reminding it to keep diversity in mind. In the statewide Coalition, the Lesbian Caucus has been a substantial force because of its numbers and political acumen.

Tensions within the Coalition over lesbian issues and homophobia reflected conflicting definitions of rape. The radicals and lesbians found the moderates' wish to avoid questions of sexuality an affront to their holistic understanding of the problem, while the moderate women were offended that, as they saw it, lesbians were using the issue of rape to promote a completely separate cause. For the moderates, rape was just a specific "social problem," that is, a crime, not necessarily a symptom of problematic gender relations. What was at stake in these contested definitions of rape was the unresolved question of whether anti-rape work was a radical political project or an ameliorative social service program. The problem, of course, was that it was both.

The relationship between OCJP and the Coalition

Although the Coalition was organized in 1980 as an autonomous movement organization it had a close relationship with the OCJP from the beginning. Only a few months after Peterson was instrumental in forming the Coalition, she was hired to manage the new Sexual Assault Program at the OCJP. The Coalition, struggling to exist with virtually no resources (they instituted a modest dues structure), eventually became dependent on the OCJP to accomplish one of its main activities, which was to put on conferences annually. By 1982, Peterson had found a way for the OCJP to fund the Coalition conferences, taking whatever money could be found in the budget at the end of the year and awarding it to a center to put on the Coalition conference. But the content of the conferences became too controversial for the OCJP to fund. The 1984 conference culminated in a change of policy, which instituted more direct control by the OCJP.

The incident around the 1984 Coalition conference occurred in a context that had been building for several years. With the state Coalition dominated by moderates and geographically centered in the north, the Southern California Rape Hotline Alliance became a forum in which feminists in the Los Angeles area movement could sustain their opposition. (Carol Nelson, of the radical San Fernando Valley Rape Crisis Service, became its chair in 1984.)

Minutes of Alliance meetings contain frequent references to concerns about the OCJP's intentions. In 1982 the OCJP terminated funding to Santa Cruz Women Against Rape because they were "uncooperative" about reporting statistics on their callers. Several groups in the Alliance felt a strong historical connection to the Santa Cruz WAR group, which had been one of the earliest anti-rape groups in the state. This use of bureaucratic rules to control how RCCs operated prompted much discussion of "the compromises grass-roots organizations must make to receive government funds" and questioning "OCJP's commitment to grass-roots rape crisis centers" (Alliance Minutes May 8, 1982). Furthering the perception of interference, the OCJP audited the East Los

Angeles hotline that year. In 1983 Alliance members expressed concern about biases they perceived operating in the OCJP. The following entry describes the experience of an Alliance member at a meeting at which funding decisions were being made:

> Emilia [Bellone] shared her experience and perceptions of her attend-ance . . . at the OCJP technical advisory sub-committee. . . . She noted that she was the only committee member present from Southern California. OCJP staff had made their recommendations on programs to be funded . . . [which] served to foster a north–south split and regional antagonism . . . (a) She [Peterson] noted a problem with data collection, particularly apparent in Los Angeles County and the south. Programs could not adequately document an incidence rate. (b) She expressed her opinion that the quality, variety, and cost effectiveness of proposals was generally much better in the northern part of the state. These programs were said to have a better con-ception of prevention, a clearer model of a prevention program, and a better plan for networking. (c) She commented on the generally poor quality of minority programs. Their limitations, according to Marilyn, related to implementation and conceptualization. (Alliance Minutes March 12, 1983)

The Santa Cruz group had been defunded for not toeing the bureaucratic line and now the Southern California groups were being criticized for not meeting agency standards for data collection, program quality, cost effectiveness, and implementation. Suspicions abounded on both sides. Nevertheless, Alliance members were not completely disengaged from the OCJP. They submitted a position paper on funding allocation procedures in 1983, and in 1984 raised questions about what was happening to all the statistics they were providing to the state. But they did not have the close working relationship with Peterson that more moderate RCCs had.

Three incidents prompted the OCJP to change its policy of funding the conferences through rape crisis centers. The last Coalition con-ference funded by an OCJP grant (of $15,000) was organized by the Pasadena hotline in 1984. With Chris Olson as its director since 1981, the Pasadena hotline had moved away from its roots in the social welfare frame and had begun to identify with the radical political wing of the anti-rape movement. Like her predecessor, Olson was very involved in the Alliance. First, although the OCJP provided the material resources to put on the conference, the organizers neglected to invite members of the agency to participate in it, which was seen as poor professional protocol. Second, some of the conference content was seen as "bizarre" and inappropriate to a state-sponsored event. Third, conflict erupted over issues about "women-only space" that made more mainstream participants uncomfortable. Peterson's summary of the events, represents the mainstream reactions to them:

[T]his is what Pasadena did, they had this conference out in the woods in a national forest by Los Angeles, and this was the most money we'd ever given, $15,000, they didn't invite us to the thing. When we asked them about it they said, Oh, we didn't think you'd be interested in coming. And then it was just a big blowup at which everybody got real upset, where they didn't want to allow men there, and then there was this argument between some of the lesbians and some of the straights about different issues . . . but it was just a big incredible thing, that nobody would ever want anybody to know public money went for. I mean it was just this incredible thing around how people really behaved inappropriately at a conference that was funded by the state. It was just incredible. . . . It had to do with the lesbian women not wanting the men to go into the dance . . . just bizarre stuff. It was after that things were on pretty sticky ground with the Coalition. . . . That was a peak period . . . it was a big embarrassment. The rape crisis center directors themselves were embarrassed about what happened, because they had taken state money and then this thing had gone on the way it did . . . staff had experienced . . . behavior and intolerance, probably as blatant as you've ever seen exhibited by people, and people were embarrassed. . . . One of them had sent a brand new staff person there and they were just embarrassed that they had experienced it.

The situation put Peterson in an uncomfortable position because she had supported giving the Coalition a free hand, and felt responsible for what its members did. She identified herself as a member of the rape crisis movement, and had a stake in how it was seen, but was also concerned about political reactions in the OCJP.

I don't think anybody has ever wanted to talk about the fact that they took state money and did it. I didn't want to know about it, because I was always a proponent of giving the Coalition the money, so when I heard it was as bizarre as it was, I didn't want to talk about it either. I didn't want to talk about it within the agency, because then it would make the rape crisis people look strange and bizarre. So I didn't want to know . . . something about the dance and men, but then they had really strange workshop titles. I mean I also didn't want anybody to see the agenda. It was like we'd given the money and everything had worked pretty well over the years, but this agenda was really bizarre. . . . [O]ne of the titles was something about the "red moon rising" or something, it had to do [laughing], I'm not sure what the analogy was, but I mean, it wasn't something that you'd want to see the light of day. . . . [A]nd we funded that under the Republican administration! I sure didn't want anybody to ever see that agenda or ever really know what went on there, just because it came off so weird.

Although this event was such a watershed for Peterson in the OCJP's relationship to the movement, evidently the organizers did not perceive it as so significant. None mentioned it specifically to me during interviews; there is one mention of "debriefing" from the conference in Alliance minutes (October 13, 1984). However, after OCJP held its own conference two months later, which combined directors of Victim Witness programs and rape crisis centers, the Alliance members considered how to "resist this 'merger'" and scheduled a discussion of "California's longterm agenda for the anhilation [sic] of rape crisis centers" (Alliance Minutes December 8, 1984).

This event highlights the conflicts in the movement and with the state agency. Support for the rape crisis organizations was increasingly generous, as long as they fitted into a mode of operation that was acceptable to the state. The agency expected its protégés to be "professional" and not embarrassing, while activists strove to maintain their political autonomy. The division, however, was not just between the state and the activists, but also between those who were feminist activists and those who adopted the social service framework, those Peterson calls the "moderates." The contested issues at the conference had developed in the larger women's movement, too. Concern with women-only space was not merely a hostile exclusion of men (although certainly some women felt that way), but an effort to provide a safe environment in which women could develop themselves apart. It was considered especially important by radicals in the anti-violence movements, stemming from their analysis of the roots of violence against women, and the view that all men benefit from violence. This premise differed from the moderate view that separated "good" men, who should be welcomed into the movement and events, from "bad" ones who caused the problems.

Instead of terminating the funding for conferences after this episode, the OCJP began to sponsor the conferences directly. This was a significant step toward coopting the movement. The conferences had been initiated by the movement, and were the main forum in which members could communicate and coordinate their work. The move reflected the strong alignment of the moderate strand in the Coalition with the OCJP and professionalization of the movement from above. The OCJP conferences virtually excluded RCCs that were not funded by it from participating. Aimed at a professional audience, they were prohibitively expensive for movement activists to attend. Staff of funded organizations, on the other hand, were required to attend, with the cost written into their grants. RCCs not connected to the OCJP were also excluded by not getting the flow of information that now connected other groups.

While producing the conferences itself gave the agency greater control over content, tensions continued to arise over similar issues, as activists chafed under new OCJP restrictions. In 1986 another episode of conflict erupted. The OCJP solicited input on the conferences from its funded centers. One way the Coalition's caucuses were able to promote their groups' interests within the OCJP's social service framework was to arrange for workshops about meeting the distinctive needs of certain clients, such as deaf women or Asian women. Such a request had been made to OCJP for a conference session that would address the specific needs of lesbian rape survivors. The OCJP approved the session, but word leaked out that the word "lesbian" would not be used in any of the workshop titles or descriptions. This created a statewide stir among lesbian activists in the movement. Eventually the activists won this battle, but only after a series of protests that created internal problems within the OCJP.

OCJP funding and bureaucratization

The flow of information upward is a standard feature of bureaucratic management, therefore rules are created which govern the regular collection of information (Ferguson 1984). The bureaucratic requirements of record-keeping and data collection were central features and points of contention in the relationship between the OCJP and rape crisis organizations. As with any major granting institution, the OCJP created a structure for accountability that the hotlines had to meet in order to receive funding. It sent monitors to visit each funded organization on a regular basis to check by-laws, operations, and records. From the bureaucratic point of view, this was just routine practice, and staff members of the OCJP in fact saw themselves as "friendly" monitors who could be resource people and problem solvers. They presented their role as auditors as a simple matter of accountability, a necessity in a publicly funded agency. However, some of the monitoring practices built into the structure of accountability could also be used to discipline centers that resisted adopting the OCJP's definition of their work. Most rape crisis centers acquiesced, at least superficially. Only one group attacked the underlying social control measures directly, and lost its funding. The OCJP's power to withhold money structured the relationship for many staff members at rape crisis centers. Some rape crisis center staff saw the monitors as the embodiment of the "Big Brother" relationship they felt caught in, and resented the implication that they need to be checked up on.

From the beginning, the kind of records the OCJP required rape crisis groups to keep was a source of friction. The conflict was rooted in issues relating to workload, autonomy, and the political uses to which statistics are put. Ironically, during its first year of existence LACAAW had planned to compile alternative statistics on rape:

> As more and more women begin calling us to report rather than the police, we hope to compile vital information for helping in the apprehension of dangerous people. The TELEPHONE LOG helps us keep track of all the calls we get, how they heard about us, and future references, etc.
>
> (Letter from Miriam Cutler for LACAAW to Bev Rosen in North Carolina January 3, 1974)[3]

But the exigencies of volunteer labor power meant that record-keeping simply was not a priority, given the amount of work to be done and the lack of compensation. Volunteers also did not want to spend time filling out forms, so requiring them to do so generated additional supervisory work for leaders or staff *vis-à-vis* volunteers in organizations that otherwise sought to minimize hierarchy. While some hotlines did at times try to keep records of calls, these were for their own immediate purposes, used for improving their own work flow. They were done inconsistently, if at all.

Record-keeping also raised the issue of autonomy for the older organizations. A central reason that many groups had not sought the earlier Law Enforcement Assistance Administration funding or even Department of Social Services grants was their resistance to allowing officials to require and use detailed records of calls they received. Confidentiality was one concern, but a more political one was how the statistics generated from hotline records might be used by these agencies. The more political hotlines simply did not want to subsidize the law enforcement system by collecting data for them. Arguments that

emerged were sometimes contradictory, because they developed from
the dual approach of the early movement, to try to improve how the
criminal justice system handled rape, and at the same time not to put
faith in the system, and sometimes to avoid contact with it altogether.

The Valley hotline chose to relinquish OCJP funding altogether over
this very issue, but the defunding of Santa Cruz WAR in 1982 demonstrated how the OCJP would use data collection to control centers. Santa
Cruz objected to the forms on which the OCJP asked centers to file
quarterly reports. The following quote is from a letter the Santa Cruz
women wrote to the magazine *Aegis*.

> Specifically, the forms required us to categorize our callers by race and
> age and to identify the type of "crime" involved (such as "rape,"
> "attempted rape," "sodomy," "rape with a foreign object," and "incest –
> number of times [etc.]"). We quickly realized that furnishing this infor-
> mation would require us to ask women who call us these questions,
> which we, for many reasons, find offensive, if not outrageous.
>
> (Mackle *et al.* 1982: 28)

After their second quarterly report in which all calls were categorized as
"rape" and age and race categories were marked "unknown," the OCJP
cracked down, insisting that the forms be filled out "correctly."

> In telephone conversations, the OCJP staff suggested that we could
> determine a woman's race or ethnicity by her accent or appearance.
> We informed the OCJP that we were unwilling to assume that we
> could accurately guess a woman's racial or ethnic background using
> these methods. We also objected to asking women to differentiate
> among fifteen categories of crime.
>
> (Mackle *et al.* 1982: 29)

Although the official OCJP position was that a counselor should try to
collect the information in a naturalistic way and that they didn't require that
she ask the caller questions directly, in fact the information was required.

The Santa Cruz women objected to the use of bureaucratic procedures like information gathering to construct a reality that was advan-
tageous for social control agencies. They felt they were being forced to
do research on crime for the agency in order to create the "success"
statistics that would be put to political purposes justifying law enforcement spending, despite the ineffectiveness of the criminal justice system
in handling sexual assault. They had a sophisticated understanding of
who has the power to define reality in a bureaucratic society:

Not having enough "evidence" to result in a conviction does not mean that the woman was not raped. It simply means that the criminal justice system is not willing to do anything about it. This abstract idea of "proof" in criminal justice system dealings with rape is based on the premise that the woman herself cannot define if or how she has been sexually assaulted, that only someone else can define or document this. (Data creates reality.)

(Mackle *et al.* 1982: 29)

The requirement of data collection imposed on the rape crisis centers reflects the attempt by the state to merge incompatible functions. While the anti-rape movement embodies a tension between its social service and political goals, the OCJP's Sexual Assault Program has a comparable conflict between social service and information-gathering to promote law enforcement goals. The state agency's demands for documentation go beyond that required for accountability and are meshed with its effort to collect crime statistics. Thus, the collection of data not directly related to providing good services permeates the day to day operation of the rape crisis centers.

By the late 1980s, RCCs still saw these OCJP requirements as impediments, but had figured out ways to live with them. As Claire Kaplan, a staff member at LACAAW, explains below, the rape crisis centers had strategies to protect the integrity of the counseling relationship itself:

There's certain information that OCJP wants. And the person counseling a person in crisis, they're not going to sit there and say "What is your race? What is the race of the person who assaulted you? How old is he?" And those are the kinds of things that they're interested in knowing. One thing . . . is they don't pressure agencies to get that, but they hope that they do. So what the counselor generally does and this is what is almost uniformly done, I think at every agency, is you write "unknown." So consequently they [OCJP] end up with no data. Partly it's just, I think, resentment that those kinds of things have to be done now. On one hand yes, [we] can understand it from the perspective of we need to know what's going on, but on the other hand, it's totally inappropriate in a therapeutic setting, you know. So we can get some answers to those questions when there's more long-term counseling, but on a hotline call, there are more urgent things to be asked. . . . I know what LACAAW has done is to say to counselors don't worry about getting it, and certainly don't use it as a script, but if you get the information, fine. But I don't know how other agencies do it, but generally I think the counseling is fairly uniform in that regard.

Contrast this explanation, however, couched in terms of what is "appropriate in a therapeutic setting," with Santa Cruz WAR's politics of knowledge analysis above. Even centers that resist OCJP interference in their work have shifted toward this therapeutic framework for justifying their approach.

Despite LACAAW's refusal to let the data collection interfere with the counseling interaction, counselors must still fill out a lengthy form to meet OCJP's requirements for documentation. That requirement directly impinges on the work of organizing the counseling, as Kaplan explains:

> [O]ne of the consequences is the person who's in charge of the hotline has to harangue people constantly to get the data and it's useless. . . . Counselors hate filling those things out, I mean, who doesn't? But often what happens is they don't, it's a real hassle. So the coordinator spends so much time just getting people to turn those things in, instead of dealing with the more important matters at hand. . . . They probably would be spending more time in being supportive of the counselors and in keeping counselors from burning out, because there are always people who drop out of the line, so a lot of time is spent filling shifts. They might be able even to do more direct services, when they're short-handed. And most of those people, like Tawnya [Jackson – coordinator of the hotline] had other projects going on at the agency [that] she was totally unable to address, especially one, distribution of the special edition of *Survivor*, because she was spending her time doing quarterly reports and trying to get the counselors to turn in their forms!

So instead of pursuing projects that promote the goals of the movement, like distributing their booklet *Survivor* to a wider audience, staff members were compelled to spend time ensuring that paperwork got done. LACAAW instituted its own social control mechanisms to try to make this thankless job easier. Counselors were required to call in with the number of calls they had received, within 24 hours of finishing a hotline shift. Then the coordinator would follow up if she did not receive the requisite number of reports from the counselor. These practices, necessitated by the relationship with a state agency, have moved LACAAW far from its collectivist origins.

The OCJP has become progressively stricter about documentation, as Kaplan explains:

> [T]hey've been cracking down on documentation. And a couple of agencies had to give money back . . . because they didn't have the

documentation. It doesn't mean they didn't do the calls, it just means that people don't turn in their forms. And OCJP, prior to that, had not really been that tight on it. But they came down and they actually counted, by hand, every form, and we're talking hundreds.

The Santa Cruz resistance to OCJP was articulated at an abstract political level, addressing a broad critique of the processes of social control in society. The concrete level of day to day practices, as reflected in the effects on LACAAW described above, are what constitute those processes.

Although the Santa Cruz group was geographically removed from Southern California, their experience had far reaching impact on rape crisis activists all over the state. Groups rallied behind them to protest the OCJP's action, but also took a cue from the incident, realizing that serious insubordination on this level would have dire consequences. Centers who shared the Santa Cruz women's objections to the requirements developed various strategies for managing the situation, including the "manufacture" of records for statistical purposes. This is a form of resistance whereby they maintain the appearance of cooperating in the bureaucratic game and therefore don't lose funding. However, the existence of this kind of resistance does not mitigate the consequences of the imposed bureaucratization of rape crisis work. Through the funding relationship, centers have been absorbed into the information/ service bureaucracy of the state.

Such relationships are rarely without contradictions; political stands taken with good intentions can conflict with *realpolitik*. The issue of racism, which was integral to the resistance to data collection, was an example. An early argument for not working within the criminal justice system was that it was historically racist, and therefore not the solution to rape. One category of information the OCJP wanted collected was the race or ethnicity of both the client and the assailant. Resisting this requirement became a *cause célèbre* in the movement, as activists argued that it was invasive of the counseling interaction to ask for such information and it was racist to assume that you could "tell" what race or ethnicity a person was over the phone. In the course of arguments over this between the OCJP and members of the movement, however, women of color in the movement eventually took the stand that they *wanted* this information collected because it was one way for them to tell whether women of color were getting adequate, or proportionate, services compared to whites. Thus, the intersection of race produces a conflict of interest between white women and women of color over how to use the state.

CONCLUSION

The major effect of OCJP funding on the anti-rape movement was to institutionalize the social service definition of the work that had previously been only one side of a dual mission. The feminist political agenda of relating violence against women to women's oppression was marginalized, ridiculed, and suppressed by various means. One method was to give more power to centers that fitted the agency's definition of doing "good" rape crisis work. This was accomplished through appointments to committees, evaluations of grant proposals, and informal communication and strategizing with "sympathetic" people in the movement. Differences within the movement were exploited so that the schism was not "OCJP versus the rape crisis centers," but the "moderates versus the radicals." Groups that "learned to be political," as Contreras put it, were rewarded.

The second method of consolidating the social service perspective was to absorb what had been movement organizations into the state information/service bureaucracy. The crucial material power of funding agencies in a grants economy gives them the ideological power to define what is important work, shaping the services that organizations provide. "Neutral" bureaucratic requirements of accountability give them power to withdraw the resources if grant recipients are not compliant. The state insures that its needs for information are met in exchange for funding services to citizens.

Bureaucracy has become pervasive, with far-reaching political consequences. Efforts to create alternative, more humane institutions are thwarted through the exercise of routine bureaucratic procedures that appear politically neutral by virtue of their cultural hegemony and the ideology that they are rational. As Ferguson (1984) points out, bureaucracy's "claim to fame, the efficient use of resources," is contradicted by its own tendencies to create additional supervision. In this case, the state's effort to accomplish a political project of collecting crime data by imposing that requirement on the rape crisis centers ended up not being rational. The incompatibility of rape crisis services with data collection foils the attempt to be efficient by combining them. Rape crisis centers have maintained the integrity of their service provision goals by only partially feeding the OCJP's appetite for statistics. But this process of managing the demands for information creates work for center staff that robs them of time to carry out the broader political and service goals of the movement.

The rape crisis centers varied in how self-consciously they resisted incorporation into the disciplines of state bureaucracy, but all of them in some way challenged the state at the intersection of their local definition of the work and bureaucratic rationality. Having gained enough legitimacy to be considered a constituency, feminists tried to change the terms of the contract, but the pervasive bureaucratic character of our society made this practically impossible. While gains have been made in getting the state to respond to important feminist concerns, such as violence against women, the deeper feminist project of reconstituting society has lost ground.

Chapter 7

The expansion of racial diversity

The effects of state funding and oversight of rape crisis services were contradictory. The role of the state in expanding ethnic and racial diversity in the anti-rape movement further illustrates how such contradictions emerged, and exemplifies the historical contingency of state–movement relations. In the previous chapter I explored how state funding promoted a more conservative form of rape crisis service through political and bureaucratic means. During these years, state money also furthered one of the more progressive goals of the movement, to become multiracial and multicultural, and to expand services to all women, but the kinds of organizations it created were much more bureaucratic than earlier grassroots groups. This chapter examines the problem of racial and ethnic diversity in the anti-rape movement and shows how racial diversity in the local movement was facilitated by the state's involvement in establishing two new Black rape crisis centers in the mid 1980s.

FEMINISM, RACE, AND RAPE

Despite collectivist feminist roots in the civil rights movement and the new left of the 1960s, the women's liberation movement remained dominated by white and middle-class women. Evans (1979) attributes this to the historic conjunction of the birth of feminism within the new left just at the time when the Black movement was becoming separatist. This legacy, combined with the general level of racism in society, has made multiracial organizing, feminist or otherwise, difficult. The Black civil rights movement of the 1950s and 1960s is the exemplary social movement of post-World War II North American history. It sparked renewed interest among social scientists in social movements, leading to the revival of that field in sociology. It also began a cycle of protest that gave rise to the new left, the anti-war movement, the new feminism and numerous smaller movements which were influenced by its ideals as well as its style of protest. Consequently, most recent progressive or radical movements recognize their historical debt to the civil rights movement and give at least lip service to the notion of being multiracial, but in practice this has been difficult to achieve.

Explanations for the absence of women of color from the women's movement range between interpersonal racism of white activists and institutional racism. Giddings (1984) offers an explanation that puts both forms of racism in historic context. She addresses three factors that disturbed Black women about the new feminist movement: one was that as the movement grew it included more traditional middle-class women who did not have the same racial and class consciousness that more radical women had; second, was the fact that the rise of the women's movement "coincided with the deterioration of the Black movement . . . it appeared that the predominantly White women's movement was going to reap the benefits that the Black movement had sown"; and third, was the "shrill tone" the movement adopted toward men (Giddings 1984: 308–9). Many Black women who were interested in feminism in the early 1970s agreed with Black Panther Kathleen Cleaver, that Black and white women would have to work in separate organizations, coming together in coalitions, because the problems each group of women faced were different enough that they could not be solved in the same organizations (Giddings 1984: 311). Thus, the early anti-rape movement arose in a context of the distrust Black women felt for white feminism, and the beginnings of Black feminism (for example, the National Black Feminist Organization, active mainly on the East Coast, was founded in 1973). The problematic pre-dominance of whites in the feminist movement affected the anti-rape movement as well.

Long before the anti-rape movement the issues of race and rape were linked. From the 1880s through the 1950s lynchings of Black men were justified on the basis of their threat to white women's virtue. Although Ida B. Wells investigated over 700 lynchings and found that accusations of rape had been made in less than one third of them, the myth of Black men's proclivity for rape became ingrained in our culture (Davis 1981; hooks 1981; Giddings 1984), manipulated to keep both Black men and white women in their places. Lynching, rather than rape, became the focus of Black women's activism against violence.

Incidents that linked race and rape caused further disjuncture between white feminists and Blacks during the early movement. First, as the nationalist phase of the Black movement crested, several male leaders, most notably Eldridge Cleaver in *Soul on Ice* (1968), called for the raping of white women as a political act. Second, Susan Brownmiller, in her pathbreaking book on rape, *Against Our Will* (1975), echoed the racist justification of lynching in her eagerness to prove the seriousness of rape.

Nevertheless, some Black women picked up the issue as they became active in feminist work. In 1973 Roz Pulitzer, a Black member of the Manhattan (New York) Women's Political Caucus, which was lobbying on rape issues, said she did not expect Black women to get very involved in the issue of rape then. Like Kathleen Cleaver, she felt that

> The splits between the concerns of white women and our concerns was so great that strategically we had to have a black organization to give the women's movement credibility in our own communities. Every group must go through its period of self-identity . . .
>
> (New York Radical Feminists 1974: 243)

Pulitzer went on to say:

> At the same time that the black woman does not want to be another foot on the black man's head, she is trying to point out that a lot of the interactions that go on between black men and women are very oppressive. It's a very difficult situation to deal with. You're caught up in the reality of these things being wrong, and you're caught up in the reality that it is a racist society too – it's almost as if you have to take sides.
>
> (ibid.: 245)

But Pulitzer, who had been instrumental in forming a Mayor's Task Force on Rape in New York City in 1973, hoped that Black women would take what white women had learned and use it to set up rape counseling and public education in the Black community. In Los Angeles it took more than ten years for this to happen, and when it did, the impetus came not from grassroots Black feminist groups, but Black community organizations responding to the OCJP's call for proposals.

WOMEN OF COLOR AND THE LOCAL ANTI-RAPE MOVEMENT

The early 1980s were a period of increasing awareness of racial and ethnic issues in the anti-rape movement. Although there were relatively few women of color in the movement, the formation of the statewide Coalition brought them together, and provided the forum in which to raise issues about doing rape crisis work among African-American, Latina and Chicana, Asian, and Native American women. The Women of Color Caucus gave formal recognition to the group within the Coalition's structure, insuring representation on a regional basis. The regional structure of the Coalition provided the means for women of color in Southern California to meet.

The East Los Angeles Rape Hotline, founded in 1976, was the earliest, and one of the few anti-rape organizations that was not predominantly white. It was founded by Latina women concerned about providing bilingual and culturally appropriate services in the largely Latino/Chicano/Mexicano area of East Los Angeles county. Being one of the few bilingual hotlines of any kind, they were kept busy with all kinds of community services. Their connection to the other local anti-rape organizations waxed and waned over the years. Although East LA was always a member of the Southern California Rape Hotline Alliance, often months would go by without having a representative at meetings. In the early years, going to the Alliance meetings to be attacked for not being "feminist" enough was demeaning and uncomfortable. After 1979 when the Alliance grew and the statewide Coalition provided a forum for meeting other women of color in the movement, things improved. These two coalition organizations came to be places where things got done, not just talked about.

Another ethnically based rape hotline also existed by the late 1970s, although it was less connected to the movement. In 1978 Nilda Rimonte started a project to provide rape crisis services to Pacific and Asian immigrant women in Los Angeles. Although Rimonte participated in the Alliance regularly, the Center for the Pacific-Asian Family, as the hotline was called, was not a grassroots organization to the same extent as other hotlines. Because it was set up to serve many language groups (Vietnamese, Korean, Laotian, Cambodian, Filipino, and others) counselors were generally staff members. They also ran a battered women's shelter, so the rape hotline was only one project of the organization. Nevertheless, Rimonte was a central figure in raising ethnic and racial issues in the anti-rape movement.[1]

By 1982 racism was becoming an explicit issue in the movement. The issue of race was central, even if in contradictory ways, in the dispute with the OCJP over data collection, its most dramatic event being the defunding of Santa Cruz Women Against Rape. Later that year the East Los Angeles hotline was audited by OCJP. Although they were told that the OCJP planned "to very carefully scrutinize all rape crisis centers receiving funds" (Alliance Minutes June 12, 1982), the fact that they were singled out seemed to carry racist overtones. Hotlines had begun to treat racism as a serious topic in counselor training and the Women of Color Caucus (also referred to as the Third World Caucus in some documents) was very active.

The National Coalition Against Sexual Assault (NCASA), the national equivalent of the statewide coalition, had also begun to pay attention to this subject. Beverly Smith, a nationally known Black feminist, was a keynote speaker at its 1984 conference and made the analogy that "lynching is to racism as rape is to sexism," suggesting that the cultural context makes such acts possible (Roth and Baslow 1984: 56). Smith thus tried to transform the historic connection between race and rape into a positive one by comparing the two crimes rather than setting them in opposition to each other.

By 1983 the Women of Color Caucus had made a connection between OCJP funding criteria and problems of rape crisis centers serving Third World people:

> Emilia Bellone and Teresa Contreras reported on the work of the Third World Caucus, especially with regard to OCJP funding criteria and how they affect programs serving third world peoples. Currently, allocations are based primarily on numbers of victims served by particular programs, and some moneys [sic] are set aside specifically for "new and innovative" programs. This forces programs like Pacific-Asian and East L.A. to spend time and energy divising [sic] new grant proposals, when money is most needed for basic services – which must include proportionately more time spent in community education and outreach, rather than "victims served" or "hours per victim".
>
> (Alliance Minutes January 15, 1983)

An Alliance committee prepared a position paper for the OCJP on funding allocations. Their central criticism was that using the number of victims served as the key allocation criteria caused "inequities in the distribution of funds, which especially handicaps ethnic minority rape crisis centers" (Position Paper in Alliance files). The paper went on to say:

> One concern stems from the fact that in order to provide rape crisis services in ethnic minority communities, a great deal of time and effort has to go into doing strong outreach and community education. Although in recent years there has been a marked increase in awareness and information about sexual assault for the general public, much of this has not permeated ethnic minority communities. Many factors affect this – language barriers, racism, distrust of educators and the media, etc. . . .
>
> (Position Paper: 1)

The paper goes on to point out several related problems: traditional coping strategies among some cultures that discourage going outside the family for help; the need for materials to be translated to reach non-assimilated people; and the extra hours of work required both for outreach in ethnic communities, and to provide adequate services to individual survivors. They linked class issues with those of race and ethnicity.

> Typically, more time must be spent with a survivor who has fewer personal resources. These survivors tend to be ethnic minority women. Often, a non-assimilated ethnic minority survivor requires translating and interpreting, transportation, overnight shelter for herself and possibly children, and counseling to significant others in addition to the usual counseling and advocacy services. So, if a rape crisis center serves a predominantly ethnic minority population, the "average" number of hours of service provided to each survivor is much higher than for a center that serves a predominantly white population.
>
> (Position Paper: 2)

Grant proposals for "innovative" programs had been the centers' only strategy to increase funding for special outreach to certain populations. The East Los Angeles Rape Hotline had used it to create some exceptional programs. A major issue for East LA was how to include families, especially the men, in their services, which was essential in order to gain legitimacy in the Latino community (Alvarado, Contreras, interviews). In 1983, through a grant for innovative projects from the OCJP, they produced a *fotonovela* about a family in which a teenage girl has been sexually assaulted by her uncle. The storyline upholds the cultural value placed on the family, but modifies it so that the young girl's integrity is not sacrificed (Alvarado, interview). They also had an innovative theater program for education in rape prevention. These programs were successful for reaching their community, but were costly to the organizations in the time spent creating new programs and did not solve the problem of needing more money for basic services.

OCJP response

Although the Alliance committee that wrote the position paper did not get a direct response, Marilyn Peterson at the OCJP began pursuing avenues of additional money for "high crime" and "minority" areas.

> I was always trying to think of new angles to get money. . . . So I came up with this idea, well, let's look at it in terms of high crime area and

minority representation, and mainly with Republicans you talk high crime. Why don't we do a survey of the high crime areas of the state and see if they're covered and if they're not, which I knew, that they weren't, I said, let's develop an anti-rape program. We called them the "target," they [higher echelon OCJP staff] always called them the "special emphasis" because they didn't like the word "targeting." I called them the target area rape crisis centers.

The OCJP studied the rates of rape reported by police agencies and rape crisis centers in communities across the state, assuming that the rate of under-reporting was consistent. They then surveyed the availability of services in the community by district attorneys' offices, law enforcement, hospitals, family service agencies and so on. In addition to a high crime rate, the poverty rate was factored in, because areas with few resources tend to have fewer social services. According to Peterson, the survey was a necessary formality – a bureaucratic justification for what she already knew was needed: "So everything pointed out the fact that ... Compton needed something and the Rosa Parks area needed something, so we put out the RFP, we knew they'd win, and they did."

An item in the Alliance minutes in September 1984 records when the target grants became known to organizations in the movement:

> There are target grants available from OCJP. A 1982 study of crime stats showed 8 areas in crisis – money for under and nonserved areas. Starting money is $25,000. Four areas in S. Calif. are South Central LA, Central LA, WLA, ELA.
>
> (Alliance Minutes September 8, 1984)

Initially only four of the eight areas were awarded the special grants. The East LA hotline was one that was conspicuously left out. During the processing of proposals and grants, however, two factors combined to increase the amount of money available. First, the request for proposals went out at an unusual time of year in relation to the fiscal calendar. The late start on implementing some of the grants saved money which enabled the OCJP to fund four additional programs. Second, while this was going on, the OCJP received over a million dollars of federal Victims of Crimes Assistance (VOCA) money and decided to use half of it to augment the "target" programs. With the extra money four additional programs were funded in the state, bringing the total to eight. The grants were for $125,000.

Two new rape crisis centers

The "target" money was awarded to some of the existing rape crisis centers in Los Angeles, including LACAAW and East LA, but its most significant effect in the county was the establishment of two new programs located in predominantly Black areas, South Central Los Angeles and Compton. The lack of services in South Central Los Angeles resulted from both geographical and cultural factors. Women in these areas could theoretically use one of the existing hotlines, but geographical distance made providing in-person services like hospital accompaniment more difficult. The primarily white hotlines did sparse outreach to the Black community. But furthermore, women of color in the movement were developing a theory of service provision that recognized that women in crisis were most likely to feel comfortable and use services if they were provided by someone like themselves (Dubrow *et al.* 1986; Kanuha 1987; Lum 1988; Rimonte n.d.). This notion reflects the influence of the peer counseling roots of rape crisis work as well as increasing awareness of cultural issues. For outreach to succeed, it was important for services like rape crisis to be *of* the community, which the white hotlines were not. Thus, homogeneous organizations of different ethnic groups were more effective.

The first of the new hotlines, the Rosa Parks Sexual Assault Crisis Center, actually began in late 1984, in anticipation of the target funding that did not begin until the fiscal year 1985–6. Avis Ridley-Thomas, the woman who was instrumental in the founding of Rosa Parks, was at the nexus of several networks that led to it. She had been working for the Victim Witness Assistance Program out of the city attorney's office since it was establised in 1980. Because of her work there she had been recommended by Assemblywoman Maxine Waters to be on the State Sexual Assault Services Advisory Committee (SAC), the committee that advised the OCJP on funding for rape crisis services, training for prosecutors, and funding for research. Ridley-Thomas became chair of the committee, which at first had very little money to give out. Hers was another voice, in addition to the Alliance members, raising the issue of underfunding of minority areas. It was clear from her knowledge of South Central Los Angeles that this area had the highest rate of reported sexual assault in the state, and no community-provided services.

A long-time activist in the Black community, she started trying to organize the women's groups to take this on as a project, but none that she approached felt they could cope with such a project in addition to their other work. But her husband, Mark Ridley-Thomas, was the director of the local branch of the Southern Christian Leadership Conference, the Martin Luther King Legacy Association, and became interested and they applied for and received an OCJP grant to start a rape crisis service. Thus, Avis Ridley-Thomas' position in the funding agency, her involvement in service provision to victims, and her relationship to the SCLC converged to create a place for the new service.

The Compton YWCA was the second new organization to start a rape crisis program in a predominantly Black community. When the OCJP called for proposals for the target funding, the city's police chief encouraged the YWCA director, Elaine Harris, to apply for it. Compton, one of the small cities that compose Los Angeles county, is located south of South Central Los Angeles. Although the rate of home ownership is high, so is the poverty and crime rate. As in many of the economically abandoned areas of the county, gangs are an important source of social identity for young people, which, combined with their involvement in drug dealing, has created a violent environment. The Compton YWCA, which, unlike the independent Pasadena YWCA, is a satellite of the large Los Angeles YWCA, has struggled to be a community resource in this context. In addition to traditional Y programs ranging from fitness to music, they offer a Minority Women's Employment Program, Job Board, support group for single parents, a food program for needy families, drug diversion counseling, and a support group for families of incarcerated people. With crime and violence a major social and political issue in the community, they had a cooperative relationship with the police, which led to the application for the target funding. The YWCA had numerous resources, including experience with grant proposal writing, that could be enlisted in starting the Sexual Assault Crisis Program.

Consequences of founding: a different approach

The way in which these two new rape crisis programs were started differed markedly from the orgins of the existing organizations, which had consequences for the nature of the movement and relationships between the new organizations and the older ones with which they interacted in the Alliance and the Coalition. All of the older organizations had been founded out of some kind of grassroots process and with some connection to the wider feminist movement. Even Pasadena, which was the least grassroots in its founding, was led by a charismatic woman who nurtured it along with few resources because she believed in it, and the organization became more politicized in a feminist sense over time. The stands on feminism differed among the older organizations, but just on the basis of their timing during a period of feminist activism, most activists associated what they were doing with the women's movement at some level. The Rosa Parks and Compton programs, by contrast, were founded with substantial state funding and without strong links to contemporary feminism.

That is not to say that the parent organizations were simply social service agencies. Both the SCLC and the YWCA had roots in grassroots social movements, but had long since become established, "becalmed" organizations with hierarchical leadership and bureaucratic structures. The women who were hired to direct the programs were social service administrators, not activists. Nevertheless, many of the women who worked in the new organizations were drawn by the opportunity to work with Black women. As Joan Crear, a staff member at Rosa Parks, said:

> Personally, I got involved because I was very much interested in women's issues, in particular Black women, and I didn't feel that there was a forum in my community for them. I know there was resistance to the whole notion of violence, women's issues, feminism, and I wanted to work in an environment that advocated on behalf of Black women. As for the Rosa Parks Center, it seemed like a good place to start, and I envisioned the center as a place where eventually, while we're funded to deal with sexual assault, that it's very difficult to separate sexual assault from just what it means to be a woman in the universe, so it gave me an avenue to do that kind of work.

Monica Williams, director of the Compton YWCA program, said:

> I had a genuine concern for women's issues and rights and moreover, I think I had a real concern for living, since I live in this community [Compton] now, a real concern for Black women. I think our image has always been of [being] strong and persevering and you can take it all, and it doesn't make a difference, and I started to notice that most of the women who were assaulted, that it wasn't a priority for them, that they couldn't see that they were hurting, too. And that usually their first concern was their children, or their home or their husband, or how'm I going to make ends meet, so for me it's just, it's a challenge.

The chance to combine work for the community and for women was attractive to these women. Drawn by their interest in combining working with women and for the community, and influenced by the articulated feminism of the other women they met through the Alliance, these

women began to see themselves as feminists, but their primary interpretive framework was community service.

The community action framework, very much a part of the mission
of both parent organizations, provided a rationale within which to fit the
provision of rape crisis services, which replaced the feminist impetus of
the older groups. The SCLC linked the rape crisis service with their
philosophy of non-violence. The YWCA had a long history of programs
to help women and girls in crisis, and many Y's around the country
sponsored rape crisis services. Additionally, the fact that the special
emphasis grants addressed racial and ethnic inequity in service and
funding resonated with the national YWCA imperative, adopted in
1970, "to thrust our collective power as a women's movement toward
the elimination of racism wherever it exists and by any means necessary." Thus, these organizations brought to the work their own ideological understanding of what they were about.

Despite being oriented to an activist ideological perspective, the new
centers were more influenced by the OCJP's definition of rape crisis
work than the older organizations. Founded with OCJP grants, they had
not gone through the grassroots stage of scraping together precious
resources from their communities and therefore did not have the
independent community roots that other groups developed through that
process. When the Compton YWCA director applied for the grant, she
was not aware of the program at the Pasadena YWCA; the new program
was set up solely on the basis of the OCJP's published guidelines and
the Y's experience with community services. This differed from the
history of support and information-sharing in the older movement
organizations. As a consequence of their dependence on the OCJP they
were more bureaucratized from the beginning and less suspicious of the
OCJP. Monica Williams, the director of the Compton YWCA program,
expressed a positive attitude toward the Office of Criminal Justice
Planning:

> I have a very good relationship with our funding source. . . . Now
> some people say, maybe we have that because of the amount that
> we're funded. But then again I think that's where that issue comes up.
> They're our funding source. I need them. Without them, I don't have
> a job, and 6 or 7 people don't have a job, and my community goes
> unserved. They give me money, I do what they ask and expect with
> that money, no more no less, and I maintain open lines with them. I
> don't take issue with them about how they do their job, that's not my
> responsibility.

This contrasts sharply with the contentious history that members of the Alliance had with the agency, but was similar to the feelings of many less radical rape crisis people around the state.

Bureaucratic contradictions

Nevertheless, the community context in which the new services were being provided posed contradictions with the state's bureaucratic concerns and practices. The special grants that led to the founding of Rosa Parks and Compton were intended to adjust for problems in the delivery of services, such as "hazardous working conditions, an absence of complementary service providers or agencies, high cost of providing services, lack of alternative funding sources, geographical and/or economic conditions; and unmet need for culturally and/or ethnically appropriate services" (OCJP *Guidelines*: 33). These new organizations were therefore encouraged to design programs that met the basic guidelines *and* incorporated the specific needs of their communities. The sponsoring organizations, the YWCA and the Southern Christian Leadership Conference, were both practiced at responding to their communities and developed emphases that differed from other programs. For example, the Rosa Parks staff discovered a great need for dealing with the intertwined problems of incest and alcoholism and started support groups around this issue.

In Compton, the ways in which appropriately serving the community confounded the standardized guidelines is even clearer. Here, rape crisis workers confronted the reality of gangs on a daily basis as part of the community context in which they served. For example, when they held an educational or support group meeting they had to monitor what gang colors the young women were wearing so as to avoid confrontations among participants. Some of the survivors they counseled were victims of gang-related rapes. Furthermore, because basic survival was often the presenting problem of the women served, they evolved a broader approach to support and counseling. As Williams said:

> Example, a woman may come in or call in for various reasons. She has no place to go, she has no job, she has no support, she has no money, she has no food, she's been beaten, and after you finish meeting all those needs, or try to meet all those needs, then she may say, by the way, during all this, I was being raped. So the immediate needs have to be met. So that makes our community different than other communities. A person wants their basic needs first. It's a lot

easier to discuss things when you're full. So that we see people who, when they come in with their children, and their children are running around and the person is on edge, we may find out that she just hasn't eaten in a few days. And we may have to pool together money and give her everybody's lunch, or take them to lunch, and days later, maybe months later, the person will say, by the way, I did come in because I was raped, but since you brought up the other things, I do need a place to stay, and I do need a job, and I can't go to the police. So – the needs are different.

Approaching rape crisis work in such a holistic way did not conform to the requirements of the bureaucracy that provided the funding. In spite of the director's positive view of the OCJP, she also expressed frustration that often very labor intensive work was not being counted towards funding:

A lot of what we do cannot be documented. That there's no place on that form for this woman called and she's standing outside with three kids and she don't have no place to go. [Because the form asks about] rape! So you know you just, it's almost like you end up having this group that's so concerned that it's very difficult for us when a woman calls and says she's battered, not to tell her to come here for counseling, even though that's not what we're supposed to do. When she says, but I'm right up the street, I don't want to go to the shelter, I just want to talk to somebody, and a staff person like Irma or Roslyn will spend hours with this person and afterwards come in and say, god, she's feeling better, and I think this, and I'm going to take her over to the shelter, and . . . it fits no place. It's just something you did. It was an "information and referral."

Given the OCJP's increasing demand for documentation and the fact that funding was allocated on the basis of "numbers of victims served," providing additional services in the community which did not fit the OCJP criteria put a strain on the organization's resources. Although the OCJP's recognition of "special service delivery problems" through the target funding seemed to take into account the class as well as racial dynamics that affect these communities, its requirements were not adjusted for that reality.

These accounts graphically point out the intersection of class issues with those of gender and race in the actual operation of rape crisis centers. The kind of problems organizations confront differ according to their clientele. Although all of the centers serve a wide variety of women, the Compton Y's location in a relatively impoverished community in which services are scarce means that its sexual assault center routinely deals with problems others groups may confront only occasionally. Like the older hotlines, in which the demands of the work they chose shaped many of the movement's policy decisions, running a rape crisis center under these different conditions produced different approaches. In this setting, rape could not be isolated as a separate issue. For these women of color, and particularly poor women, rape appears as one kind of incident in a larger series of attacks – emotional, physical, and economic.

Women at these rape crisis centers tackled anew the problem already faced by the East LA and Pacific-Asian centers: that getting clients connected to their services was more than a simple issue of publicity. It also involved changing the cultural ethic around seeking help. The challenge of successful outreach to their communities was one of the issues that prompted the Alliance position paper on how funding allocations affected ethnic hotlines. Despite the high rates of sexual assault in these communities, there was not a mobilized citizens' group demanding the services. Once the services were available, women from both Rosa Parks and Compton had to work on legitimizing the idea of seeking a support group or some kind of therapy from the outside, a relatively new idea in the Black community. Ethnographic studies of Black communities have illuminated the extent of informal networks among members of even the poorest communities which provide both material and emotional support (e.g., Liebow 1967; Stack 1974), but the pursuit of more formal support through counseling is new. Avis Ridley-Thomas, founder of Rosa Parks, talked about the social pressure to "strain up," meaning to be tough and take the hard knocks, which works against seeking outside help with emotional or psychological problems. Williams elaborates:

> I think we work on empowerment a lot more because of the community we serve. It's difficult for a person to sit in a group and talk about their rape and the rapist and go through all of the psychological changes without first understanding that they have some other problems too. So that what's been helpful is for Black women to see other Black women to say I understand what it's like, to have to worry about the kids and him, and this and this and this and this. And that most of our support system I guess since the beginning of time, has been through the church, and through our family members, so that now, with things, economics and everything, we're pretty spread out, families are not always living close to each other, everybody is not

involved as closely with the church, so I think over the last 15 or 20 years we've made great strides socially and economically, but I think emotionally we've been pretty neglected. . . . [T]he former sources of support are gone. Now you see more of us putting children in child-care and daycare, whereas before we had mothers and sisters and aunts, and you know, the extended family. So that now, we're kind of [little rueful laugh] socialized a little more, so that we're running into the same things that other people are running into. We say we're stressed. Before we just said life was tough.

As Williams points out, changes in Black communities, including the loss of traditional sources of emotional, social, and material support, have made Blacks more open to getting support through social service agencies.

Victims' rights

The broader emergence of a crime victim's rights ethic in the U.S. was the bridge by which rape crisis services came to the Black communities. The Victim Witness Program was started about the same time as state funding for rape crisis services and was also administered by the OCJP. The program, which provides services to victims and families of victims of violent crime (counseling, financial compensation and restitution), originated largely in district attorneys' offices in an effort to humanize the process of testifying for the prosecution of crimes, and thus produce better witnesses. This activity within state agencies merged with a growing network of grassroots victims' rights groups in the 1980s. Unlike rape crisis, the Victim Witness Program had strong insider support from district attorneys, probation and police departments, which had a lot of clout at the OCJP. The two programs fought an ongoing battle within the OCJP because of several moves between 1981 and 1986 to place the Sexual Assault Program under the umbrella of Victim Witness. Both Marilyn Peterson and the rape crisis centers resisted this; for Peterson it was an organizational power struggle; the rape crisis centers saw it as a further threat to their autonomy.

Part of Peterson's fight to strengthen the Sexual Assault Program's position was to try to increase its share of funding. This was largely unsuccessful because of the political strength of the district attorneys, but also because the budget division of approximately 75 per cent to Victim Witness and 25 per cent to Sexual Assault reflected the statistics on people served. Failing to get the budget divided differently, Peterson looked for creative ways to increase rape crisis funding, and the target grants were one such strategy that succeeded. So in an immediate sense, competition with Victim Witness for funds resulted in the funding of Rosa Parks and Compton.

More generally, the movement for victims' rights helped legitimize the culture of therapy. People of color are more likely to be victims of violent crime in our society, so much of the outreach by the newly established Victim Witness programs in the early 1980s was to Blacks, according to Avis Ridley-Thomas. Seeking help for emotional traumas became more acceptable, not only in state-supported services, but also in grassroots victims' groups such as Loved Ones of Homicide Victims or the Black Coalition Fighting Back Serial Murders, two groups working in Los Angeles in the mid-1980s. While these groups are only loosely connected to the rape crisis organizations, they contributed to a climate in which reaching and helping sexual assault victims was less alien than it might have been earlier.

CONTINUING ISSUES OF RACE AND ETHNICITY

Despite the target funding, which provided substantial resources to expand services to "minority" women, "number of victims served" remains the key criteria for funding allocations. The problems raised by the writers of the 1983 Alliance Position Paper, that this criteria is inherently biased, have not been solved. Williams' account (pp. 139–40) provides an indication of the extra hours required to serve women whose crisis involves more than just sexual assault. This creates an ongoing struggle for centers that serve small numbers of women, because they are constantly at risk of losing their funding. In 1986 rape crisis centers were given the chance to recommend one of several alternate funding formulas. However, the formula most of the Alliance members agreed on was disadvantageous to the Pacific-Asian hotline, which sparked a commitment from the group to continue pressing for new allocation criteria (Alliance Minutes December 15, 1986). This issue is unresolved.

The dynamics of interpersonal racism and homophobia

Interpersonal racism continued to be an issue within the movement. Although the movement became more diverse both in perspective and membership, the dominant subculture within the local movement was white feminism, generally to the left of liberal feminism, and strongly influenced by a lesbian perspective. The combination of feminist jargon and political viewpoints, and the high number of lesbians in leadership positions, created an alienating environment for many of the Black women in the movement. Black lesbians were not visibly organized in the local movement, perhaps because of their small numbers in general and their absence from staff positions.

The dynamics of racism in the movement were intertwined in a complex way with homophobia and differences of political perspective. White activists in the movement were predisposed generally to accept women of color because they believed it was right. But their theory about what women of color should be about – they should be radical because they are oppressed – did not always fit with reality. Black women hired into the movement tended to identify with the social service orientation, thus the more conservative side of the movement, which created tension with the more politically oriented women who dominated the Southern California Rape Hotline Alliance. Joan Bendy, a Black staff member at the mostly white Pasadena hotline, explained the resulting dynamic: the problem of white women feeling so afraid of expressing racism (or being accused of it) that they would not openly disagree with a woman of color in meetings. This led to an undercurrent of distrust rather than genuine interaction.

Bendy correctly predicted that Black women would not tell me much about the Women of Color Caucus because I am white. She felt there was a strong "us–them" feeling in the group, which she faced because she worked at a white rape crisis center. She also felt she was an outsider because she was older than many of the other women and held different views from them. Other African-American women both from the Compton and Rosa Parks centers and LACAAW told me how important the Women of Color Caucus was for them as a source of support. Tawnya Jackson, a LACAAW staff member and chair of the caucus, articulated the range of issues it deals with:

> I think it serves a really important function in a lot of different ways. . . . I think there are special needs and issues. I think that a lot of women at their agencies are the only woman of color there. I think people always like seeing a familiar face. You know, if you can imagine working someplace where you're the only person that wasn't Black. . . . It gives those women an opportunity to come together and to be with people that look like them and may under- stand things about them without having to explain, even if it's just . . . someone knows what you have to do to your hair! . . . Just what it's like that people may project certain things about you, make assump- tions . . . or someone's real anxious because they're doing in-person

counseling, and they have anxiety because they're afraid that if it's a white survivor she's not going to want to talk to them because they're Black. Someplace where they can come and talk about what's that like. Where they can come and have support for whatever's going on at their center. . . . Basically we talk about issues that are of concern to us, as women of color doing this work.

Because a substantial number of the white women involved in the movement were lesbians the racial differences were compounded by homophobia. Homosexuality is even more hidden in the Black community than in the general society. Black women were not alone in the anti-rape movement in their discomfort with the openly lesbian presence. As I discussed in the preceding chapter, this also surfaced in the statewide Coalition, often between centers outside the major urban areas, which tend to be more conservative, and those from Los Angeles and the Bay Area. However, locally, the fact that racial and sexuality differences overlapped exaggerated the schism. Both sides felt they had a moral cause for offense when someone from the other side slipped. Both racism and homophobia are extremely difficult topics to address at the interpersonal level, so it is not surprising that tensions surfaced, despite the fact that all of the centers include these topics in their volunteer and staff training.

These tensions affect both interpersonal interactions and organizational processes. Differences in lifestyle led to varying concerns among women in the movement. Several Black women mentioned that they wished there were more support in the Alliance for dealing with husbands and families while working in rape crisis. This concern was shared by straight white women in the movement; working with rape victims arouses feelings of anger toward men that puts stress on intimate relationships with them. Black women, newer arrivals to the movement, felt an absence of support on these issues outside of their caucus meetings.

Lesbians did not share this concern because their partners were less likely to be threatened by their working with survivors of male violence. Furthermore, lesbians active in rape crisis centers had another framework through which to interpret violence against women: that it represented not just sexism, but heterosexism. The multi-leveled commitment that feminist lesbians held to promoting women's well-being meant that they formed a core of activists in the anti-rape movement, not only in Los Angeles, but elsewhere (Taylor and Whittier 1992; Taylor and Rupp 1993). Many previously straight women came out while working in the anti-rape movement, partly because it was a supportive environment in which to do so. But this also meant that lesbians in the movement, who were primarily white, created an oppositional culture that was not always comfortable for those outside it.

Black women, like some Chicana women earlier, sometimes felt marginalized by being outside the shared reference system of white feminists. As Teresa Contreras of ELA put it:

> I'm fairly sure that some of us felt threatened by the jargon, the politics, the feminist politics, and the real assertiveness of the women involved in the rape crisis movement and their confrontational style was totally contrary to the Chicano style.

In interviews some Black women noted that they did not really understand what "feminism" was, and yet felt expected to know and support its precepts. Being thrown into the Alliance and the Coalition where this was the political vocabulary could be intimidating and alienating. Over time, however, some came to put the name "feminism" to their own positions. Joan Crear, for example, was tentatively identifying herself as a feminist at the time I interviewed her, after working in the anti-rape movement for over two years.

> So for me it has evolved . . . and it has become important for me to say "I'm a feminist" to other women in my community, but I work on a definition where it doesn't sound like it's such a big thing, because I believe that most women, or a lot of women are under . . . some of the things that feminism encompasses. . . . [F]or me it means to want to be or to demand to share power in relationships, so I don't know if that's an appropriate term, because when I think about sharing power within relationships I have to look at that in terms of sharing power with my children, my boss, whether male or female, and so it means . . . I wish we didn't have to use "feminism", that I could . . . take responsibility for things that happen in my life. . . . I see myself as an adult woman, as an adult.

While the older, predominantly white organizations taught feminism in some form to new volunteers through the training process, women who came to work at the newer organizations did not come into such a system. However, by participating in the Alliance and Coalition they were exposed quickly. Under these conditions feminist ideology could be intimidating and alienating. White feminists who took their feminist analysis of the issues for granted were not always very sympathetic.

Not all women of color live in South Central or East Los Angeles, so the emergence of ethnically-based rape crisis centers was only one step toward serving all women and having a multiracial movement. Therefore the predominantly white hotlines continued to be concerned about recruiting women of color, but their strong stances on feminism and homophobia posed a dilemma. For example, Rochelle Coffey, director of the Pasadena hotline, acknowledged that "getting women of color involved . . . [has] been a big challenge that we have been more successful at some times than at other times". She went on to say:

> It's the whole issue of lesbian visibility and feminist philosophy and women of color being on the line, and it's been one of those things where we have decided that we need to maintain a position of integrity. Rather than stop having the lesbianism or the feminism, we maintain it and the women of color who can deal with that we will certainly do outreach there, and certainly some education stuff, but it's been difficult. What's been helpful, actually, what's been great, is both Compton and Rosa Parks coming into existence and the fact that Pasadena has always worked real closely with those two groups. . . . That's helped, because it's given us some credibility with women of color and they are able to say to their friends in Pasadena, this is an OK place to be and you're gonna have to deal with the fact that they're lesbians, they're OK women.

Despite these conflicts, women in the Alliance, Black and white, lesbian and heterosexual, worked together. The predictions from the early 1970s that women of color would need to establish their own organizations in order to become active in feminist causes seems to be borne out still. Racially and ethnically homogeneous organizations apparently are more likely to succeed individually and working in mixed coalitions when they have powerful common interests, but independent bases. In the context of the anti-rape movement's work of providing direct services, the social geography of Los Angeles contributes substantially to these conditions. Residential segregation means that ethnically-identified rape crisis centers can divide the city into service areas without competing with each other.

The expansion of racial diversity in rape crisis work, especially the inclusion of Blacks, was facilitated by state funding. Although a multi-racial movement has long been a goal of the anti-rape movement, its achievement through state-initiated rather than grassroots organizations has been fraught with contradictions and tensions. The following characteristics represent two different kinds of organizations:

new	old
state-funded	originally grassroots
bureaucratized	resistant to bureaucracy
community oriented	feminist
Black	white
predominantly straight	substantially lesbian

All of these were potential and actual sources of tension and conflict that was often multi-layered and complex. This particular constellation of characteristics was produced by the intersecting dynamics of gender, race, and class relations, which can only be understood in historical context.

Whether states coopt or facilitate social movements is historically contingent on particular political forces, and in the historical period described here, both processes occurred. Without state funding, the new Black anti-rape organizations might not exist. But more significant is the further infusion of a bureaucratic orientation into the movement, because the new organizations bear the stamp of their origins. However, the contradictions of such bureaucratic relations continually appear. The disjunctures women at Rosa Parks and Compton experienced between the local conditions and the centralized definitions of their work inspired them to resist the OCJP's control in some ways. This added a new source of resistance in addition to that of the older feminists to state demands on the movement.

Chapter 8

From stopping violence to managing rape

Stopping violence against women is ultimately a project of changing gender relations, because rape, battering, incest, and other violence are rooted in the power men have over women. Both gender structures and consciousness must be changed. The feminist anti-rape movement focused on changing consciousness – redefining women's rights to their bodily and psychological integrity. Changing consciousness led to rape prevention education, along with the provision of services for victims of rape. Although more structural changes were the ultimate political goal of many in the movement, day to day crisis work became the most visible and central aspect of its work. This tendency was promoted and institutionalized by the ways in which state funding was offered and managed.

Feminist demands and state responses converged at the point of what happens after the fact of violence: having rape taken more seriously, having laws that do not blame the victim, having fairer standards of judging "facts" in sexual assault cases, having stricter punishment of attackers, and the subject of this study, providing services to victims. These goals are more or less amenable to state action. The state funds prevention services, but at much lower levels than it funds crisis intervention. In the context of the pervasive social construction of gender the limited rape prevention work represents a very modest effort to change gender relations. This suggests that the state is enmeshed in gender relations, not outside them, and incorporates feminist goals only in limited ways. Because of the focus on after-the-fact treatment, I call the kind of responses made by state agencies "managing rape."

In Los Angeles the anti-rape movement's central orientation was transformed from a political agenda of changing consciousness to a social service agenda of helping victims manage the trauma they experience. This history shows the dynamics of change within feminist movement organizations and in their relationships with the state agencies they encountered.

Despite the trend toward assimilated, moderate, individualistic service provision, I found a strong thread of resistance from the feminist political elements in the movement. Thus I see rape crisis work as contested terrain between different factions in the movement and the state.[1]

From the beginning anti-rape activists combined the desire to help women through a tough experience with the political work of helping them to redefine the meaning of that experience. This merging of political and service work was most pronounced in the earliest organizations, where it emanated from the women's liberation branch of feminism. Within a feminist paradigm, this blend made complete sense, but practically, these orientations lent an uneasy tension to the movement's goals and strategies. Once the commitment to providing services took hold in the movement, it remained constant (cf. Burt, Gornick and Pittman 1984) and shaped the course of the movement. As the movement expanded activists increasingly varied in their commitments to a feminist political ideology. Those with more radical views feared that the movement was "selling out," being diluted, and becoming careerist, as a social service consciousness displaced the critique of gender relations in the movement's ideology. Activists committed primarily to providing good services felt pride that they maintained and expanded services in the face of material and political obstacles. These tensions, which characterize the anti-rape movement across the country, were played out in microcosm in the Los Angeles movement.

The trend toward a social service agency orientation, promoted and consolidated by the anti-rape movement's involvement with state agencies, is the most prominent characteristic of the changes in the movement during its first fifteen years. Involvement with the state began early, but escalated in California when most rape crisis organizations became reliant on OCJP funding for survival. The resulting shift in orientation encompassed both ideological challenges to the movement and reduced autonomy. Rape crisis organizations have changed their work in response to state agencies' application of everyday bureaucratic processes, backed up by the ultimate threat of lost funding.

Programs the state supports must be implemented and managed through some state bureaucracy. The political decision to locate the Sexual Assault Program in the OCJP had specific consequences for the movement. The anti-rape movement in California benefitted from being connected to law enforcement rather than social services during a time when social spending was shrinking. During the Reagan years social programs suffered deep cuts, while money for law enforcement flowed freely. Increases in funding for the OCJP's Sexual Assault Program had little to do with support for feminist principles or rape crisis work. They were largely a result of an effort to crack down on "crime" as the agency decided to enforce penalty payments by convicted criminals in the state. This contrasts poignantly with states like Massachusetts, where rape crisis funding was located under social services, and was cut during the same years. Instead, in California funding expanded dramatically, but it was accompanied by increased regulation by the state agency. This might be a simple case of cooptation were it not for the movement's resistance to absorption into the state.

Despite its apparent success, evidenced by long-lived organizations that have relatively stable funding and expanded programs, the anti-rape movement has been characterized by profound ambivalence and contradiction that continue to be sources of tension in the movement, sometimes overt political contention, sometimes as the backdrop for disagreements or decisions. Two clusters of issues are the focal point for these tensions: one is feminist views of women, violence, and the state, and the other is the relationship of feminism, bureaucracy, and the state.

FEMINISM, VIOLENCE, AND THE STATE

Feminist activists in the anti-violence movement have been ambivalent about the relationship between violence against women and the state. The liberal view of the state as the appropriate institution to control violence is in tension with a radical analysis of the state as using violence repressively to uphold power relations, including oppressive gender relations. The varying approaches to the police in the Los Angeles movement exemplify this tension. Activists were influenced by their ideological perspectives and by their gender, race, and class. Liberal middle-class white women pressed for the police to do their jobs more effectively, assuming and expecting police responsiveness. In contrast to middle-class white women's reflex to call the police when in trouble, Black and Latina women had experiences of police racism, including harassment, trivializing their complaints, threats of deportation, and assault, so they were more likely to view the police as another potential threat rather than to assume protection. Even middle-class white women, however, experienced the disjuncture of police inaction when it came to violence against women. For some, this was radicalizing, and led to a critique of gender policing by the state. An early response was to see the anti-rape movement as a substitute for the criminal justice system and its failures, but that was a relatively short-lived strategy. Black and Latina women helped bring these perspectives together: to be neither pollyanna liberals who think the police just need fine-tuning, nor to reject them out of hand, but to use political pressure to demand that the police change and live up to the stated (liberal) principles that they supposedly represent.

Two disjunctures intersected in the movement: for white women, between their expectation of police responsiveness and police inaction on violence against women; for women of color, between knowing the lack of police responsiveness and the desire to demand this as a basic right. The anti-rape movement demand for police responsiveness *on this issue* became the dominant approach because it addressed both these concerns. For women in communities with less police protection to start with, the political pressure to take rape seriously became a catalyst for improving police service generally – for example, in Compton.

Although action based on the liberal view of the state became the dominant mode for practitioners in the movement, theoreticians have continued to develop the radical critique of the state. For example, Hanmer (1978) and MacKinnon (1983, 1989) have argued in different ways that the state is responsible for promoting violence against women by institutionalizing male dominance and not punishing the violence men use to enforce it. There has been some divergence between everyday politics on the frontlines where service provision occurs and feminist political theory that analyzes the larger power relations. Theory has taken a more radical direction while the movement's practice has become more conventional.

It might be tempting to pin this issue on a split between theory and practice, but it is only partly that. The tension was also produced by change over time and ideological variation among practitioners. The debates that I have analyzed in this study demonstrate how ideological variation was one factor that affected change in the movement's practice. Activists who came into the movement with a liberal view of the state and law as "potentially principled" (MacKinnon 1983) were more inclined to work with the police and courts than radicals who saw the state as inherently repressive. Yet even the latter ended up having to engage with the state. The differences between the founding leaders of LACAAW and Pasadena, and the direction in which the LACAAW women moved illustrate this.

The most compelling conceptual contribution of the anti-violence movement has been its success in redefining rape as violence. Earlier cultural understandings of rape were primarily sexual, essentially presuming that men's uncontrollable lust caused them to rape. "Good" women were construed as innocent victims, while women whose social position or behavior was not pristine were blamed or not believed. The feminist redefinition of rape as violence attempted to downplay the sexual aspect of the crime both to get it treated more seriously and to eliminate blaming the victim. Yet in this very move they placed responsibility squarely with the state as the institution responsible for controlling violence, which had implications for the movement's strategies.

An example of the divergence between practice and theory emerges from this process. While women in the movement are still working to convince the public that rape is violence, MacKinnon (1989) has reframed rape as sex, replacing the issue in its gender political context and expanding its significance beyond being exclusively an issue of public social control. But this theoretical next step has not been adopted by the movement. A general indictment of heterosexual sex as violence is not strategically realistic for the movement, and just as significantly, it does not make sense to many activists themselves. Thus, while radical feminist theorists have carried notions of sex, the state, and violence to their logical conclusions, women working in the movement hold more circumscribed views. An analysis that attributes direct responsibility to "the state" for causing violence against women is not alien to activists, but was not in the forefront of their analysis. Theoretically sophisticated radicals in the movement see and feel the ideological contradiction, but for most women whatever ambivalence they felt was overcome for practical reasons. First, the strong association between violence and the state is practically inescapable in modern society. Second, state-related agencies were the most likely source of resources.

Furthermore, the social structure of the state made it practically impossible to compete with its police functions and far easier to perform social service functions. The strategic implications of radical theory of violence against women and the state are for women to enforce collectively the social control practices neglected by male dominated state institutions. Indeed, the anti-rape movement experimented with such forms of action in its early days. But confrontational tactics made the movement a target of state power when men sued the anti-rape groups for slander. Being labeled as deviant vigilantes also marginalized the movement rather than promoting society-wide change. At the same time, the provision of personal services, considered equally important by activists, absorbed a great deal of organizational energy without carrying such costs.

Instead of a stand on "the state," activists have mobilized in relation to the particular state institutions they confront in the course of working with rape survivors, particularly the criminal justice system. From the beginning, when anti-rape activists criticized the state, police and courts were the targets. The injustice of the system that treated rape victims as criminals and let rapists off easy was the theme, rather than the state as a perpetrator of violence against women. When organizations rejected possible funding offered by law enforcement agencies, as LACAAW did in the late 1970s, it was based on how such agencies were treating women and seeing law enforcement as a generally repressive arm of the state, racist and intolerant. Later their reluctance was overcome by necessity, as OCJP funding became the standard answer to organizational financial crises.

The uneasiness some members of the movement felt about working with the state on an issue related to violence still simmers in the background, often appearing along with issues of social inequality, such as racism and homophobia. These issues are part of the political side of the movement that is less prominent now, but is maintained by feminists for whom fundamental social change is the impetus for their work. When ambivalence about the state's real motivation or commitment to stopping violence against women is expressed, the movement's historical roots in the women's liberation movement show. But for the most part, getting the state to fulfill its function of managing violence is a more accessible goal than implementing a broader critique of the state. Thus, practical politics about the issue of violence have affected how ideological ambivalence is handled.

Many of the practical issues the movement faced – how to organize the provision of services, how to mobilize resources to support them, how to make decisions together – hinged on translating ideology into action. In this process a contradiction emerged between the movement's anti-bureaucratic values and the pervasiveness of bureaucratic practices in the society in which they operated. The conflict was most pointed in relation to state agencies.

FEMINISM, BUREAUCRACY, AND THE STATE

Women came into the anti-rape movement with differing orientations toward the state, largely determined by either radical or liberal political views. Factions developed according to different understandings of what can be accomplished through the state, and whether real alternatives were available. In the early 1970s there were differences between LACAAW, Pasadena, and East LA in the extent to which they were willing and able to build connections to state institutions in their work. While LACAAW started off being the least willing ideologically, they ended up being quite successful in getting connected to programs that furthered the organization's survival, for example, the NIMH funding. For Pasadena the financial reward was not as high, but the eagerly-built network that included local officials was important for the hotline's success. East LA developed ties to state political figures, but was not able to translate that into substantial material support. The organizations started in the 1980s were more polarized on this issue, reflecting changes in the movement. The Valley group eschewed law enforcement funding altogether, but was less adamant about other kinds of state involvement. The Rosa Parks and Compton organizations were intimately tied to the state from their founding. Since all of the surviving organizations (the Valley hotline folded in 1986) receive substantial state support, their differing stands on the questions are largely matters of ideology. Where this matters most is in whether they approach their relationship to state institutions as adversaries or colleagues.

A benchmark of different attitudes toward the state is whether activists see their work as part of the system or an alternative to it. Women with social welfare backgrounds were influential in improving the services the movement provided, and also in building links to state bureaucracies, beginning with mental health centers. While some activists maintained the view of their work as an alternative to the system, others began to see it as a supplement to the system. This image of rape crisis services as part of the system contributed to its partial absorption into other state-supported services. As the work became more imbued with a social welfare orientation, the distinctive political content was submerged. Techniques were adopted from social work in order to improve counseling. Along with these positive features also came an increasing orientation to other public institutions to which clients could be referred if necessary. Case management thus became part of the repertoire for dealing with women who sought help (cf. Gusfield 1982; D. Smith 1990).

The ascendance of a social service orientation, increasing bureaucratization, and involvement with state agencies were developments that occurred in tandem and mutually reinforced each other. In each organization, people debated how to carry out their goals, developing a consciousness about what it meant to relate to the police, hospitals, media, and each other in particular ways. External forces defined their perception of their choices. The expediency of more conventional structure often was related to being more attractive to a funding agency. Despite experimenting with collective structure, they adopted bureaucratic features when those seemed imperative.

Bureaucracy as a mode of organization was an ideological issue for feminists of the early 1970s, who saw hierarchical and highly regulated organizations as problematic, and sought alternatives in the form of collectivist structures. The demise of collectivist organizations is often attributed to shortcomings inherent in their structure. But there are really two separate processes at work, collectives folding and collectives being transformed into more bureaucratic organizations. Both processes are evident in this study. The Valley, which chose not to surrender its collectivist structure, was confounded by problems that seem to be inherent in collectives, such as limits on the practicable size of the group, the difficulty of bringing in new members, and the time-consuming decision-making process. But they were also affected by larger historical changes in the women's movement. As Taylor (1989) suggested, the women's movement has gone into "abeyance." By the 1980s, there were fewer radical women willing to put in the amount of time necessary to operate a group in the collectivist style. The aging of the activist cohort politically socialized in the 1970s, and the lack of a vibrant countercultural women's movement to provide new activists with the same vision, combined to produce the "burnout" that ended the organization. The same context made it difficult to mobilize the necessary material resources when other more mainstream groups operated from a more solid financial base.

In addition to these historical factors pressing on the movement, my study suggests that other external factors also promoted bureaucratization of women's organizations. For the groups that transformed their structure, the periods of rapid change were prompted by interactions with outside institutions. Practicing the feminist critique of bureaucracy began to break down because bureaucracy was so pervasive in the society they were trying to change. LACAAW provides a telling history of a feminist group that actively eschewed bureaucratic organization, but came to adopt many of its features in order to stay viable as an organization. The search for resources outside the group led LACAAW to connect with a community mental health center through a governmental grant. This external relationship first prompted adoption of more formal procedures. Resembling a bureaucracy makes operating easier in the context of a bureaucratic society. Thus, it is important to recognize the power of the social context in promoting accommodation toward conventional structure, rather than seeing its pervasiveness as somehow natural.

The critique of bureaucracy has left its imprint on the organizations with feminist roots. Flattened hierarchy and the personal and informal style of management now found in most of the rape crisis centers are the organizational legacy of that period of feminism. Bureaucratization of these organizations is relative, meaning they adopted more formal structure, defined separate jobs, and experienced increased regulation of their practices.

Increases in bureaucratization tended to occur in bursts, often prompted by increased involvement with state agencies. Most of the groups I studied sought access to the state through various means, including lobbying legislators. Eventually the result was the relatively stable funding from the OCJP. This has posed a dilemma for the movement's feminist ideology: when the movement has become "successful" in relation to demands made on the state, what happens to its analysis? This quandary is not unique to the anti-rape movement, but plagues all progressive movements that become a part of what they had been critiquing (cf. Rupp and Taylor 1987). Success in getting funding entails organizations turning more of their energy toward the state, as maintaining the relationship with the funding agency takes time and work. They become faced with one of the contradictions associated with bureaucratization, in which maintaining the organization takes precedence over the purpose for which the organization was originally designed. Has the work of promoting and maintaining funding for rape crisis services become the surrogate for action to stop violence against women? To say that is what has happened in the anti-rape movement would be an inaccurate oversimplification, but there is an element of that process going on. Their original purpose was to stop rape, or at least reduce it, but their time is now spent meeting, and documenting how they have met, the service goals narrowly defined by their grant contract. Time spent on bureaucratic routines robs the leaders of time for developing the political agenda of the movement.

The material necessity of a relationship that entails internal accommodation to the state's mode of operating reinforced a focus on service provision, because that is what the organizations were being "paid" to do. Accommodation increased as state involvement became a permanent feature of the organizations' material base. For example, LACAAW's early short-term funding from the NIMH did produce the first structural changes, but not to the same degree as the later funding from OCJP. In the course of a permanent arrangement new regulations were added and the organizations lost more of their movement character.

Practically speaking, attempts to work outside the state have proved difficult and not feasible on a long-term basis. Organizations that have held too closely to this goal, like the Valley, have folded. Creating alternative institutions that both provide services and promote a political analysis depends on a certain social–historical context (i.e., a broader movement cycle in which support for alternatives to the establishment is widespread) and a time during which the problem they seek to address is undergoing redefinition. Part of the quandary referred to above is that if the movement succeeds in redefining the problem, it is likely that mainstream institutions will become involved in responding. Organizations that retain a separatist stance in relation to the responding state appear unreasonable. The price of autonomy is diminished resources.

Autonomy has been a constant theme in feminism, whether at the individual or institutional level. Much of the resistance to state-imposed bureaucratization reflects concern with maintaining autonomy. The closer connection to bureaucratic state structures threatened rape crisis centers' autonomy because it placed regulation of their work with an external agency. The actual change required in structure and practices may have been small, since the existing organizations that got OCJP grants had instituted some formality in their organizations prior to the funding. But these requirements were seen very differently, since the initial adoption of conventional structures was often token, and most importantly, they were controlled by women in the movement. For example, a board of directors was necessary for obtaining non-profit status, which helped in raising money. Few other trappings of conventional organization (formal division of labor, job descriptions, systematic record-keeping) were adopted until required by funding agencies. It was the imposition of structures and the idea that they would be monitored for compliance that elicited resistance from movement members.

A distinctive characteristic of a movement organization is its ability to be in flux, to adapt to the changing needs of the situation. Although the rape hotlines became somewhat formalized, many people running them still saw themselves as activists in a movement and the more settled social service agency framework implied by required structures conflicted with this sense of themselves. That is why, although it can be argued that some of the structures served some good social purpose, even ones that the activists supported, they chafed at their loss of dissenting status and real autonomy.

One infringement on the movement's terrain was in the state's usurpation of the power to define the issue. In the process of translating what the rape crisis centers did into terms compatible with the state's bureaucracy, the problem of rape itself was redefined. The movement had succeeded in influencing society to see rape as violence against women rather than a sexual act in which the woman might be implicated.

Although this basic notion gained legitimacy with public officials, their interpretation was filtered through institutional perspectives to yield a new version of the idea. In order for the state to respond, the problem was defined in such a way to produce "clients" (Ferguson 1984) of two state systems.

For mental health agencies and related programs (including the OCJP, which funds services to victims, although it is a law enforcement agency), rape has been redefined as an individual psychological trauma. In this view rape crisis services deserve public support because the movement succeeded in defining rape as violence, but it is an individual problem, not a personal experience with political implications in the feminist sense. The movement developed the notion of the rape *survivor* in order to express concern with empowering women. Use of this term points to changed consciousness as a continuing goal. But the state still classifies its clients as victims, which entitles them to remedies the state can provide. Furthermore, in California and other places where a law enforcement agency administers rape crisis programs, services to victims are intended to improve the prosecution of crimes, a goal that does not always complement the needs of the victim (*cf.* Schecter 1982).

Within the criminal justice system women hardly even gain the status of client. They remain merely witnesses to their own rapes, who serve at the behest of gatekeepers of the criminal justice system. Although rape has been legally redefined, evidence is mixed about how that is actually affecting prosecution. Some research suggests that the meaning of rape has been sufficiently broadened so that more incidents are resulting in prosecution, especially in terms of rape by familiars rather than strangers. This reflects the movement's success in influencing legal changes in how sexual assault is defined, and in changing attitudes among law enforcement and prosecutors and juries about what is acceptable behavior for women and men. If so, this development contains the seeds of a broader critique as the movement pushes at the boundaries, problematizing what in the past have been regarded as normal gender relations in dating and marriage. Although the boundaries of cases that appear in district attorneys' offices have expanded, the problem of women being blamed for being raped has not disappeared. Despite the vaunted attention acquaintance-rape has been given recently, few of these cases are successfully prosecuted and outcomes have not changed, though the reasons criminal justice agents give for rejecting cases may have changed (Frohmann 1991).

In the electoral sector of the state, rape crisis services have gained sufficient legitimacy to be considered a basic service that should not be denied to communities that have not produced grassroots mobilizations to provide them. A few state legislators, notably Alan Robbins and Maxine Waters, have been significant in pursuing legal changes and creating the current programs. These efforts served to gain them legitimacy with feminist and minority constituents by bringing services to communities that did not have them. Inevitably, demands made on politicians get defined within the limits of conventional politics. In the late 1980s the Republican Deukmejian state administration congratulated itself on the dramatic increase in funding and expansion of services during its term when much of this was the unintended consequence of other policies.

All of this leads to much more talk about the problem of rape, but little real change. Feminist success in changing ideology about rape was filtered through bureaucratic structures to yield a new version of what the problem of rape is about. Rape became depoliticized in the sense that the feminist analysis of gendered power relations was removed from the picture. In place of the goal of ending violence against women, rape crisis services now help the state to manage it. They are therefore absorbed into the regulatory functions of the state. Because this is done under the humanistic mantle of providing services to women who have experienced very real trauma does not lessen the importance of understanding the ideological and organizational cooptation of the movement.

Institutional power to define issues, practices, problems, and solutions was a strong force in changing the nature of rape crisis work as it became more closely regulated by state agencies. Members of the movement have fought that trend by attempting to create legitimate space for their own definitions of their work. For example, they worked to have their own methods of certifying trained volunteers recognized by law. The threat of the state taking over that function prompted members of the Alliance to articulate, coordinate, and regularize their own practices. Thus, external pressure pushed them to become more systematic and to have written guidelines for their work, hallmarks of bureaucratic organization.

Connection to and regulation by a centralized state agency contributes to the removal of how work is defined and carried out from the local, situated context in which it is done. The struggle over autonomy is one manifestation of this disjuncture. Another appears in how the needs and everyday realities of doing rape crisis work in particular communities is ignored by the official guidelines and regulations for doing the work. This disjuncture between bureaucratically defined and everyday reality (D. Smith 1990), was clearest among organizations serving women of color. The bureaucratic definitions of the situation are biased toward white and middle-class definitions of social contexts. The organizations were expected to be able to provide discretely defined services related to rape, ignoring how women's experience of rape was enmeshed in other aspects of their social context, such as poverty, racism, or lack of legal documents. This remains, despite, and within the context of, special efforts to fund "minority" programs. It is a fact produced by the separation of local action from the places where the work is defined. Activists still attempt to meet their local needs, but are not compensated within the system of rewards that enables them to provide services in the first place. They must therefore scramble to bridge the gap between the local situation and policies made elsewhere.

However, that rather pessimistic summary is only part of the picture. Feminists continue to work on pressing the boundaries of what the state allows by finding ways to expand services, expand the meaning of violence, and reach women who are most victimized and have least access to recourse. LACAAW, for example, has recently developed services for deaf women by bringing feminists from the deaf community into the organization. It also continues to press the state on its terrain: for example, trying to affect the funding allocation formula used by the OCJP. Maintaining the critical movement stance sometimes has meant covert resistance to bureaucratic requirements. On other occasions it has demanded overt political conflict.

IMPLICATIONS FOR THEORY AND PRACTICE

What are the implications of understanding the tensions that characterize the anti-rape movement and transformation it has undergone? In the sections below I will briefly summarize how my findings inform theories of social movements, feminism, and the state.

Informing social movement theory

In the area of social movements, my study has implications for understanding the dynamics of social movement transformation and relations with the state. First, openings to win concessions from the state may occur while the movement is insurgent, but the metamorphosis from challenger to polity member is based on accommodation to certain measures of legitimacy. The evolution of the anti-rape movement from being a radical branch of the women's liberation movement to being an accepted part of service provision occurred as it adopted more moderate goals that could be translated into state-supported programs. Adopting more formalized structure and becoming more oriented to direct service provision rather than direct political action were features of the change.

Second, the processes of professionalization and bureaucratization that have been the focus of analysis of social movement organizations in recent years are produced by external as well as internal forces. The development of these features in anti-rape movement organizations was promoted both by people trying to cope with providing services on a voluntary basis, and by interaction with the state, which required accommodation to certain practices. Two areas where this process is visible are in the record-keeping and data collection requirements, and in the pressure on rape crisis workers to develop their own credentialing system or have one imposed by the state.

My study therefore suggests directing more attention to the dynamic between internal and external sources of bureaucratization in social movement organizations. Classical and recent explanations of bureaucratization emphasize internal processes, e.g. Zald and Ash's (1966) work on oligarchical tendencies in social movement organizations. But I found it was neither the loss of a charismatic leader nor an oligarchy, but the dialectic between the problems of collective leadership and external pressures on the organizations that produced the move toward professionalization and bureaucratization.

Bureaucratization was a solution to the contradictions the organizations faced because it gave the movement better access to resources, the lack of which were at the root of the crisis. Orienting toward the state as the likely source of funding required forging an organizational structure that would be acceptable to the state. As the relationship with the state became more permanent, further trappings of bureaucracy were imposed on the movement organizations. Tension arises between the supposed autonomy of a social movement organization and an increasingly satellite-like relationship to the state, in which state agencies regulate the activities of the group. Social movement organizations are oppositional, but state bureaucracies do not easily incorporate that stance. Thus they attempt to recast these social movement organizations as agencies themselves.

Third, my findings demonstrate the interaction between cultural processes in movements and structural questions of organization and strategy. How issues were framed by the activists continued to influence their stance toward the state and the strategies they adopted in relating to it. Despite state pressures toward conformity, feminist anti-rape groups resisted and often operated in ways that reflected their ideological commitments while appearing to accommodate state requirements (Matthews 1994). The maintenance of an oppositional culture within the rape crisis centers was essential to their organizational identities. As Patricia Giggans, the executive director of LACAAW in the late 1980s put it, "We're not just a little service agency." Identifying themselves as part of a movement meant that even years into the institutionalization process, rape crisis activists felt a responsibility to take certain political stands, not to view themselves as representatives of the state agencies that funded them. As a result they pushed the state agencies toward new interpretations of the work they were doing.

Feminism

How is our understanding of feminism informed by this example? First, this case exhibits how feminist action is rooted in the local situation rather than dogmatic ideology. Most of the groups were flexible, according to the demands of their environment, their resources, and their goals. This points to a lesson in understanding the diversity of feminist projects globally and in different communities and time periods locally. No one universalistic theory of feminist practice can be applied to concrete local and historical situations.

Second, differences among women, especially those based on race and class, are currently of great interest both to activists and theorists. This story contains lessons about the nature of "diversity" in feminism. Women of color were not always "radical" by white feminist standards. Their approaches stemmed from different cultural contexts, social positions, and the integration of racial or ethnic group concerns. For Chicanas the need to uphold the value of the family and include men, for African-Americans the historical connection of rape, racism and lynching, and for Asian women understanding the value of privacy and the needs of immigrant women – these concerns shifted the issues around which mobilization took place. The locally situated nature of the work becomes even more apparent when looking at the differences that have developed among organizations located in different communities.

Additional differences stemmed from the relative social positions of women who became involved in the movement. Until recently, white women who worked for rape crisis centers were more likely to be choosing a socially relevant alternative job, whereas for women of color these jobs have been professional steps. Since the system is not likely to radically change and Black and Latina women have more to lose by not succeeding within the system, women of color in this movement have tended to work less contentiously with the state. Thus, structural occupational barriers that affect women differently by race have an impact on diversity in the movement.

Third, feminist activism is subject to the influence of the surrounding culture and social relations. Feminist separatism is not a real option except for a few, any more than other forms of separatism are for other movements (e.g., monasticism in Christianity). Those broader influences will transform feminist projects. For example, bureaucracy encroached on anti-rape groups, not only from the state, but simply through the culturally accepted modes of operating. Collective structure and practice was an alternative frame feminism created, but the existing and more dominant frame of bureaucratic structure tended to encroach on this dissenting one. Similarly, in the provision of services, the social welfare orientation tended to overpower the feminist political definition of the problem.

Fourth, contrary to the polemics of movement participants, the reality of movement activism involves a path that is neither "selling out" nor separatism, especially in relation to the state. Instead, women are working with such institutions and actively resisting. This characterization avoids condemning women who want to accomplish something by labeling them as self-interested, but also points to the risks involved. Strategically for feminists this is a path worth exploring and developing, as it is inclusive, yet critical. This kind of critical engagement is also a useful concept both sociologically and politically because it lends itself to assessing the ways in which women work with institutions like the state, and ways in which they resist.

The state

What are the implications of this study for understanding the state? First, women's demands have resulted in institutional responses that do make a real difference, but not always in the way feminists have wanted. My study is a further example of the flexibility of the state in absorbing new ideas and granting new rights, while at the same time not essentially changing social relations. What are the limits? There are no predetermined limits on how far state institutions will go, but the limits are produced by the interplay of changing political forces. Creating the OCJP Sexual Assault Program was not just a token response to feminist demands but was the incorporation of a new notion into other developing programs that fitted in with the state's framework. The newly legitimate idea of rape as violence combined with the growing recognition of victims' rights to produce the political space for state-funded rape crisis services.

Second, in the course of responding, state agencies reformulate demands into issues they are willing to address. Thus the OCJP was willing to address rape as a crime problem and as a problem for the individual victim, but not as a reflection of problematic gender relations. The social service aspects of the movement's work were more amenable to adoption by state agencies than the feminist political agenda. The social service agenda could be incorporated into a program, and as the state responded to that, activists responded by shifting their emphasis in that direction, too. Thus, a different perspective on the problem is produced by the interaction between the movement and the state.

Third, services are overseen by bureaucratic organizations of the state. Various bureaucratic requirements either control directly or are used to control the agenda of the organizations that are connected to the state. My study shows how record-keeping and data collection by the state were seen as interfering with the movement's agenda and how these apparently innocuous requirements represented a more profound reformation of the movement's purpose. I have developed the complex and subtle ways in which bureaucratization is both a backdrop and a political tool in relations between the state and the movement.

Fourth, my study suggests the breakdown of boundaries between different sectors of the state. The line between law enforcement and social service provision was blurred in the OCJP's Sexual Assault Program. The acknowledged social control functions of law enforcement were ostensibly softened by a victim-sensitive ethic, while therapeutic services for victims evoked social welfare programs that have a regulatory undercurrent (e.g., Piven 1971). Victim services mediated through state programs have a social control aspect aimed not so much at individual women, but at feminist attempts to change gendered power relations. Efforts to understand state power therefore must be sensitive to the functional fluidity of state agencies and examine the innovative ways in which social control can be deployed.

The anti-rape movement has had an impact on the state and its treatment of violence against women, but in limited ways. The existence and level of state funding for the movement's programs is evidence of concessions won, but the requirements of the state in return, especially the challenge to the movement's autonomy, represent the limits of success. The extremely high rate of violence against women and the continued evidence of prejudice on the part of police officers, district attorneys, and judges is also a reminder that victory is yet to come.

Services to survivors of violence will probably continue, perhaps becoming increasingly routinized as they become entrenched in state bureaucracies. The feminist component of the service institutions will continue to push the boundaries of what is possible when working in concert with the state, but the extent to which they are able to articulate opposition and resist cooptation depends on the existence of a broader feminist movement. Only in that context will new activists continue to emerge who have a feminist vision of rape crisis work as a broader project than just managing victims of violence.

Appendix A

Interviewees

The following people generously gave of their time to be interviewed for this project. The women's names are grouped by the organization with which they were primarily involved. For the three oldest organizations, LACAAW, Pasadena, and East LA, I note the period in which the person first became involved by the following codes:

E = early	c. 1972–8
M = middle	c. 1979–82
L = late	c. 1983–7

LACAAW

Joan Robins	E
Patricia Hoffman	E
Hope Blacker	E
Barrie Levy	E
Almut Fleck (Poole)	M
Judy Ravitz	M
Krysia Dankowski	M
Joan Sutherland	M
Claire Kaplan	L
Patti Giggans	L
Jennifer McLaren-Owens	L
Tawnya Jackson	L

PASADENA

Grace Hardgrove	E
Chris Olson	M
Rochelle Coffey	L
Joan Bendy	L
Doris Boyington	L
Joan Cashion	L

EAST LOS ANGELES

Irene Mendez   E
Connie Destito   E
Teresa Contreras   E–M
Yolanda Ochoa   M–L
Elena Alvarado   L

SAN FERNANDO VALLEY

Carol Nelson
Lynn Magnan Donovan

ROSA PARKS

Avis Ridley-Thomas
Ayofemi Folayan (Stowe)
Joan Crear

COMPTON YWCA

Monica Williams
Andrea Stewart
Elaine Harris

PACIFIC–ASIAN

Nilda Rimonte

INDEPENDENT

Betty Brooks

SANTA MONICA RAPE TREATMENT CENTER

Gail Abarbanel

OCJP STAFF MEMBERS

Marilyn Peterson
Linda Bryan

Appendix B

Interview schedule

INTERVIEW: RAPE HOTLINE PARTICIPANT

Name _____   Date of interview_____

Hotline _____   Date of involvement_____

I want to ask you about two aspects of the same thing: one is your own story as an involved participant, how you got involved, when, why, etc., and then the organization's story from your point of view, how it runs (or ran), how and why it got started, etc.

Questions about the individual

When did you get involved in rape crisis work?
How did you get interested in it? What brought you into it?
How did you choose this hotline to work with?
Did you know other people in this group before you joined? Through what context?
In what context do you see other people who belong to the organization outside of the organization?
What type of participation did/do you have?
How do you feel about your hotline work? What is it like for you to work a shift?
How often do you take shifts? How busy is it? How do you feel?
If no longer active, why not?
Were you always involved in the same organization, or several? Tell me about it.
What other movements have you been active in?
Were you in specific organizations? Which ones? How have you found rape crisis work similar or different from that involvement?
Can you recall what else was going on in LA around the time of your hotline work that involved women?
Do you consider yourself a feminist?
What does "feminism" mean to you? Is there some branch or kind of feminism that you identify with more than others?
(If identifies as feminist:) Do you see your hotline work related to your feminism? How?

Were there other concerns that brought you into rape hotline work, for example, other people- or issue-oriented work? How did these influence your involvement with the rape crisis work?

Questions about the organization

How is the organization set up? How is it structured?
Is the work of running the organization divided formally?
What about the founding of the organization? Who were the founding members? How did they get together? What was the purpose of founding the organization? What was the organization like when you joined?
What was involved in the training? (For trainers) How was the training planned and conceptualized? Purpose? What was important to incorporate? Has the content changed over time? How and why?
Are women who use the service brought in in any way? Has this changed?
How is the organization structured?
Who takes care of administrative work (mailings, bills, finances)?
How is/was communication handled among members (formal and informal)? Is there a clear leadership? How is it chosen? Is anyone paid staff? What do they do? How is their input different from volunteers?
How does the hotline survive financially? Where do funds come from? Has this changed?
What is the usual path that participants take through the organization? Does everyone work on the hotline; are there other activities that some people do?
Does the hotline do any work with the local police? Describe. Who initiates this sort of work? Who makes the decisions about how it is done?
Does the organization have a connection to the OCJP? What do they do for the hotline? What requirements do you have to meet?
Are there other ways that the hotline deals with local or state government? Do you make welfare related referrals?
How has the organization changed over time? What do you think about the changes?
Were there issues of debate within the organization? Recurring issues? Ones that were particularly significant to you?
Is the hotline connected to other organizations?
What is its relationship with e.g., the Alliance, shelters, NOW, other organizations? Are these connections formalized in some way? Are they informal? How are they maintained?
What groups does the hotline refer people to? How are these selected, screened?
Do you know people in other women's organizations; other hotlines? Do you know them through organizational links or informal ones? (Probe for informal and formal connections.)
Are you active in any other feminist groups? Are other people in the hotline also involved?
Who else would you recommend that I interview?

Questions asked of at least one member (leader) of each organization

Are there paid staff members who work for the hotline?

How many?
What do each of them do?
Did the organization start with the same size of staff? If not when did the numbers increase, and in which positions?
How is funding acquired to pay staff members? How were new positions justified?
How is the organization structured? What is the division of labor?

Demographic information

Age_____

Sex _____

Race/ethnic identity _____

Class identity _____

Educational background _____
High school
Some college
College graduate
Graduate or professional degree
Self educated

Occupation(s) (last 5 years)
Annual income
under $5000 $21,000–$25,000
$6000–$10,000 $26,000–$30,000
$11,000–$15,000   over $30,000
$16,000–$20,000
Parents' occupations
What part of LA do you live in?_____

Zip code _____

Marital status _____

Do you have children? _____

If yes, ages of children?_____

Notes

INTRODUCTION

1 Two very useful projects have studied larger samples of rape crisis centers. Janet Gornick, Martha Burt, and Karen Pittman surveyed a national sample in the early 1980s. The five reports on different aspects of rape crisis centers are available from The Urban Institute in Washington D.C. Patricia Yancey Martin, Diana DiNitto, Diana Byington, and Sharon Maxwell studied 25 rape crisis centers and 105 mainstream organizations involved in rape processing in Florida in the mid-1980s, producing a large number of papers and reports (see bibliography).

2 It could be argued that I made one exception to this in the case of Compton, but I regard the YWCA as having a strong community orientation, with roots in social movement.

3 A test of the success of this method of selection is that all but one of the organizations in Los Angeles County who were members of the Southern California Rape Hotline Alliance as of 1987 were included. The one not included, Project Sister Sexual Assault Crisis Service in Claremont, was a relatively small organization that, at the time of my study, was not very active.

1 FEMINISM, THE STATE, AND THE ANTI-RAPE MOVEMENT: THEORETICAL UNDERPINNINGS

1 Much of the evidence for this comes from feminist legal criticism of the state's inaction and reinforcement of women's conditions of inequality, such as the extensive literature on family law (e.g., Fineman 1991). Also research on reproductive rights (e.g. Petchesky, Gordon 1988), employment discrimination and the limitations of legal remedies (e.g., Crenshaw 1989), violence against women (e.g. Estrich 1987; Stanko 1990), and social welfare (e.g., Sidel 1986).

2 This differs from Freeman's view that small groups' service projects necessarily took such apolitical directions.

3 Dobash and Dobash (1992) offer an analysis of how "the therapeutic society" influenced the direction of and response to the battered women's shelter

movement, especially in the U.S., where psychological individualism is a central cultural feature along with a therapy industry that promotes such interpretations and solutions to problems.

2 THE NATIONAL CONTEXT

1 The January–February 1973 issue contains news about groups in Phila-delphia; New York City; Los Angeles; Roanoke, Virginia; Ames, Iowa City, and Cedar Falls, Iowa; Boston; Grand Falls, North Dakota; Chapel Hill, North Carolina; and at the University of Maryland. The March–April issue reports on additional groups in Anchorage, at the University of Pennsylvania in Philadelphia, and a group at Florida State University in Tallahassee. The Washington D.C. Rape Crisis Center newsletter became the FAAR News-letter, which later became *Aegis; Magazine on Ending Violence Against Women*, published from 1978 to 1987.

2 As Camille LeGrande (1973) notes, the societal concern, reflected in courts' concern with false accusations by women who wanted sex but feared admitting it or regretted having it, reflected the rapist's perspective.

3 See Tong (1989) for an excellent summary of these debates.

3 THE BIRTH OF THE LOS ANGELES ANTI-RAPE MOVEMENT

1 The National Black Feminist Organization (NBFO) was started in 1973 on the east coast (Giddings 1984) and the Combahee River Collective in Boston started in 1974 (Smith 1983).

2 Although their structure and process was quite fluid, the women of the Westside Women's Center were self-conscious about issues of structure – according to Hoffman, they were discussing Jo Freeman's critical piece, "The Tyranny of Structurelessness," during this time, after it was published in the inaugural issue of *MS.* in 1972.

3. The first bake sale took place at the J. C. Penney's in Monterey Park.

4 SURVIVING THE EARLY YEARS

1 The NCPCR resulted from a bill introduced by Senator Charles Mathias of Maryland in September 1973 (Largen 1981). It was the product indirectly of feminist organizing, but not a coordinated national effort.

2 In Yolo County, California, the rape crisis center received $48,000 from the LEAA in 1978, which approximately tripled its previous budget from com-bined city and county funds, and permitted hiring two additional full-time and one additional part-time staff members.

3 In addition to the letters, this incident was discussed at Alliance meetings every month but two from June 1979 through September 1980. After the first six months these reports appeared as routine notations (e.g., another letter sent, no response) in the minutes, and it appeared that the issue would just fade, but after 15 months of efforts, a meeting took place with staff at the

station. The minutes note the positive outcome in the interest that media people had in helping stimulate funding for the hotlines.

4 During the 15 months that the Alliance pursued the issue, its member organizations got back on their feet. By the time they got a response, the problems in the movement Essensten had highlighted were no longer salient. In the end, they got this media organization on their side, which had been the original goal of the press conference over a year earlier.

5 In fact, the Los Angeles Police Department's PDID unit continued spying on leftist groups throughout the 1970s.

6 In later years (1986–7) a medical issue became the focal point of movement activity when the state (through the OCJP and legislation) instituted a medical protocol for evidence collection, without reimbursing hospitals adequately to cover the costs of following it. As a result, many hospitals statewide stopped accepting rape survivors in their emergency rooms. Outcry in the movement resulted in increased standard compensation to hospitals. That later incident was the culmination of the state's own ambiguous approach to rape crisis services, as it absorbed movement criticisms and instituted new rules, but failed to appropriate funding to implement them effectively.

7 Snow *et al.* (1986) use the term "master frame" to capture the pervasiveness of certain modes of social organization, and this could be applied to the bureaucratization of social movements (*cf.* Thomas and Meyer 1984).

5 THE POLITICS OF CRISIS AND A CRISIS OF POLITICS

1 The term "radical" feminist refers generally to women who believe that the oppression of women is the most fundamental source of social inequality and that men's sexual violence is a primary pillar of misogynist social systems (Jaggar 1983). Radical feminists believe that both personal and social structural transformation are necessary to overcome misogyny. While the term has remained in currency during the 1980s and 1990s, the process of delineating new feminisms has not stopped, and many of the new perspectives – cultural feminism, spiritual feminism, eco-feminism – overlap with radical feminism. See Chapter 1 for a discussion of collectivist feminism.

6 POLITICS AND BUREAUCRACY: OCJP FUNDING

1 Diana Russell, a sociologist, has been influential in legitimizing the feminist analysis of rape by her early work on the rape experience from the victim's point of view. *The Politics of Rape* included much material originally developed by the anti-rape movement, and its publication in 1974 facilitated the diffusion of such information.

2 This excerpt again reflects the ambivalence of the movement toward the police. They clearly saw themselves as an alternative institution to which women could report, but it is not clear here whether they would also be apprehending the assailants.

3 Bear in mind that although the conflict became identified with these labels that apply to a social group based on sexuality, there were lesbians who

agreed with the moderate strategy and heterosexual women who held very radical views. Indeed, the labels themselves are problematic because of the fluid nature of sexual identity over the life course.

7 THE EXPANSION OF RACIAL DIVERSITY

1 Rimonte also generated information on Asian and Pacific rape survivors through her work, which was included in the Los Angeles County Protocol on Rape.

8 FROM STOPPING VIOLENCE TO MANAGING RAPE

1 The evocative term "contested terrain" was popularized by Edwards (1979) analyzing management–labor relations. Claire Reinelt (1992), who has analyzed the relationship between battered women's shelters and state agencies in Texas, treats the state itself as the contested terrain on which activist groups struggle for resources and power. Our different uses of this term point out both its flexibility and how using different "angles of vision" reveals the contours of struggles over power that occur in various social locations.

Bibliography

Alford, Robert R. and Friedland, Roger (1985) *Powers of Theory: Capitalism, the State, and Democracy*, Cambridge: Cambridge University Press.

Amir, Menachim (1971) *Patterns in Forcible Rape*, Chicago: University of Chicago Press.

Bart, Pauline and O'Brien, Patricia H. (1985) *Stopping Rape: Successful Survival Strategies*, New York: Pergamon Press.

Bellah, Robert, Manson, Richard, Sullivan, William M., Swidler, Ann and Tipton, Steven M. (1985) *Habits of the Heart: Individualism and Commitment in American Life*, New York: Harper and Row.

Brownmiller, Susan (1975) *Against Our Will: Men, Women, and Rape*, New York: Bantam.

Burgess, Ann Wolbert and Holmstrom, Lynda Lytle (1974) *Rape: Victims of Crisis*, Bowie, Maryland: Robert J. Brady Company.

Burstyn, Varda (1983) "Masculine Dominance and the State," in Ralph Milliband and John Saville (eds) *Socialist Register*: 45–89, London: Merlin Press.

Burt, Martha R., Gornick, Janet C. and Pittman, Karen (1984) *Feminism and Rape Crisis Centers*, Washington, D.C.: The Urban Institute.

Byington, Diane B., Martin, Patricia Yancey, DiNitto, Diana M. and Maxwell, M. Sharon (1991) "Organizational Affiliation and Effectiveness: The Case of Rape Crisis Centers," *Administration in Social Work* 15: 83–103.

California Legislature History (1985–86), Sacramento, California.

Chappell, Duncan, Geis, Robley and Geis Gilbert (eds) (1977) *Forcible Rape: The Crime, The Victim, and the Offender*, New York: Columbia University Press.

Cicourel, Aaron (1964) *Method and Measurement in Sociology*, New York: The Free Press.

—— (1968) *The Social Organization of Juvenile Justice*, New York: John Wiley.

Cleaver, Eldridge (1968) *Soul on Ice*, New York: Dell.

Congressional Record (1973) Senate Bill 2422, 9-17-73, 119 (134).

Cott, Nancy F. (1987) *The Grounding of Modern Feminism*, New Haven: Yale University Press.

Crenshaw, Kimberle (1989) "Demarginalizing the Intersection of Race and Sex:

A Black Feminist Critique of Antidiscrimination Doctrine, Feminist Theory and Antiracist Politics," University of Chicago Legal Forum: 139–67.

Dalton, Russell J. and Kuechler, Manfred (1990) *Challenging the Political Order: New Social Movements in Western Democracies*, New York: Oxford University Press.

Dalton, Russell J., Kuechler, Manfred and Burklin, Wilhelm (1990) "The Challenge of New Movements," in Russel J. Dalton and Manfred Kuechler (eds) *Challenging the Political Order: New Social Movements in Western Democracies*, New York: Oxford University Press.

Davis, Angela (1981) *Women, Race, and Class*, New York: Random House.

Delphy, Christine (1984) *Close to Home: A Materialist Analysis of Women's Oppression*, London: Hutchinson.

De Silva, Lisa (1987) *The Impact of State Funding on the Political Ideology of Rape Crisis Centers in California*, unpublished M.P.A. Thesis, University of San Francisco.

Devault, Marjorie L. (1986) "Talking and Listening from Women's Standpoint: Feminist Strategies for Analyzing Interview Data," paper presented at the meetings of the Society for the Study of Symbolic Interaction, New York.

Diamond, Timothy (1992) *Making Gray Gold: Narratives of Nursing Home Care*, Chicago: University of Chicago Press.

Di Leonardo, Micaela (1987) "Oral History as Ethnographic Encounter," *Oral History Review* 15: 1–20.

Dobash, R. Emerson and Dobash, Russell P. (1992) *Women, Violence and Social Change*, London: Routledge.

Domhoff, William G. (1978) *The Powers That Be: Processes of Ruling Class Domination in America*, New York: Random House.

Dubrow, Gail, Flynn, Carolyn, Martinez, Renee, Peterson, Jane, Qayam, Seemin, Segal, Barbara and Welch, Mary Beth (1986) "Planning to End Violence Against Women: Notes from a Feminist Conference at UCLA," *Women and Environments* 8: 4–27.

Echols, Alice (1989) *Daring To Be Bad: Radical Feminism in America 1967–1975*, Minneapolis: University of Minnesota Press.

Edwards, Richard (1979) *Contested Terrain: The Transformation of the Workplace in the Twentieth Century*, London: Heineman.

Eisenstein, Hester (1991) *Gender Shock*, Boston: Beacon Press.

Emerson, Robert M. (ed) (1983) *Contemporary Field Research: A Collection of Readings*, Boston: Little, Brown.

Epstein, Cynthia Fuchs (1974) "A Different Angle of Vision: Notes on the Selective Eye of Sociology," *Social Science Quarterly* 55: 645–56.

Estrich, Susan (1987) *Real Rape*, Cambridge, Mass.: Harvard University Press.

Evans, Sara (1979) *Personal Politics*, New York: Vintage Books.

FAAR Newsletter (1974) Washington D.C.: Feminist Alliance Against Rape.

Ferguson, Kathy E. (1984) *The Feminist Case Against Bureaucracy*, Philadelphia: Temple University Press.

Ferree, Myra Marx and Miller, Frederick D. (1985) "Mobilization and Meaning: Toward an Integration of Social Psychological and Resource Perspectives on Social Movements," *Sociological Inquiry* 55: 38–61.

Ferree, Myra Marx and Hess, Beth B. (1985) *Controversy and Coalition: The New Feminist Movement*, Boston: Twayne Publishers.

Freeman, Jo (1975) *The Politics of Women's Liberation*, New York: Longman.

Friedman, K. V. (1981) *Legitimation of Social Rights and the Western Welfare State*, Chapel Hill: University of North Carolina Press.

Frohmann, Lisa (1991) "Discrediting Victims' Allegations of Sexual Assault: Prosecutorial Accounts of Case Rejection," *Social Problems* 38: 213–26.

Giddens, Anthony (1987) *The Nation-State and Violence*, Berkeley: University of California Press.

Giddings, Paula (1984) *When and Where I Enter: The Impact of Black Women on Race and Sex in America*, New York: W. Morrow.

Gilligan, Carol (1982) *In a Different Voice*, Cambridge: Harvard University Press.

Goffman, Erving (1974) *Frame Analysis*, Cambridge: Harvard University Press.

Gordon, Linda (1988) *Heroes of Their Own Lives: The Politics and History of Family Violence*, New York: Penguin.

Gornick, Janet, Burt, Martha R. and Pittman, Karen J. (1983) *Community Relations and Public Image in Rape Crisis Centers*, Washington D.C.: The Urban Institute.

—— (1985) "Structure and Activities of Rape Crisis Centers in the Early 1980s," *Crime and Delinquency* 31: 247–68.

Griffin, Susan (1971) "Rape: The All-American Crime," *Ramparts* 10: 26–35.

Grossman, B. and Kramer, R.M. (1985) *Child Abuse Prevention in a Grants Economy: An Organizational Perspective on AB 1733*, unpublished manuscript, Berkeley: University of California School of Social Welfare.

Gusfield, Joseph (1982) "Deviance in the Welfare State: The Alcoholism Profession and the Entitlement of Stigma," in Michael Lewis (ed.) *Research in Social Problems and Public Policy* 1–20, Greenwich, Conn.: JAI Press.

—— (1989) "Constructing the Ownership of Social Problems: Fun and Profit in the Welfare State," *Social Problems* 36: 431–41.

Hammersley, Martyn and Atkinson, Paul (1983) *Ethnography: Principles in Practice*, London: Tavistock Publications.

Hanmer, Jalna (1978) "Violence and the Social Control of Women," in Gary Littlejohn, Barry Smart, John Wakeford, and Nira Yuval-Davis (eds) *Power and the State*, New York: St Martin's Press.

Hill Collins, Patricia (1990) *Black Feminist Thought: Knowledge, Consciousness, and the Politics of Empowerment*, Boston: Unwin Hyman.

Hole, Judith and Levine, Ellen (1971) *Rebirth of Feminism*, New York: Quadrangle Books.

hooks, bell (1981) *Ain't I a Woman: Black Women and Feminism*, Boston: South End Press.

—— (1984) *Feminist Theory: From Margin to Center*, Boston: South End Press.

Iannello, Kathleen P. (1992) *Decisions Without Hierarchy: Feminist Interventions in Organization Theory and Practice*, New York and London: Routledge.

Jaggar, Alison M. (1983) *Feminist Politics and Human Nature*, Totawa, N.J.: Rowman and Allenheld.

Jenkins, J. Craig and Schock, Kurt (1992) "Global Structures and Political Processes in the Study of Domestic Political Conflict," *Annual Review of Sociology* 18: 161–85.

Kanter, Rosabeth Moss (1972) *Commitment and Community*, Cambridge, Mass.: Harvard University Press.
Kanuha, Valli (1987) "Sexual Assault in Southeast Asian Communities: Issues in Intervention," *Response* 10: 4–6.
Klandermans, Bert (1990) "Linking the 'Old' and 'New': Movement Networks in the Netherlands" in Russel J. Dalton and Manfred Kuechler (eds) *Challenging the Political Order: New Social Movements in Western Democracies*, New York: Oxford University Press.
Kriesi, Hanspeter (1989) "New Social Movements and the New Class in the Netherlands", *American Journal of Sociology* 94: 1078–116.
Landerman, Donna and McAtee, Mary (1982) "Breaking the Racism Barrier: White Anti-Racism Work," Aegis: Magazine on Ending Violence Against Women 33: 16–26.
Largen, Mary Ann (1981) "Grassroots Centers and National Task Forces: A History of the Anti-Rape Movement," *Aegis* (Summer): 46–52.
LeGrand, Camille E. (1973) "Rape and Rape Laws: Sexism in Society and Law," *California Law Review* 61: 919–41.
Leidner, Robin (1991) "Stretching the Boundaries of Liberalism: Democratic Innovation in a Feminist Organization," *Signs* 16: 263–89.
Liebow, Elliot (1967) *Tally's Corner*, Boston: Little, Brown and Company.
Letwin, Leon (1980) "'Unchaste Character,' Ideology, and the California Rape Evidence Laws," *Southern California Law Review* 54: 35–89.
Los Angeles Times (1972) "Rape Crisis Center Assists Victims," July 6.
—— (1973) "New York's Rape Analysis Bureau," February 11.
—— (1973) "Rape Crisis Center Set in Berkeley," March 1.
Lum, Joan (1988) "Battered Asian Women," *Rice* (March): 50–2.
McAdam, Doug (1982) *Political Process and the Development of Black Insurgency, 1930–1970*, Chicago: University of Chicago Press.
McCarthy, John D. and Zald, Mayer (1973) *The Trend of Social Movements in America: Professionalization and Resource Mobilization*, Morristown, New Jersey: General Learning Press.
McDermott, Thomas E. III (1975) "California Rape Evidence Reform: An Analysis of Senate Bill 1678," *The Hastings Law Journal* 26 (6): 1551–73.
MacKinnon, Catharine A. (1983) "Feminism, Marxism, Method, and the State: Toward Feminist Jurisprudence," *Signs* 8 (4): 635–58.
—— (1989) *Toward a Feminist Theory of the State*, Cambridge: Harvard University Press.
Mackle, Nancy, Pernell, Deanne, Shirchild, Jan, Baratta, Consuelo and Groves, Gail (1982) "Dear Aegis: Letter from Santa Cruz Women Against Rape," *Aegis: Magazine on Ending Violence Against Women* 35: 28–30.
Mansbridge, Jane J. (1973) "Time, Emotion, and Inequality: Three Problems of Participatory Groups," *The Journal of Applied Behavioral Science* 9: 351–68.
Martin, Patricia Yancey (1990) "Rethinking Feminist Organizations," *Gender & Society* 4: 182–206.
——(1993) "Rape Crisis Centers, Feminism, and the Politics of Rape Processing in the Community," unpublished paper.
Martin, Patricia Yancey, DiNitto, Diana, Byington, Diane and Maxwell, M. Sharon (1992) "Organizational and Community Transformation: The Case of a Rape Crisis Center," *Administration in Social Work* 16: 123–45.

Marx, Gary T. and Wood, James L. (1975) "Strands of Theory and Research in Collective Behavior," *Annual Review of Sociology* 1: 363–428.

Matthews, Nancy A. (1994) "Feminist Clashes with the State: The Case of State-funded Rape Crisis Centers," in Myra Marx Ferree and Patricia Yancey Martin (eds) *Women's Organizations: Harvest of the New Feminist Movement*, Philadelphia: Temple University Press.

Mueller, Carol McClurg (1987) "Collective Consciousness, Identity Transformation, and the Rise of Women in Public Office in the United States," in Mary Fainsod Katzenstein and Carol McClurg Mueller (eds), *The Women's Movements of the United States and Western Europe*, 89–108, Philadelphia: Temple University Press.

Nestle, Joan (1989) "The Sexual Imperative of Our History," Lecture at UCLA, January 19.

New York Radical Feminists (1974) *Rape: The First Sourcebook for Women*, Noreen Connell and Cassandra Wilson (eds), New York: New American Library.

Oakley, Ann (1981) "Interviewing Women: A Contradiction in Terms," in Helen Roberts (ed.) *Doing Feminist Research*, London: Routledge and Kegan Paul.

O'Connor, James (1973) *The Fiscal Crisis of the State*, New York: St Martin's Press.

Offe, Claus (1984) *Contradictions of the Welfare State*, Cambridge, Mass.: MIT Press.

Office of Criminal Justice Planning (1987) *California Sexual Assault Victim Services and Prevention Program Guidelines*, State of California.

Pateman, Carole (1988) *The Sexual Contract*, Stanford: Stanford University Press.

Piven, Frances Fox (1971) *Regulating the Poor: The Functions of Public Welfare*, New York: Vintage Books.

Piven, Frances Fox and Cloward, Richard A. (1977) *Poor Peoples' Movements*, New York: Vintage Books.

Polsky, Andrew (1991) *The Rise of the Therapeutic State*, Princeton, New Jersey: Princeton University Press.

Reinelt, Claire (1994) "Moving onto the Terrain of the State: The Battered Women's Movement and the Politics of Engagement," in Myra Marx Ferree and Patricia Yancey Martin (eds) *Women's Organizations: Harvest of the New Women's Movement*, Philadelphia: Temple University Press.

Rich, Adrienne (1980) "Compulsory Heterosexuality and Lesbian Existence," *Signs* 5: 631–60.

Rimonte, Nilda (n.d.) "Pacific Asian Survivors," Los Angeles County Protocol on Rape.

Rodriguez, Noelie Maria (1988) "Transcending Bureaucracy: Feminist Politics at a Shelter for Battered Women," *Gender & Society* 2: 214–27.

Roth, Stephanie and Baslow, Robin (1984) "Compromising Positions at Anti-Rape Conference," *Aegis: Magazine on Ending Violence Against Women* 38: 56–8.

Rothschild-Whitt, Joyce (1979) "The Collectivist Organization: An Alternative to Rational–Bureaucratic Models," *American Sociological Review* 44 (August): 509–27.

Rothchild, Joyce and Whitt, J. Allen (1986) *The Cooperative Workplace: Potentials and Dilemmas of Organizational Democracy and Participation*, Cambridge: Cambridge University Press.

Roy, William G. (1989) Personal communication.

Rupp, Leila and Taylor, Verta (1987) *Survival in the Doldrums: The American Women's Rights Movement, 1945 to the 1960s*, New York: Oxford University Press.

Russell, Diana E.H. (1974) *The Politics of Rape*, New York: Stein and Day.

Sale, Kirkpatrick (1973) *SDS*, New York: Random House.

Schecter, Susan (1982) *Women and Male Violence: The Visions and Struggles of the Battered Women's Movement*, Boston: South End Press.

Schlesinger, Melinda Bart and Bart, Pauline (1981) "Collective Work and Self-Identity: The Effect of Working in a Feminist Illegal Abortion Collective," in Frank Lindenfeld and Joyce Rothschild-Whitt, (eds) *Workplace Democracy and Social Change*, Boston: Porter-Sargent.

Selznick, Philip (1949) *TVA and the Grass Roots: A Study in the Sociology of Formal Organization*, Berkeley: University of California Press.

Sidel, Ruth (1986) *Women and Children Last: The Plight of Poor Women in Affluent America*, New York: Penguin Books.

Skocpol, Theda (1984) *Vision and Method in Historical Sociology*, Cambridge: Cambridge University Press.

Smith, Barbara (ed.) (1983) *Home Girls: A Black Feminist Anthology*, New York: Kitchen Table Press.

Smith, Dorothy, E. (1974) "The Social Construction of Documentary Reality," *Sociological Inquiry* 44 (4): 257–68.

—— (1987) *The Everyday World as Problematic*, Boston: Northeastern University Press.

—— (1990) *The Conceptual Practices of Power: A Feminist Sociology of Knowledge*, Boston: Northeastern University Press.

Snow, David A., Burke Rochford, E. Jr., Worden, Steven K. and Benford, Robert D. (1986) "Frame Alignment Processes, Micromobilization, and Movement Participation," *American Sociological Review* 51: 464–81.

Stacey, Judith and Thorne, Barrie (1985) "The Missing Feminist Revolution in Sociology," *Social Problems* 32: 301–16.

Stack, Carol (1974) *All Our Kin: Strategies for Survival in a Black Community*, New York: Harper and Row.

Staggenborg, Suzanne (1988) "The Consequences of Professionalization and Formalization in the Pro-Choice Movement," *American Sociological Review* 53: 585–605.

—— (1989) "Stability and Innovation in the Women's Movement: A Comparison of Two Movement Organizations," *Social Problems* 36: 75–92.

Stanko, Elizabeth (1990) *Everyday Violence: How Women and Men Experience Sexual and Physical Danger*, London: Pandora.

Tarrow, Sydney (1988) "National Politics and Collective Action: Recent Theory and Research in Western Europe and the United States," *Annual Review of Sociology* 14: 421–40.

—— (1989) *Democracy and Disorder: Protest and Politics in Italy 1965–1975*, New York: Oxford University Press.

Taylor, Verta (1989) "Social Movement Continuity: The Women's Movement in Abeyance," *American Sociological Review* 54: 761–75.

Taylor, Verta and Rupp, Leila J. (1993) "Women's Culture and Lesbian Feminist Activism: A Reconsideration of Cultural Feminism," *Signs* 19: 32–61.

Taylor, Verta and Whittier, Nancy E. (1992) "Collective Identity in Social Movement Communities: Lesbian Feminist Mobilization," in Aldon Morris and Carol Mueller (eds) *Frontiers of Social Movement Theory*, New Haven: Yale University Press.

Thomas, George M. and Meyer, John W. (1984) "The Expansion of the State," *Annual Review of Sociology* 10: 461–82.

Tilly, Charles (1978) *From Mobilization to Revolution*, Reading, Massachussetts: Addison-Wesley.

Tong, Rosemary (1989) *Feminist Thought: A Comprehensive Introduction*, Boulder, Colorado: Westview Press.

Turner, Ralph and Killian, Lewis (1987) *Collective Behavior, Third Ed*, Englewood Cliffs, New Jersey: Prentice-Hall, Inc.

Turner, Ralph (1989) Personal communication.

Walby, Sylvia (1986) *Patriarchy at Work*, Oxford: Polity Press.

Washington D.C. Rape Crisis Center Newsletter (1973).

Watson, Sophia (ed.) (1990) *Playing the State: Australian Feminist Interventions*, London: Verso.

Wilson, John (1983) "Corporatism and the Professionalization of Reform," *Journal of Political and Military Sociology* 11: 53–68.

Wood, Pamela Lakes (1973) "The Victim in a Forcible Rape Case: A Feminist View," *American Criminal Law Review* 11: 335–54.

Zald, Mayer N. and Ash, Roberta (1966) "Social Movement Organizations: Growth, Decay and Change," *Social Forces* 44: 327–41.

Index